MICHELANGELO

The Complete Sculpture

Self-portrait as Joseph of Arimathea, from *Pietà*, Florence Cathedral
(see pages 280–89)

MICHELANGELO

THE COMPLETE SCULPTURE

FREDERICK HARTT *Chairman, Department of Art, University of Virginia*

HARRY N. ABRAMS, INC., PUBLISHERS, NEW YORK

MILTON S. FOX, *Editor-in-Chief* PATRICIA EGAN, *Editor*
Book designed by Robin Fox

Library of Congress Catalog Card Number: 68–24045
HARRY N. ABRAMS, INCORPORATED, *New York*

Printed and bound in Japan

IN MEMORIAM

IOHANNIS POGGII

IMPIGRI PACE DISCIPVLI

IMPAVIDI BELLO DEFENSORIS

ARTIVM FLORENTIAE

CONTENTS

FOREWORD

This book is primarily intended for the general public who, I am credibly informed, do not care for footnotes. Specialists will not miss them. Graduate students may occasionally have trouble hunting down references, but in the present age of vast anthologies designed to spare anyone the torment of going back to original documents, sources, and commentaries, maybe a search will do them good. Accordingly, individual scholars are mentioned in the text only when their discoveries are both recent and revolutionary, or when their personal suggestions to me have not yet been published.

The occasional translations of passages from Michelangelo's writings are my own. I am aware that in certain crucial words my rendering differs from that of other recent translators. In all these translations I have kept as close as I could to the exact Italian phrases at the expense of idiomatic English but not, I hope, of intelligibility.

In a book of this nature there is no room for contested attributions in whose validity the author does not believe. In recent years the majority of these have been fairly well settled by scholars. The perplexing problem of the statues on the Piccolomini Altar in the Cathedral of Siena, however, remains at issue. It cannot reasonably be denied that Michelangelo was paid for these four statues, under the assumption that he carved them. In all probability the four blocks sold to Baccio da Montelupo are not to be identified with these statues. Yet the quality of the statues themselves is so far below that of any other known work by Michelangelo as to cause me to doubt seriously that he did more than furnish an assistant with the necessary drawings, supervise, and make an occasional direct intervention. The recent proposal that an unfinished male statue formerly in the Boboli Gardens is really a fifth Captive for the group in the Academy has not, as far as I know, won general acceptance.

Like all recent students of Michelangelo's art, I am beholden in innumerable ways to the massive contribution of Charles de Tolnay, whose six volumes will remain for many years to come the standard treatment of the great artist's work and the problems surrounding it. My special indebtedness includes a number of black-and-white photographs published here, but originally taken under Dr. de Tolnay's supervision, and the measurements of the individual works of sculpture, which I have derived from his catalogues. The respect which Dr. de Tolnay's achievements deserve—and have received throughout the world—should not prevent me from underscoring the single general issue on which I regretfully part company with him, the interpretation of meaning. Dr. de Tolnay is the most eminent surviving exponent of the Neoplatonic group, and my opinion of the validity of their contentions is a matter of record in this book and elsewhere.

And now a word on a still more delicate subject. The effects of a great scholar's teaching are more evident, it seems to me, in the independence of his pupils' judgment than in their docility. My reverence for the ideas and writings of Professor Erwin Panofsky is, I think, sufficiently well known to prevent misconstruction of any of the following pages, even when it has become necessary to take issue with some of the more preposterous assumptions of those who find complete Neoplatonic cosmogonies in Michelangelo's Christian works, or when, more regrettably, I have had to comment on perplexing personal attacks. These pages, and indeed the foregoing sentences, were written and sent to the publisher in the full expectation that Professor Panofsky would, if he liked, be able to reply to them with his customary erudition and wit. It would be no tribute to his memory if I were now to alter any statement that I believe to be true.

I am happy to add my name to the lengthening list of those students of Michelangelo's work who accept as authentic the beautiful wooden *Crucifix* for Santo Spirito so dramatically rediscovered in 1963—in its original home!—by Dr. Margrit Lisner. To Professor Earl Rosenthal I am indebted for having sharpened my eyes to the implications of the original high placing of Michelangelo's *Moses* for the strange proportions of that masterpiece, a matter which Dr. Rosenthal has investigated with exemplary thoroughness.

The publishers have been most generous in their aid to this book, supporting the European trip essential for my study and financing the splendid new photographs, which include all the colorplates and many of the black-and-whites, especially the views and details of the Louvre *Slaves*, never before so well photographed. Mrs. Barbara Adler has been, as usual, tireless in her efforts to solve knotty production problems, and Mrs. Sophia Kozak typed the book with flawless accuracy, all one hot summer.

Now that the book has been completed, I notice that many intense memories of the great master's works crowd upon my mind—none more personal than the weeks I spent thirty-seven years ago learning about the subtleties of Michelangelo's form in the defeating attempt to copy the *Brutus* in clay, and none more poignant than that moment twenty-six years ago when, in the substructure of a Florentine villa still shaken by the nearby explosions of enemy shells, I climbed over an immense crate to gaze down through its bars at the agonized face of the *Aurora*.

F. H.
Old Ordinary, Charlottesville, Virginia
July, 1968

If my rude hammer forms the hard stones
Into human semblance, now this shape, now that,
And taking its motion from the minister who guides, watches, and holds it,
Follows the movements of another,
That divine hammer which in Heaven lodges and stays,
Others, and especially itself, with its own motion makes beautiful;
And if one can make no hammer without a hammer—
From that living one every other is made;
And since the blow is the more full of strength
The more it lifts itself above the forge,
Above mine, that to heaven has taken flight;
So my unfinished work will fall short
If now the divine workshop does not give me
That help to make it which is alone in this world.

Sonnet by Michelangelo, written about 1528

Stone was Michelangelo's life. It was his friend, his enemy, and his enduring love. In poem after poem, many times quoted, he tells us how the statue is there inside the stone, and how it grows as the stone shrinks. He sought out perfect stone in the wildest mountains, only to abandon it in St. Peter's Square. He cut it, beat it, loved it, hated it, finished it with infinite care down to the most minutely calculated tensions, hesitations, and curves, left it in rugged masses. It was his triumph and his defeat. He carved it for seventy-five years. He was born with it and died with it. In the very process of bringing shapes out of the "hard and Alpine stone" he could find metaphors of life, love, and death, discern the will of God, and foresee redemption.

On Sunday, March 6, 1475, Michelangelo Buonarroti was born at Caprese, high in the Apennines. This little village, consisting of a few rough stone houses clinging to the ruin of a medieval castle, has changed little since Michelangelo's day, and there is no special reason why it should. To the rare visitor who ventures so far, Caprese presents a world of stone—barren, brutal, and desolate. The castle and its houses cluster in a depression in the mountaintop, so that, from every point of view, the eye is blocked by stone. Of course the infant Michelangelo, hardly more than a month old when he was carried away from Caprese, could have had no memories of the place, but he seems to have set a certain store by the fact that he was born there. At one time he jokingly told his friend Giorgio Vasari, the first art historian, on whom we depend for so much of our knowledge of the Renaissance in general and Michelangelo in particular, that his genius was first nourished in the rarefied air of the mountains of Vasari's Arezzo (Caprese is today in the province of Arezzo). And, probably during the days when he was picking his way through apparently hopeless stones in the attempt to bring a mighty order into the chaos of the unfinished St. Peter's, he wrote:

> *From the high mountains and from a great ruin*
> *Hidden and circumscribed by a great rock,*
> *I descended to discover myself in this pit,*
> *Against my will in such a stoneyard.*
> *When with the sun I was born, and by whom the heavens destine . . .*

The first two lines describe Caprese with perfect accuracy. The fragment leaves much to conjecture, but not the artist's vision of himself, nor his connection with the very mountain masses of Tuscany, and with the sun and the surrounding sky.

Michelangelo also let Vasari know that, taken to the family farm at Settignano, a village of stonecutters to the northeast of Florence, he had drunk in his love of carving tools with the milk of a stonecutter's wife, hired as his wet nurse according to Italian custom. Much will be made of this memory in these pages, with no pretense of knowing how psychologists would use such a fact, but in the conviction that a childhood memory so resolutely repeated by a great artist in his old age must, true or false, have had a certain bearing on his work—the more so since the process of freeing the image from the surrounding matrix of stone held so passionate a meaning for Michelangelo, and also since both the theme of nursing and the depiction of masculine identity submerged in a maternal bosom recur at striking moments in his imagery.

The letter—now securely dated in the spring of 1547—that Michelangelo wrote to Benedetto Varchi, the humanist who delivered two lectures on the artist's poetry before the Florentine Academy, must be requoted here, no matter how familiar it may be:

> So that it may appear that I have received, as I have, your little book, I will answer something to it as you ask me, although ignorantly. I say that painting seems to me the more to be held good the more it approaches relief, and relief to be held bad the more it approaches painting: and therefore I used to think that sculpture was the lantern of painting, and that between the one and the other was that difference which there is between the sun and the moon. Now, since I have read in your little book, where you say that, speaking philosophically, those things which have the same end, are the same thing; I have changed my opinion: and I say, that if greater judgment and difficulty, impediment and labor do not make greater nobility; that painting and sculpture is the same thing: and so that it should be so held, every painter should not do less sculpture than painting; and likewise, the sculptor [no less] painting than sculpture. I understand sculpture, that which is made by force of taking away; that which is made by way of adding on, is similar to painting: enough, that one and the other coming from the same intelligence—that is sculpture and painting— one can get them to make a good peace together, and leave so many disputes;

because there goes more time than in making figures. He who wrote that painting was more noble than sculpture, if he had understood so well the other things
he has written, my maidservant would have written better. Infinite things, still
not said, there would be to say of similar sciences, but as I have said, they need
too much time, and I have little, because not only am I old, but almost in the
number of the dead: therefore I pray you to hold me excused. And I recommend
myself to you and thank you as much as I can and know how for the honor is
too great you do me, not appropriate to me.

Michelangelo's sarcasm is an eloquent witness to his opinion of painting and its defenders,
and to his true conviction that sculpture was the more noble *because* it was more difficult. The
battle with the stone made it so: clay modeling ("adding on") was not sculpture; only stone
carving ("taking off") deserved that title.

It is interesting to observe in this respect that Michelangelo was the first stone sculptor
in history who, as far as we know, never (except for his early *Crucifix*) succumbed to the age-
old temptation of polychroming his sculpture, in whole or in part. Even Donatello applied
gold and colored stones at times. Michelangelo left the stone unadulterated by color from
any source. Yet, as can be seen in the plates of this book, color is very important to the understanding of Michelangelo's sculpture—the color of the marble itself, made as rich and resonant
as possible. No sculptor ever paid closer attention to such matters than Michelangelo, in his
finished works. In fact, even in some works which have not yet received their final polish, the
strokes of the chisel are already so deployed as to bring out a soft radiance in the structure of
the marble.

But Michelangelo did not like the optical effects employed by Donatello and his followers
in the preceding century any more than he enjoyed working in bronze based on clay modeling.
There are no deliberately sketchy surfaces in his sculpture, no attempts to create the illusion
that a veil of hazy atmosphere intervenes between the eye and the object. The smoothed masses
have a deep, inner glow which comes from careful and prolonged polishing, and seems the
counterpart of firm muscles and silky skin. And as for the unfinished masses about which so
much foolishness has been written, there is no evidence to support the contention that the
artist consciously intended them to look that way. The last three lines of the sonnet rudely
translated at the beginning of this chapter give Michelangelo's own ideas on the subject
clearly enough. That he suffered from an inner compulsion which prevented him from bringing
a large proportion of his work to completion, that he overrated his ability to the extent of
taking on more work than he could have completed even in five lifetimes as long as his can
scarcely be denied—but that is another story. Such was his sense of form that no slightest
touch from any instrument held in his hand could fail to carry conviction, power, and beauty;
this does not mean that the unfinished works we like so much today would not have been
brought to complete, polished perfection if "circumstances" (always adverse with Michelangelo) had permitted.

All this brings us to the question of how the sculpture of Michelangelo was actually done.
Romantically attractive as the idea may have seemed to certain critics in the past, sculptors
in the sixteenth century did not simply attack the block of stone without preparation, and
liberate the statue living inside. In general the pose, and frequently the details, of a figure
were first studied in a series of drawings, ranging from quick sketches in pen, charcoal, black
chalk, red chalk, lead point, or some combination of these media, to elaborately shaded and
modeled analyses of various anatomical features. The sculptor then made a small model (figs.
1–6). Nothing, of course, prevented him from making such a model without preliminary
drawings, and Michelangelo may sometimes have done just that—we have no means of
knowing. But we can fairly doubt that he ever followed a hard and fast routine, particularly if
he was working under the spell of a great new idea, or was pressed for time.

Despite Michelangelo's vehement disclaimer in the letter to Varchi, such models must
have been done, at least partly, "by way of adding on," since the medium was often clay,

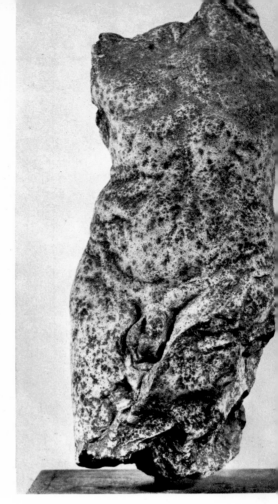

1. *Model for Slave*, Tomb of Julius II
1513–16. Terracotta, height 11¼″
British Museum, London

2. *Model for Slave* (back view of figure 3)

3. *Model for Slave*
Tomb of Julius II
1513–16. Clay
Casa Buonarroti, Florence

which permitted major changes easily. Clay also had the advantage of drying by itself, so that models could be carried about and shown to patrons. Most modeling in clay was done with tools of wood or bone. Benvenuto Cellini describes these procedures in detail, telling how sculptors kept the models covered with damp cloths when they were not working on them, to keep them from drying out, as was indeed the custom until the recent invention of plastic films, which are now used to hold in the moisture. Also, it appears that a little cooked flour was mixed with the clay, partly to make it dry more slowly, partly to reduce its brittleness. Drapery was not modeled in clay but literally applied to it, by dipping pieces of cloth of the desired weight in a thick slip of clay, and arranging them in folds to harden on the surface of the nude figure. This procedure tells volumes about the appearance of draped statues in the Renaissance. Wax was also used for the models, mixed with a small quantity of pitch, which gave it a dark bronzy color and made it eventually harden and toughen.

   The third step—which it may be presumed that Michelangelo often skipped—was the creation of a full-scale model in clay. An armature or framework had to be constructed (this is still done), and this armature, made of wood during the Renaissance, was then covered with such simple materials as tow, or even straw, to bulk it out and to reduce the need for large amounts of heavy clay. Naturally by this time all major decisions had been made, as once the armature had been constructed, nothing could be changed without serious, perhaps even disastrous, results. The final layer of clay, if the calculations had been exact, could be fairly thin. On this layer the delicate play of muscles and drapery could be worked out in detail (figs. 252–55).

   The sculptor was then ready for the attack on the stone—with a very clear idea of every

4. *Model for Female Victory*
Tomb of, Julius II
1513–16. Clay, height 13⅜"
Casa Buonarroti, Florence

5. *Model for Slave*, Tomb of Julius II
1513–16. Wax. Casa Buonarroti, Florence

6. *Model for Crossed-Leg Slave*
Tomb of Julius II
1513–16. Wax, height c. 4½"
British Museum, London

form and every relationship, already expressed in three dimensions, so that he knew with some exactitude what he was going to have to do. Devoted as he was to the perfect quality of the marble he wanted for his sculptural vision of human beings of more than natural power and beauty, Michelangelo went to the quarries and selected the marble himself. This was not an easy task. Frequently a mass of marble would seem white and perfect from outside, only to divulge, as it was cut, either cracks (such as the fissure running across the face and shoulders of the *Rebellious Slave;* figs. 140, 141, 143) or, worse yet, gray or blackish veins (such as disfigure the cheeks and forehead of the otherwise flawless *Bruges Madonna;* colorplate 5), doubtless causing Michelangelo acute distress. Such veins were not only ugly but extremely hard to work. Many a chisel was broken in the attempt to subdue them. Sometimes, as in the first version of the *Christ Holding the Cross,* the sculptor considered the obstacles insuperable and abandoned the statue. It may be supposed, however, that small flaws were often eliminated by slight changes in the predetermined plan. Michelangelo's contracts with stonecutters usually stipulated that the marble be very white and free from any flaws.

Michelangelo provided the quarrymen with clear outline drawings of the blocks he wanted, accompanied by exact dimensions (in Florentine cubits), and sometimes the drawings even showed how the statue was to be cut, in order to lay to rest any doubts in the stonecutters' minds about the basic requirements of the block (fig. 7). Apparently, once the block arrived at his workshop in Florence or Rome (perhaps after many adventures—see page 126) he drew the principal view of the figure to be carved directly on the surface of the marble with a piece of charcoal. This must have been a very rough drawing, as the marble itself had been only split out of the quarry with drills and its surfaces were not smooth; but the outline would hold the positions of the major masses of the figure, and could readily be incised into the marble once the sculptor started to carve. Cellini speaks of this process, and refers also to the other principal views; so, although Michelangelo is not precise on this point, we can fairly assume that he made similar drawings on the sides of the block as well, particularly if he intended the work to be seen from several different positions. In many of his statues the side views, even the adherence of the figure to the original faces of the block, can still be discerned (especially in the *Bacchus*, fig. 66). The back view, however beautiful, must have been residual. The sculptor, if he wished, could enlarge his work directly in stone by a system of proportional squares drawn on the surface of the block, corresponding to the squares in a little wooden device set up against the model. According to Vasari, the projections would begin to emerge from the stone and continue round the statue as the stone receded, for all the world like a wax figure in a basin from which the water is gradually drained.

Starting with the principal view, then, the sculptor assaulted the block with a hammer and a pointed chisel, known as a *subbia*. Both Cellini and Vasari are eloquent on the necessity of proceeding at the start as if one were making a high relief, and are caustic about sculptors who start the block from all sides at once, only to discover that the side, back, and front views will not meet in the statue itself. Such a refusal, of course, induces great despair: the inept workman is compelled to piece out his statue with added marble, "which patching," Vasari says, "is for bunglers, and not for excellent or rare masters; and is a most vile and ugly thing and of the greatest blame." Needless to say, Michelangelo's marble shows no traces of such errors.

By a careful examination of subsequent illustrations, the reader will discover many places where the trace mark of the *subbia* is still evident, marching across a surface in parallel grooves so as to block in major masses, which at that stage would have suggested hardly more than the possibility of life. Figure 270 shows the original, relatively even surface of the block at the front and on the top, and the channels left by the *subbia* as it proceeded, splitting off chunk after chunk. The resultant broad planes became in turn surfaces for a kind of draughtsmanship with the *subbia*, which was then employed to make a series of holes connecting into a dotted line. Now it is this line, let us say this continuous profile, which contains the essential magic of Michelangelo's sculpture. For in his art, form is basically a product of contour. In this same illustration one can clearly distinguish how the left elbow was profiled by a series of these little holes, which must have been produced by hammering the *subbia* directly into the stone at intervals. Along this line, then, as under the upper arm, the *subbia* was used to chip away the marble. Between the upper and lower arm can be seen a mass of marble, outlined by the little holes and ready to be chipped off in this way. What Michelangelo does, then, is to drive the contours relentlessly around the figure, first by means of the line of holes, then by chipping, so as to free it from the reduced block.

At this stage, one would imagine that a sculptor might feel compelled to free the entire roughed-in figure before starting to finish it. Not Michelangelo! Generally he started the next phase with a toothed chisel—usually the torso—while some portions of the figure were still roughed in with the *subbia*, others merely blocked in, and some major masses still encased in the original block of marble. Again and again one finds all three supposedly successive stages coexisting in the same work: evidence, perhaps, of Michelangelo's impatience to see the body muscles actually heaving under his hands. Vasari describes a chisel with one notch, and therefore two teeth, that was called the *calcagnuolo*, and another much finer chisel with two notches, or three teeth, the *gradina*. From the traces visible in Michelangelo's unfinished surfaces, he seems to have preferred the *gradina*, with which, Vasari tells us, sculptors "go over all with gentleness, shaping the figure with the proportion of the muscles and the folds, and hatching it in such a manner, by virtue of the aforesaid notches or teeth, that the stone shows admirable grace."

At this juncture the sculptor often removed the hatchings with a smooth chisel. But there is no evidence that Michelangelo ever used one, possibly because he was able to carry the *gradina* to lengths beyond the capabilities of lesser masters. The astonishing results of this

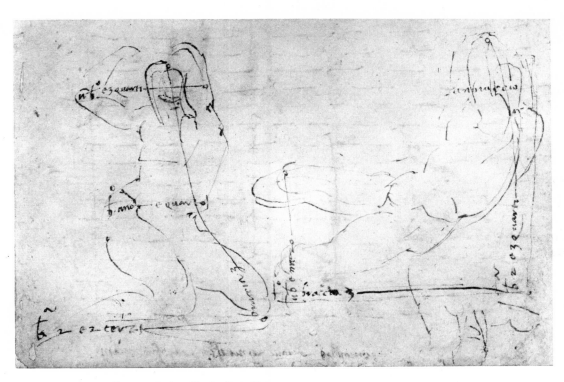

7. *Drawing of River God in block of marble.* 1520–25
Ink, 5⅜ × 8¼". British Museum, London

tool in his hands can be seen especially in the breathing surfaces of the faces of the *Medici Madonna* (figs. 242, 243) and the *Victory* (colorplate 15; figs. 282, 283). Finishing was done with the *lima*, or file, which created a unified surface texture. This had eventually to be polished with pumice and, finally, a buffer made of wheat straw. In the polished sections of Michelangelo's work, he achieved a remarkably high gloss, very unlike the soft, sometimes slightly granular surface preferred by late Quattrocento sculptors in Florence. This smooth sheen was clearly intended to function as an artistic counterpart to the rich smoothness of muscular flesh, and to suggest all the energy and suppleness of healthy muscles.

One of the most surprising yet essential aspects of Michelangelo's artistic procedure, which has not been sufficiently recognized by scholars, is that he seems to have started work on all his great sculptural projects not with the statues but with the enframing architecture and the secondary ornamentation. In the Medici Chapel and in the Tomb of Julius II these abstract elements were carried to the highest point of completion, with each detail minutely calculated to produce its exact effect of richness or barrenness, dainty grace or distressing tension, before the statues were roughed in, sometimes even before the marble for them had arrived. One might have expected the reverse: the usual conception of Michelangelo as an inspired and even violent artist would presuppose the creation of the statues first, to be surrounded by frames made to fit. His obsessive delight in the beauty of ornament, sharpened to a hair, was as characteristic of Michelangelo as was his inability to bring any of his great sculptural undertakings to completion, and his paralysis of will before certain figures, or portions of figures, which have remained forever in initial or intermediate stages.

Equally important is the fact that so many of the figures do not fit the spaces for which they were planned. There seems never to be room for the feet. Time and again myopic scholars have complained that the figures seem to be sliding off, or could not possibly have been planned for such a spot because the dimensions do not jibe, or that the figures would never have projected in such a manner if Michelangelo himself had put them there, rather than some clumsy

pupil. The fact seems to be that a conflict between the figure and its enframement is basic in Michelangelo's art, and is sometimes deliberately planned in his architecture, as in the staircase hall of the Laurentian Library (fig. 8), where coupled columns are at war with their surrounding masses of stone, which project as if to overwhelm them.

After Michelangelo's first entrance on the stage of European monumental sculpture, with the 1505 project for the Tomb of Julius II (fig. 15), his workshops at any given moment must have presented a fantastic spectacle—of delicate ornamental pieces, carved down to the finest detail, in the glowering presence of vast, rough personages, dimly and partially visible as they struggled to free themselves from their encasing masses of rough marble.

Something most important about Michelangelo's nature is undoubtedly revealed by his repeated use of the phrase "pietra alpestre e dura" (stone Alpine and hard) to characterize the marble with which he worked. The mountains around Carrara and Seravezza are still known today as the Apuan Alps, and apparently Michelangelo thought of his marble always in terms of its mountainous origin. There is a well-known account by Ascanio Condivi, his friend and official biographer, of the great sculptor's dream of carving an entire peak in this range into a colossus looking out to sea. Anyone who has seen these glittering summits reflected in the blue Tyrrhenian Sea, or has even enjoyed their jagged profile on a clear afternoon from Florence, will sympathize with Michelangelo. There is a streak of grandiosity in most of us that reacts warmly to dreams of elevating the mean and transitory existence of humanity to a nobler plane and a more lasting substance. Michelangelo often stated this. To Vittoria Colonna he wrote:

> *How may it be, lady, that one sees*
> *By long experience, that the live image*
> *In hard and Alpine stone lasts longer*
> *Than its maker, whom the years reduce to ashes?*
> *The cause inclines and cedes to the effect,*
> *Whence by art nature is conquered.*
> *I know, since I experience it in beautiful sculpture,*
> *That time and death do not hold faith to the work of art.*

And from the chasms and peaks of these marble mountains he wrote, "I have undertaken to raise the dead in trying to domesticate these mountains and bring art to this village."

This was written at the moment that Michelangelo was trying desperately to quarry marble from a site which had as yet yielded none. He cared for sick workmen with parental tenderness, and was horrified when a stonecutter perished in a rockslide. Yet the major disaster of these fruitless years overseeing the quarrying of marble for the façade of San Lorenzo—a project later abandoned—was the loss of one of the six great columns. A dishonest blacksmith had sold the sculptor iron rings that were hollow, and in consequence he had to watch the column roll from its broken ring to be smashed into a thousand pieces in the bottom of a ravine.

As the years of Michelangelo's childhood in the dark and narrow Via dei Bentaccordi (whose curves follow the plan of the old Roman arena) are wrapped in almost total obscurity, we can have no exact knowledge of the symbolic meaning of stone in his inner life. We know only that he lost his mother at the age of six and his stepmother at twenty-two, and that he grew up in a family of males (father, uncle, and four brothers), subject to the inevitable rivalries and jealousies inherent in such a situation. These emotions were later to erupt in letters of alternating violence and affection. It may be that both the receptivity and the hostility of stone in Michelangelo's imagination, represented feelings originally provoked by members of his family. Such feelings were not lessened by the stupidity and cupidity the family usually betrayed. Michelangelo's perpetually impoverished father, Lodovico Buonarroti, fancied himself a Florentine gentleman and considered art beneath the family's social status, precarious though that was. However, after vainly punishing the boy for drawing in school, he gave in and apprenticed him not to a sculptor but to a painter, the conservative and highly successful

Opposite page:
8. Corner of Vestibule
Laurentian Library. 1533
San Lorenzo, Florence

21

9. Drawing for bronze David and for arm of marble David. 1501–2
Ink, 10⅜ × 7⅜". The Louvre, Paris

Domenico del Ghirlandaio, leader of the most active shop in Florence. Michelangelo was thirteen by then—which was rather elderly for an apprentice in those amazing days—and he must have known what he was about, as he drew a small salary rather than having to pay for instruction. In addition to learning the techniques of painting, he certainly learned a great deal about drawing in the studio of this meticulous draughtsman, and also about sculpture and ornament. The backgrounds of Ghirlandaio's frescoes and panel paintings are full of beautifully executed ornamental detail, imitating carving in stone.

After only about a year, Michelangelo was able to get out of his three-year contract in 1489 and move into an exalted society—that of the Medici themselves, uncrowned rulers of Florence. Across the street from the monastery of San Marco, which had been rebuilt half a century before by their munificence, were the Medici gardens, which were replaced in the later six-teenth century by the Casino Mediceo, now occupied by the Court of Appeals. Under a loggia and in the garden walks were magnificent works of sculpture, including the Medici collection of Greek and Roman (mostly Roman) statues, reliefs, and fragments. Here a "free art school" flourished under the guidance of the sculptor Bertoldo di Giovanni, a pupil of the great master Donatello who had died more than twenty years before. This too seems paradoxical, as Bertoldo was a specialist in bronze, which Michelangelo always claimed was not his profession. In fact, of all the great bronze commissions he undertook, only two, a bronze *David* (see pen sketch, fig. 9) and the colossal statue of Julius II for Bologna, were ever executed, and these have disap-peared. The three works we know from that time, the *Mask of a Faun*, now lost, the *Madonna of the Stairs* (colorplate 1; fig. 39), and the *Battle of Lapiths and Centaurs* (colorplate 2; figs. 40–47), are all in marble.

Such control of marble and tools could never have been learned from Bertoldo. The boy's real teachers were sculptors long since dead, such as Donatello himself and Antonio Rossellino, whose exquisite, supple surfaces he imitated with great care in his early works. He can have had little interest in the misty, blurred atmospheric renderings of Desiderio, or the complex open profiles—all legs and arms—of Antonio del Pollaiuolo and Andrea del Verrocchio. These were based on clay modeling, and Michelangelo always maintained in his sculpture the com-pactness of the original block. Until his last, sedentary years, Michelangelo was often on the move, traveling about Italy, and was thus able to see and study works of sculpture in many places. It must have been fairly easy to get around the country, in spite of customs barriers at the frontiers between the various Italian principalities and republics. Before he was twenty-five Michelangelo had visited Bologna, Rome, and Carrara, and in between these centers, so important for his work, he must of necessity have stopped in Pisa, Pistoia, Siena, and Orvieto. In 1494 he even fled to Venice.

In city after city he must have expanded his knowledge of sculpture: from the works of Jacopo della Quercia (fig. 11) and of many of the great sculptors of the thirteenth and fourteenth centuries, especially Nicola Pisano and his son Giovanni (fig. 12), and Lorenzo Maitani (fig. 13). In Florence, and later in Rome, he saw many a work of classical sculpture that we know,

10. ANTONIO FEDERIGHI
Holy Water Font
1462–63. Marble
Cathedral, Siena

11. JACOPO DELLA QUERCIA
St. Petronius,
from lunette over central portal of façade
1425–38. Marble, height 85″
San Petronio, Bologna

12. GIOVANNI PISANO
Sibyl, from pulpit
1301. Marble, height 24⅜″
Sant' Andrea, Pistoia

13. LORENZO MAITANI
Damned Soul
Detail: *Last Judgment* relief on façade
c. 1310. Marble
Cathedral, Orvieto

14. APOLLONIUS,
SON OF NESTOR
Belvedere Torso. C. 150 B.C.
Marble, height 62⅝"
Vatican Museum, Rome

and many now lost to us. In each case what interested him was the same: the pose of the human figure, the intensity and power of its movement, and the quality of its flesh. The mighty fragment of Hellenistic sculpture known as the *Belvedere Torso* (fig. 14) was Michelangelo's favorite work of ancient art. In the tonus of the muscles and particularly in the tension of the diaphragm, he could find, translated into physical terms, that inner warfare, that battle in the soul which was his deepest concern. For, according to his writings, the "beautiful and mortal veil" of human flesh clothed the movement of the spirit but reflected the divine will.

Aside from bringing him into contact with ancient art and letters, the life of the Medici circle was important to Michelangelo in many ways, for he lived in the Medici Palace on the Via Larga (the present Via Cavour). The table of Lorenzo the Magnificent was remarkably informal, and suffered from no stratification. Whoever came in first sat next to Lorenzo, and so on down the line, until all the empty places were filled. Michelangelo sometimes found himself sitting above Lorenzo's sons: Piero the Unlucky (who was to succeed Lorenzo briefly); Giuliano, later to become the Duke of Nemours and to be the subject, much idealized, of one of Michelangelo's greatest statues (colorplate 11; figs. 169–77); and Giovanni, who became Pope under the name of Leo X. The adolescent artist at this time must also have acquired some knowledge of ancient literature and philosophy, at least in translation, from the humanists who frequented what was in effect a princely court. Also, and this point is seldom mentioned, he must have cemented the personal relationships which were the basis of his first great commissions in Florence. It is noteworthy that the *St. Matthew* and its companion Apostles—never executed—and the *David*, and the *Doni* and *Taddei Madonnas* were all ordered by the powerful Arte della Lana (guild of wool manufacturers) and its members; and that the *Bruges Madonna*, whose original patron remains unknown, was bought by a Flemish wool merchant. One wonders whether these personages dealt at the Medici Bank, whose central office was situated in the palace, and only a block away from the Cathedral for which the *St. Matthew* and the *David* were designed.

The death of Lorenzo in 1492 brought this happy situation to an end, and Michelangelo went back to his father's house in the family neighborhood of Santa Croce, although he returned to the Medici Palace for a while. But Piero de' Medici was not up to Lorenzo's statesmanship or taste. He treasured Michelangelo—just as he treasured his Spanish servant who could outrun a horse—and commissioned him to do a colossus in snow. This was the period of the Santo Spirito *Crucifix* (figs. 48–54) and of the young man's study of anatomy from corpses furnished him by the prior of Santo Spirito. This study can scarcely have been scientific. Only one or two drawings and no notes have survived. Michelangelo's anatomy is seldom completely reliable: what makes his figures so overpowering is his instinctive feeling for what the human body can do rather than a medical knowledge of its exact structure. During this time a larger-than-lifesize block of marble was bought by the young artist for a statue of Hercules, which has since disappeared. This seems to have been his first work of major dimensions, and it must have given him a grand opportunity to display his new understanding of the body.

After the Bolognese interlude (figs. 55–64), in which the young man found his own identity in spite of the powerful shadow of Jacopo della Quercia, he returned briefly to Florence. Again, the work he did during these months, chiefly the *St. John the Baptist* and the *Sleeping Cupid*, is now lost to us. There is no telling what either was like, but the *Cupid* was of such quality that it was passed off in Rome as a genuine work of ancient art. In that run-down, ruinous, and murderous city, under the rule of the infamous Borgia family whose chief sat on the papal throne as Alexander VI, Michelangelo arrived in 1496. This was the first of his infinite number of trips to the city where, eventually, he was to pass the last thirty years of his life. Travel in the Renaissance was much easier and more rapid than we imagine: post horses would take a traveler from Florence to Rome in two days, and over the Apennines to Venice in three. In Rome, the imperial and papal city, Michelangelo's art expanded rapidly. The *Bacchus* (colorplate 3; figs. 65–73) and the *Pietà* (colorplate 4; figs. 74–80) belong to this time; he studied works of ancient sculpture as fast as they were retrieved from the earth, as well as acquiring the beginnings of his immense knowledge of Roman architecture. In spite of contentions that Michelangelo "was converted" late in life, his letters at this time already abound in references to divine protection and requests for prayers. Sincere faith was not favored at the court of a Pope who, it is sometimes claimed, entertained seriously the intention to convert the papacy into a hereditary monarchy. The young artist wrote a bitter sonnet which may date from these years; especially since in it he refers to "the Moor" (the nickname of Alexander VI):

> *Here they make helmets and swords from chalices,*
> *And the blood of Christ is sold by handfuls,*
> *And Cross and thorns are lances and shields,*
> *And even Christ's patience fails.*

Christian feeling of piercing intensity runs through the sad melodies of the *Rome Pietà,* and no wonder. The child Michelangelo had been brought up almost in the shadow of Santa Croce, citadel of Franciscan piety, and in the years just before his departure for Rome he had been so impressed by the great Dominican preacher Savonarola that, according to Condivi, even in old age the great master never forgot the sound of Savonarola's voice.

But the first tremendous burst of power on the part of Michelangelo was touched off by the commission for the marble *David,* the *St. Matthew,* the marble and tempera *Madonnas,* and the colossal fresco of the *Battle of Cascina.* In these works both religious poetry and an expanding vision of the power and beauty of the human frame were inspired by the critical situation the newly restored Florentine Republic had to face. Michelangelo's imagery was quickly recognized by the Florentine leaders as a major spiritual force in their gallant, but alas hopeless, attempt to reconstruct the power and unity of the state, threatened by a host of enemies from without and within. In this atmosphere of urgency and heroic endeavor, Michelangelo's new race of titans was born—and, it should not be forgotten, his grave and sweet Madonnas acquired their special protective meaning. Lingering traces of fifteenth-century idiosyncracies of line and surface are rapidly thrown off. The sculptor emerges as a truly universal genius, able under divine guidance to communicate the revived message of human freedom and dignity, through the rich, ancient vocabulary of powerful human forms in action. And even this repertory is salted by the pungent observation of local types and individual peculiarities which always prevents Michelangelo's art from falling into the deadly trap of false idealism that swallowed so much sixteenth-century sculpture. His Madonnas are not Greek goddesses, but Tuscan women; his knobby *David* is no Apollo, but a tough young Florentine.

This brief and fecund period, from 1500 to 1505, during which the young artist rivaled his older compatriot Leonardo da Vinci and inspired the younger outsider Raphael of Urbino, was doomed by the same forces that eventually overwhelmed Piero Soderini's Second Republic. In 1503, after the twenty-six-day pontificate of Pius III, the papal throne fell into the waiting hands of Cardinal Giuliano della Rovere, by methods that will not bear close inspection. Nonetheless this powerful individual, nephew of Pope Sixtus IV who had built the Sistine Chapel and caused it to be decorated by the most important painters of the 1480s, was, as Pope Julius II, to revolutionize Rome, the papacy, and Italy. First he attempted to bring law and order into a city still suffering the effects of Borgia rule, then to reform the papal court, then to reconquer the border towns which had revolted from papal government or had been captured by neighboring Italian states. His ten-year rule saw the emergence of the papacy as a contender for power on the European stage, achieving eventually the expulsion of the French invaders from northern Italy and the beginning of the Lateran Council, aimed at the "reform of the Church in head and members." What might have been accomplished, had this military and political genius and religious enthusiast been succeeded by a pontiff of comparable endowments, is anybody's guess. Perhaps Martin Luther would have found less to complain about; and perhaps the Spanish in the South would have gone the way of the French.

At any rate, dead or alive, the mighty Ligurian was to dominate Michelangelo's life in one way or another from the moment the thirty-year-old sculptor was called to Rome in 1505 to

15. GIACOMO ROCCHETTI. *Copy of Michelangelo's design for Tomb of Julius II*
c. 1505. Ink, 20⅝ × 13⅜". State Museums, Berlin

design the Pope's tomb on an unprecedented scale until the day forty years later when the artist, now seventy, was at last able to lower the curtain on what his biographer Condivi calls "the tragedy of the Tomb."

The Rome of Julius II was a strenuous place. What with the destruction of so much of Old St. Peter's to build the new, and the driving of the great avenue that is still called the Via Giulia through the thickly populated quarter along the Tiber, it was noisy to boot, and filled with clouds of dust from the demolition and the new construction. None of this had started, of course, when Michelangelo arrived, but the years during which he was at work on the

27

16. *Active Life,* drawing for 1505 project,
Tomb of Julius II. Ink and bistre, 16½ × 11″
British Museum, London

17. *St. Paul,* drawing for 1505 project,
Tomb of Julius II. Ink, 15⅜ × 10¼″
Musée Condé, Chantilly

Sistine Chapel were those of the alternating defeats and triumphs of the warrior Pope, and of the growth of his vast building projects under the direction of his favorite architect—and Michelangelo's sworn enemy (or so we are told)—Bramante. Inspired by the Pope's fiery vision of a heroic Italy united under the leadership of a rededicated papacy, Michelangelo, Bramante, and Raphael in separate ways worked out a style converting the elements of the Florentine High Renaissance into a majestic unity, at once dynamic and harmonious. As in its Florentine phase, the new style in Rome was short-lived, but its achievements are reckoned high on the list of human triumphs, vying in power and beauty with classic Greece and Gothic France.

No one really knows why the first project for the great Tomb was abandoned (figs. 15–17; see page 126). In any event, Michelangelo left Rome for Florence in April, 1506, with the declared intention of never working for that Pope again. By November Julius had become a power to be reckoned with very seriously indeed. In a stunning political and military upset, he had reacquired Perugia without striking a blow, outflanked the Florentine Republic to the east (utilizing the tunnel of the ancient Roman emperor Vespasian to negotiate the Marchigian pass into northern Italy), and entered Bologna in triumph, in a chariot with a purple canopy. From this vantage point he could summon the recalcitrant sculptor with a new authority, and did so. Piero Soderini, Gonfaloniere (flagbearer) of Florence for life, clearly had no wish to risk papal displeasure, and sent Michelangelo to Bologna. On November 29 he met the Pope, to use his own phrase, "with a rope around his neck," and was pardoned.

There was no more talk of the Tomb, however. Julius wanted Michelangelo to make a colossal bronze statue of himself, to be placed over the doorway of San Petronio, the principal church of the city, as a sign of papal triumph. Complaining that bronze was "not his profession," the sculptor set to work, writing to his family to pray for him. He needed their prayers. Living conditions were desperate, the city was overcrowded, the wine bad, and as the year 1507 ripened, the heat became unbearable. There was trouble with the assistants, too: one had to be dismissed, and another left with him. In January the Pope visited Michelangelo's studio behind San Petronio, and was apparently well satisfied with the portrait. By April the statue was finished in wax. An expert in metalwork had to be summoned, and this was none other than Master Bernardino, armorer of the Florentine Republic. In July the casting began, but half the metal remained in the kiln, and the statue was complete only up to the waist. The whole kiln had to be dismantled to extract the bronze, and then rebuilt. A few days later the statue was recast, this time successfully. The laborious job of finishing and chasing the work lasted until March of the following year, when Michelangelo was finally able to leave for Florence—he hoped for good.

We have no idea what the statue really looked like. Its life was short. In May, 1511, the Bolognese threw off the papal yoke temporarily, and in December, at the order of the Bentivoglio family, the colossal statue was destroyed by dint of opening a hole in the wall of San Petronio and pushing it off from behind, to be smashed on the stones below. The bronze fragments were sent to the Pope's arch-enemy, Alfonso d'Este, to be melted down for cannon to fire at the papal troops. The lost statue may possibly have borne some relation to Michelangelo's ideas for the statues on the second level of the 1505 version of the Tomb (figs. 16, 17; see page 119), and perhaps to the *Moses*, started by Michelangelo only two years after the destruction of the bronze. We can certainly imagine the figure as dramatic and intense, carrying a book and keys, and blessing with extended hand. Of course the statue was beardless, since the Pope did not grow his famous beard until the winter of 1510–11. The destruction of this colossal work must be reckoned as one of the major artistic losses of the Renaissance. The bronze *David*, which the master worked on intermittently from 1502 to 1508 and finally left for a pupil to complete, would also have given us an insight into his attitude toward bronze, but it too has disappeared (fig. 9).

The four and a half years from April, 1508, to October, 1512, during which the great sculptor was occupied entirely by the supposedly unwelcome task of painting in fresco the ceiling of the Sistine Chapel, were by no means lost to sculpture. For at last he had a chance to try out his ideas on the interrelation of architecture (simulated in this case) and the figurative arts (fig. 18). This opportunity certainly had some bearing on later projects for the Tomb of Julius II and the Medici Chapel. And the very process of painting on such a grand scale and at such speed brought about an essential change in his attitude toward form. The linear precision of the early sculpture was hardly the best introduction to pictorial art. Of necessity such exact formal definition relaxed as the great undertaking proceeded. The forms outgrew their frames, the surfaces became larger and more easily rendered. Although Michelangelo never was to be a painter's painter, nor even a painter's sculptor, when he returned to sculpture in 1513, after Julius' death, the Louvre *Slaves* (colorplates 8, 9; figs. 134–43) and the *Moses* (colorplate 10; figs. 144–52) certainly show the effects of the immense pictorial experience, in their expanded form and richer play of surface.

Despite the sculptor's attempts to speed up the work on the Tomb of Julius II by making models (figs. 1–6) to enable assistants at least to block in the statues, the project was interrupted a second time in 1516 under circumstances still far from clear (figs. 19, 133). Probably Michelangelo really wanted to undertake the façade of San Lorenzo, although he protested later that he had been forced to do it against his will. It would have been a marvelous thing, and a triumph for the great artist in the Florence he loved so deeply. It must be remembered that

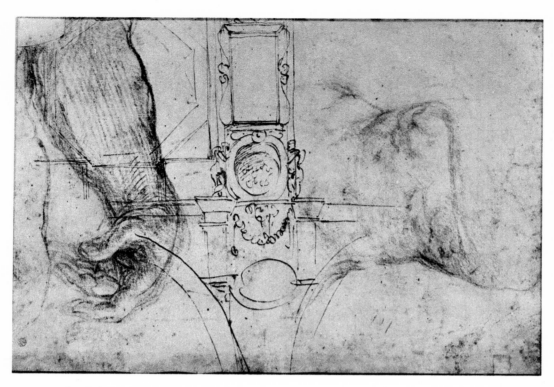

18. *Sketch for Sistine Ceiling.* 1508–10
Ink and black chalk, 9⅞ × 14⅛″. Detroit Institute of Arts

among the major churches of Florence at this time, only San Miniato, Santa Trinita, and Santa Maria Novella had complete façades. Just how the façades of San Marco and the Santissima Annunziata then looked is not known, but that of the cathedral was completed only to the level just above the portals (dismantled later in the sixteenth century), and the façades of San Lorenzo, Santo Spirito, the Carmine, and Santa Croce had not even been started. The only Renaissance work among them was the façade of Santa Maria Novella, which had had to accommodate Renaissance ideas to a Gothic first story. The masterpieces of the first generation of Renaissance sculptors, Donatello, Ghiberti, and Nanni di Banco, all had to be fitted into Gothic niches, or into Renaissance niches inserted in Gothic buildings. Only Giuliano da Sangallo had tried to imagine a Renaissance façade with Renaissance sculpture, and that in connection with the same project for San Lorenzo.

Against this background one must set Michelangelo's great idea—a towering structure composed of architecture, colossal statues in marble and bronze, and reliefs in bronze, springing complete from the same creative intelligence. He called it "a mirror of architecture and sculpture for all of Italy," and this it would most certainly have been. The work would also have taken him the rest of his life. For there were to have been twelve heroic standing statues in marble, six seated ones in bronze, six lifesize figures in high relief, and eleven large and four small reliefs in bronze, as well as the architecture itself, every detail of which was designed by Michelangelo, quarried under his supervision, and would have been carved in his workshop. By January, 1518, a contract became necessary; it provided for the completion of the whole work in the unrealistic span of eight years. Let the visitor to Florence, contemplating the blank mass of masonry that serves San Lorenzo for a façade, picture how Michelangelo's two-story dream would have looked—its lofty columns, its grand pediment and doubtless dramatically posed and sharply projecting statues in marble and bronze, and its rich bronze reliefs, all catching the morning light (San Lorenzo, like St. Peter's in Rome, is not oriented; the façade is at the east end). No richer or grander project could be imagined, and none that

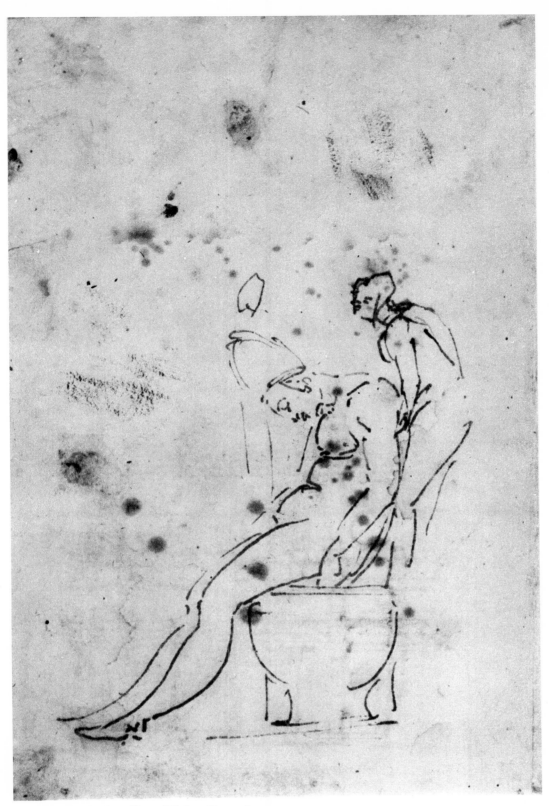

19. Sketch for Effigy of Julius II. 1516–17
Ink, 8⅝ × 5⅝″. Casa Buonarroti, Florence

would have enabled the master to leave so powerful an imprint upon the very center of his beloved city.

Of the whole vast design nothing remains, save for the foundations, a wooden model (without the wax sculptures made for it), and a few sketches. In another volume the author will make the first attempt to reconstruct the iconography of the façade, and to connect some existing drawings for unknown sculpture with its ideas. Most of the years between 1516 and

1520 were spent at Carrara, and later at Seravezza and Pietrasanta, where he had to open new quarries and build a new road in order that the marble might come from territory controlled by Florence. Then, probably due to the new project for the Medici Chapel, proposed in June, 1519, and actually commenced on November 4 of that year, work on the façade was called off. Suddenly in March, 1520, after the Medici Chapel had been under way for more than four months, the contract for the façade was annulled and all the marbles abandoned. Small wonder that the artist claimed he had suffered "great damage and humiliation." Men have committed suicide for less. Looked at from the present point in time, the tragedy of the façade seems worse than that of the Tomb, of which at least we possess nine statues and a finished monument of sorts.

Michelangelo was not the only man in Florence to suffer on such a scale under the Medici tyranny, which maintained the outward semblance of the Republic, but was kept under stern control from the Vatican, first by the Pope's brother Giuliano de' Medici, duke of Nemours, and even before his death in 1516 by his nephew Lorenzo, Duke of Urbino, who actually ruled as Captain General after 1515. When Lorenzo died, in 1519, Cardinal Giulio de' Medici, Pope Leo X's first cousin, later to be Pope himself under the name of Clement VII, governed the state. No one had as yet dared assume the title of Duke of Florence, but the citizens were under no illusions. The dreadful Sack of Prato in 1512, just before the triumphal return of the Medici, had given them an idea of what they might expect if they rebelled. As Pope, Leo X visited Florence in splendor in 1515, and by then it was abundantly clear that the cradle of European liberty and of the Renaissance was now merely a province of papal Rome. Liberty in the Renaissance sense was gone, and intellectual and commercial activity stagnant. The alliance of the papacy and Medici political power seemed impregnable.

Under these conditions it is no wonder that a new style was growing up, or rather bursting out, in Florence, under the gifted and disoriented artists of a new generation, especially the painters Pontormo and Rosso Fiorentino, both of whom took many of their cues from Michelangelo. With no ideals left to believe in save power—and that the uncertain authority of a worldly and vacillating Pope, totally unequal to the challenge from Martin Luther and opposed to any liberty for Florence—the grand harmonies of the High Renaissance must have seemed to such artists not only impossible but even ludicrous. The new style of this so-called Mannerist crisis (and the term Mannerism, however inappropriate, is probably here to stay) took shape around the towering figure of the embittered and disillusioned sculptor. Now forty-five, he complained of feeling old—a complaint we will read in his letters for the next forty-four years—and of lacking energy or strength to work. Since November, 1519, he had been absorbed with the construction and decoration of the funerary chapel for the entombment of the recently deceased members of the Medici family (figs. 20, 21; see page 168) at San Lorenzo, whose grim and featureless front must have tormented Michelangelo every time he passed it.

This project dragged along for the next fourteen years, interrupted by the third expulsion of the Medici from Florence in 1527. Under the Third Republic Michelangelo was able for a while to return to the Tomb of Julius II (see page 250); he was then himself caught up in the death struggle of Florentine liberty, as governor of the Florentine fortifications. His designs for these, still preserved, show an astonishing combination of military inventiveness and artistic beauty; characteristically enough, they were not executed. In order to protect his by now considerable fortune from requisition by the government of the Republic to aid in the financing of its defense, Michelangelo suddenly fled Florence in September, 1529, "in the greatest disorder," according to a contemporary account, and for a second time took refuge in Venice. For a while he wished to go to France, but King Francis I's offer of a house and a pension arrived in Florence too late, so we are spared a repetition of the useless end of Leonardo da Vinci. After repeated insistence on the part of the Republican leaders, Michelangelo returned to his home in November, underwent a symbolic punishment, and again took up his doomed work on the fortifications. The siege soon began; in August of the following year Florence was betrayed to the Medici and the liberties of the Republic were at an end.

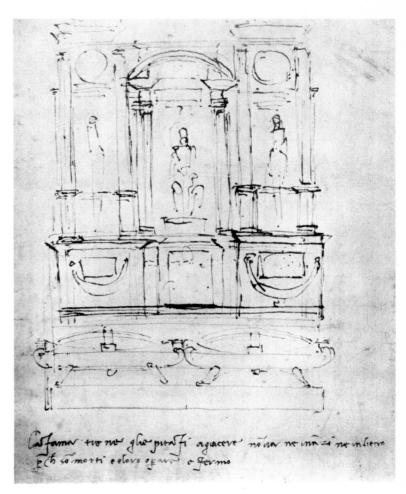

20. *Sketch for Medici Tombs.* 1520–21
Black chalk, 11⅝ × 8½"
British Museum, London

21. *Sketch for Medici Tombs.* 1520–21
Ink, 8½ × 6⅝"
British Museum, London

Michelangelo's defense of the Republic brought down on him the wrath of the Medici governor of the defeated city, Baccio Valori, who actually arranged for the assassination of the great artist. At this moment the long-suffering Giovan Battista Figiovanni, canon of San Lorenzo, who had every reason to complain of Michelangelo's behavior during the construction of the Medici Chapel, came to his rescue and hid him, thus preserving not only Michelangelo's life but all his yet unborn works. Soon the Pope let it be known that he would pardon Michelangelo, but he did not reappear. By November, however, Michelangelo had accepted the Pope's offer of protection, and, however unwillingly, resumed work on the Medici Chapel. Four years later, after the death of Clement VII, the artist decided he need never again return while Florence was under Medici control, and this project was left incomplete. One can hardly conceive of his producing work for the Chapel of the conviction and harmony of the Sistine Ceiling and the first two projects for the Tomb of Julius II—and he did not. For all its formal beauty and spiritual intensity, the Medici Chapel is essentially tragic, and is generally felt to be so. Only the wonderful *Medici Madonna* promises the release to have been provided by the never-executed frescoes. These must have included a *Resurrection*, to which the Chapel was dedicated (figs. 22, 23). Michelangelo expressed his opinion of his Medici patrons in a devastating sonnet, lumping together Clement VII, sarcastically characterized as "major Medic of our ills," and Cardinal Ippolito among "the others who deny Christ." In a masterpiece of comic writing, he turned down the Pope's absurd suggestion for a colossus forty cubits high to be erected in the Piazza San Lorenzo behind the Medici Palace.

22. *Study for a Resurrection.* 1513–16
Black chalk, 16 × 10⅝″. British Museum, London

23. *Study for a Resurrection*, for Medici Chapel. 1520–25(?)
Black chalk, 9½ × 13⅝″. Royal Library, Windsor Castle

Still, he had to work for these people and to glorify them. His position was humiliating enough after the fiasco of the San Lorenzo façade, but it became intolerable after the defeat of the Republic. In the tortured poses, desperate hesitations, struggling architectural elements, and involved linear convolutions of the Chapel, not to speak of the closely allied treatment of the Laurentian Library (which he also executed at San Lorenzo for the Medici Pope), the relation of the new style to the artist's situation and to the prevailing mood of Florence becomes clear. Yet nowhere in these works does the great master's superb masculinity ever countenance a retreat into a world of such reverie as that inhabited by Pontormo, or into the vicious fantasies of Rosso. The Republic had surrendered, but not the sculptor. The fierce intensity and poignant grief, not only in the expressions but in the lines and shapes of the works from this strange period (fig. 26), render it as moving as are the unrecapturable harmonies of a happier time in the Rome of Julius II.

After the Medici Chapel Michelangelo produced only five works of sculpture—two statues for the Tomb of Julius II (figs. 285–90), the *Brutus* (figs. 291–93), and two *Pietàs* (figs. 35, 294–314)—in thirty years of residence in Rome. The man who had so proudly signed his contracts for works of painting as "*Michelangelo scultore*" now repeatedly warned his nephew, Lionardo Buonarroti, not to put the word "sculptor" on the outside of letters, but to address him as "Michelangelo Buonarroti"—so he was known in Rome. True, for the first sixteen years the artist's working time had been chiefly absorbed by the huge pictorial commissions assigned to him by Pope Paul III, the *Last Judgment* and the Pauline Chapel. But there are undoubtedly other reasons for his apparent renunciation of his craft.

One reason may have been his new acceptance into one of the highest Roman social groups, the constellation of prelates and *literati* centering around Vittoria Colonna, member of a princely Roman family and widowed Marchioness of Pescara. Frequenting such lofty circles, the aging artist may indeed have felt it necessary to emphasize that he had never been a sculptor or a painter "like those who keep shops." This, of course, was literally true. You could not have entered Michelangelo's establishment and ordered a portrait, a Madonna, or a crucifix as you could have from, let us say, Pollaiuolo or Verrocchio. But Michelangelo went further, insisting that his poor old brother Sigismondo quit farming and move back to Florence, because he was ashamed to have it known he had a brother behind the plow. He even gave away the Florentine cubit he had asked his nephew, Lionardo, to send him, because on its arrival he found it was made of brass, like one that a mason or a carpenter might use. Only during these last years did Michelangelo rediscover the legendary origins of his family in the noble house of the Counts of Canossa.

But there is a deeper reason, easily understood but, like so many important things, not so easily defined. After the onset of his intense passion for Tommaso Cavalieri, whose physical beauty he extolled in many a sonnet and letter, Michelangelo never again carved an ideal male nude, and only two male nudes of any sort, both representing Christ—slender, emaciated, detached from any standards of physical perfection or muscular prowess. His vast pictorial compositions overflow with nudes, but all are rugged, thick-waisted, and barrel-chested; their faces alone are ideally beautiful. The beautiful nudes are relegated to a private sphere: the drawings of the legends of Ganymede and Phaeton, of the allegory of Human Life, of the archers shooting at a terminus, of the torment of Tityos—all of these works were intended for Cavalieri himself.

The role of three-dimensional form in Michelangelo's imagination is now assumed by stone architecture, on a colossal scale. During these years Michelangelo was so fragile and so racked by pain that it was difficult enough for him to climb the stairs in his own dwelling, much less visit the building sites, especially those which required him to cross Rome on horseback. Much of the work had to be supervised by means of drawings, reports, messages, and written instructions. Yet in his seventies and eighties Michelangelo designed the majestic rebuilding of the Capitoline Hill and its palaces (towering above his home in the Macello dei Corvi) as a center for Roman *imperium*, the completion of the Palazzo Farnese in a more powerful new style, the revamping of the great hall of the Baths of Diocletian to make the

24. GIOVANNANGELO MONTORSOLI. *St. Cosmas*
1533–34. Marble, height 7′ ½″
Medici Chapel, San Lorenzo, Florence

25. RAFFAELLO DA MONTELUPO. *St. Damian*
1533–34. Marble, height 7′ 4″
Medici Chapel, San Lorenzo, Florence

grand Renaissance church of Santa Maria degli Angeli, and the construction of the fierce Porta Pia as a gateway to the Roman walls. He made magnificent designs for the national church of the Florentines in Rome, San Giovanni dei Fiorentini, and a new plan for the Gesù, mother church of the militant Jesuit order. Although these plans were never executed, the ideas behind them had a formative influence on European architecture for two centuries. And finally, in an immense expansion of his formal and spiritual imagination, he redesigned St. Peter's itself, and carried out, before his death, much of the new building in shapes whose mighty simplicity and muscular power embody all the beauty and grandeur with which he once invested the human body. On this superhuman scale, the colossal statues of the twelve Apostles he imagined for the twelve columnar buttresses of the great dome would have been merely auxiliary elements in the cosmic composition. At last he had created his colossus looking out to sea. In the intensity of his desire to complete St. Peter's he refused all entreaties to return to his beloved Florence. Is it mere imagination to see in the shape of this dome, so different from all preceding domes, the suggestion of a maternal breast? One can also understand how, when he was rebuilding St. Peter's, hemmed in by hills, he was reminded of his birthplace Caprese, ringed by stone.

In Vittoria Colonna's circle, it has been shown that justification by faith was one of the chief topics of conversation and thought. Her convictions and those of her associates, with

36

their suggestion of Lutheranism, skirted perilously the pit of heresy, and one unfortunate cleric was pushed over the edge. Yet the burning faith this group fostered and maintained, closely allied to that of the Italian and Spanish mystics, was one of the prime elements in the Counter Reformation, and was to lead toward the great Catholic triumphs of the seventeenth century. This faith fills the last religious drawings of Michelangelo with their unquenchable desire for divine love (fig. 35)—and the last sculptures as well, from the monastic austerity of the *Active Life* and the *Contemplative Life* (figs. 285–90) to the oceanic intensity of the *Florence Pietà* (Frontispiece; figs. 294–304) and the ultimate release of the *Milan Pietà* (colorplate 17; figs. 305–14). In these last works in stone Michelangelo's warfare is accomplished. Sinking into the grave, he is released from it. The artist who lamented that he was "so close to death, and yet so far from God," triumphs over the one and is reabsorbed into the Other.

26. The Brazen Serpent, possibly for Medici Chapel
1520–25(?). Red chalk, 9⅝ × 13¼". Ashmolean Museum, Oxford

27

28

29

Sculptures by PUPILS OF MICHELANGELO: Tomb of Julius II
San Pietro in Vincoli, Rome. *27. Sibyl.* c. 1542. Marble, height c. 69″
28. *Madonna and Child.* c. 1537–42. Marble, height c. 66″
29. *Prophet.* c. 1542. Marble, height c. 69″
30. *Effigy of the Pope.* c. 1532–42. Marble, length of sarcophagus c. 72″

30

31

32

31–34. JACOPO DEL DUCA. *Termini*. Tomb of Julius II. c. 1542
Marble, height 35″. San Pietro in Vincoli, Rome

33

34

35. Studies for a Pietà. 1550–55(?)
Black chalk, 4¼ × 11″. Ashmolean Museum, Oxford

THE COMPLETE SCULPTURE

I. THE MADONNA OF THE STAIRS

Marble; 21¾×15¾″
1489-92
Casa Buonarroti, Florence

This tiny Madonna, the only work in low relief known to have been carved by Michelangelo, is also probably the earliest of his sculptures that survives. According to the account by Giorgio Vasari, Michelangelo made the relief during the years when he was living in the Medici Palace and working in the Medici gardens. He was therefore between fourteen and seventeen years of age when he conceived and executed this little masterpiece. Apparently the relief has never left Florence. After the artist's death, it became the property of his nephew, Lionardo Buonarroti, who gave it to Cosimo I de' Medici, grand duke of Tuscany; Cosimo II, however, returned the relief to Michelangelo the Younger, Lionardo's son, in 1617, and it has been in the Casa Buonarroti ever since. The marble surface is in almost perfect condition, but the border has been broken at the upper left and right corners.

36

colorplate 1

37

The Virgin is seated in absolute profile on a simple cube of stone, her wide-eyed gaze directed straight forward as she draws her mantle gently around her sleeping Child, whose face is pressed against her uncovered breast, at which He has apparently been taking nourishment. A stairway, consisting of five steps and an unmolded stair rail, almost fills the background to the left of the Virgin. Two children appear at the top of the steps, a third leans over the balustrade, and a fourth is behind the Virgin to the right; all are occupied in stretching out an enormous cloth. Modern scholars agree that this is no mere depiction of an intimate scene of family life. The stair rail suggests the beams of the Cross, the flattened steps remind us of the ladder, the cloth resembles a shroud. It has been shown that the sleeping Christ Child, in Italian representations of the Madonna and Child, invariably foretells the death of the adult Christ. The four children here recall the number of the Gospels; the five steps, the mysteries of the rosary. The background scene thus suggests the reason for the prophetic solemnity of the Virgin's gaze. Detached from the world around her, Mary contemplates, as in a vision, the future sacrifice of her Son.

The *Virgo lactans* (the Madonna nursing her Child) was a well-known subject during the later Middle Ages and the Renaissance, especially in Tuscany. Moreover, innumerable examples of Madonna images were said to have favored their worshipers with drops of milk. The milk of the Virgin, nourishing the body of Christ, was held to symbolize the true doctrine of the Church, which brings forth the body of Christ in the Eucharist. Michelangelo's gracious Madonna, seated on an altarlike block, illustrates beautifully St. Augustine's characterization of the Virgin as "nurse of God and of our life." There may also have been a second, more personal, level of symbolism, for Michelangelo, as we have seen, attached great importance to the fact that he had been nursed by a stonecutter's wife in Settignano.

The balanced serenity of Mary's pose and the classic beauty of her face have frequently suggested the influence of Greek sculpture, especially of grave stelae, and a rude copy of such a stele was actually in the Medici Palace. The extreme delicacy and refinement of the drapery surfaces was probably influenced by more elaborate and finished classical works in the Medici collection, now lost or dispersed. But there is nothing classical in the rigidity and tension of the Madonna's erect back, or in the passion latent in her face and exploding in the muscular back and twisted arm of the child. These factors, and the extremely low relief, justify Vasari's remark that in this work the adolescent sculptor wanted to "counterfeit the manner of Donatello." This is, in fact, as close as Michelangelo ever came to imitating the famous *rilievo schiacciato* ("flattened relief") of the great fifteenth-century sculptor, and even here he managed the imitation without adopting the optical effects for which Donatello had invented this peculiar form of relief, emulating methods of drawing and painting in order to suggest atmospheric values. These values meant little to Michelangelo, always obsessed with the pursuit of form, so that in those areas which are finished he produced a degree of surface polish seldom if ever found in the work of Donatello.

Michelangelo must actually have seen the even tinier *Madonna with Angels* by Donatello (*Shaw Madonna*, now in the Museum of Fine Arts, Boston), and have followed closely the head type and the exact movement of the veil from above the forehead in a graceful S-curve downward and over the shoulder. But he Hellenized the features and made the entire figure infinitely more imposing—gave her, as Vasari said, "more grace and design." It is interesting that he, unlike Donatello, did not allow the Virgin's halo to pass behind the narrow border,

38

but brought it out to overlap the frame. The Child has no halo at all, possibly because it would have interrupted grotesquely the exquisite interrelationship of head, mantle, and breast that the youthful artist was at such pains to define.

Although the feet of the Madonna are less than convincing, Michelangelo has worked out with great subtlety the interplay of the fingers and folds and the shimmering quality of the minutely rippled drapery surfaces, and has endowed them with a translucency not seen again in his work until the mystical drawings of his late maturity and old age. He has also contrasted most sensitively the firm perfection, even crispness, of the surfaces and contours of the Virgin's neck and breast with the swelling, muscular shapes of her infant Son's back, shoulder, and right arm.

In this earliest known work, probably done well before the boy's seventeenth birthday, his mysterious reluctance to finish a piece of sculpture is already abundantly evident. In fact only the drapery (and not all of that) and the anatomical passages have received their final polish. But marks of the toothed chisel are still visible on the Virgin's cheek, very clear on her left foot, and they are so pervasive throughout the background as to give it a deceptive suggestion of just those optical effects Michelangelo would surely have eliminated if the work had been carried to its final stage. The head of the Christ Child is still rough, and the figures, and above all the heads of the children in the background, are scarcely more than blocked in. The instinctive feeling for the rhythmic motion of the figure as the prime determinant of a work of art unites these earliest human beings made in Michelangelo's extreme youth to the last ghostly drawings made in his old age, when his hand could scarcely hold the pencil.

There are, in fact, quite a number of elements in this little work which foreshadow the great masterpieces to come. The muscular back of the Child and the peculiar twist of His arm and hand are spectacularly reused in the back of the *Giorno* in the Medici Chapel (color-plate 12; figs. 182, 184, 186). The Madonna is herself a prototype not only of certain of the Sibyls of the Sistine Ceiling but of the *Medici Madonna* (figs. 236–38). The shroud will reappear, held by nude youths in the background of the *Doni Madonna*, and sustaining the body of Christ in the London *Entombment*. In the form of continuous bands of cloth, it will uphold the ten medallions in the Sistine Ceiling. The broad, easy movement of the background figures foretells some of the grandest motives of the *Last Judgment*. Far more important than any configuration of individual elements, however, are the peculiar combination of grace and grandeur, infinite sweetness and passionate strength, and above all the sense of the majesty and universality of human destiny that mark this surprisingly small relief as a great work by Michelangelo. It is hard to imagine the feelings of those who first saw it. Could they have had any presentiment of what was to come?

2. THE BATTLE OF LAPITHS AND CENTAURS

Marble; 33¼ × 35⅝″
c. 1492
Casa Buonarroti, Florence

Like the *Madonna of the Stairs* (colorplate 1; figs. 36–39) this too is an adolescent work, done during Michelangelo's sojourn in the gardens and palace of Lorenzo the Magnificent. It never left Florence. Although the artist once entertained the idea of selling it to Federigo Gonzaga, duke of Mantua, the relief remained in the possession of the Buonarroti family. It certainly represents a more advanced stage in the boy-artist's development, with its astonishing command of the anatomical and dramatic resources of the human figure. Perhaps it was done for Lorenzo himself (the Gonzaga envoy negotiating unsuccessfully for its purchase said it was made "at the request of a great lord"). According to Michelangelo's friend and biographer

40

Condivi, the work was "finished" just before Lorenzo's death. It was, however, never truly finished in any portion; the demise of the artist's great patron may provide an explanation accounting for this.

The legend of the disastrous wedding feast of the Lapiths (at which their centaur guests, inflamed by wine, attempted to carry off the Lapith women, including the bride, thereby provoking a pitched battle with all available weapons) is preserved in several accounts. The principal narration is in the *Metamorphoses* of Ovid, known in detail to the learned circle in which Michelangelo moved. Even if he could not read Ovid in the original, at least one Italian translation existed. Both Condivi and Vasari, who are frequently mistaken in spite of their

colorplate 2

48

personal friendships with Michelangelo, believed that the relief represented a different legend, the battle of Hercules and the centaur Nessus over Deianira; this is unlikely, since Michelangelo's representation does not correspond to that story. In all probability the composition was inspired by Ovid's tale, probably suggested to the boy by the poet Angelo Poliziano.

Characteristically enough, however, Michelangelo selected only a few elements from the elaborate story, and none of the figures can be identified with certainty. Moreover, although the figures are for the most part violently struggling and suffering, and many brandish clubs and what may be rocks (or possibly would have been weapons if the work had been completed), none of the horrifying details on which Ovid gloats for page after page is represented. In this respect Michelangelo already reveals himself as at once deeply Christian and intensely human. Ovid's audiences must have enjoyed the crushed skulls, gouged-out eyes, and spattered brains in his endless narrative much as they relished the slaughters of the arena. His whole life long, Michelangelo never represented such things. Here not a weapon or missile connects with its intended victim, just as in the Sistine Ceiling David's sword does not touch Goliath, and in the *Last Judgment* not a single torment is depicted. For this artist, even at a juvenile stage, the physical damage inflicted by one person on another pales in comparison to the spiritual suffering of those on whose bodies we can discern no wounds.

In Michelangelo's relief all that remains of Ovid's account is a group of struggling figures, mostly male (only one is undoubtedly a woman). Most interesting of all, the centaurs themselves, so fascinating to Michelangelo's contemporaries Botticelli and Piero di Cosimo, are so humanized that one hardly notices the horse part. Of approximately twenty figures, only three can be identified as centaurs, and those with difficulty. The monstrous apparently interested the artist as little as did cruelty.

What he has done is to pit will against will in the form of physical interaction. The struggling, twisting, wrestling, hair-pulling figures are less suggestive of classical literary sources and classical representations of combat than of medieval depictions of the Last Judgment. In fact the figure holding his head at the lower left is drawn in part from one of the damned in the late-thirteenth-century *Last Judgment* by Nicola and Giovanni Pisano, on the pulpit of the Cathedral of Siena.

In the relief as Michelangelo has composed it there was no room for the setting and the accessories described in detail by Ovid. Not even the cavern would have appeared, for the sculptor has cut away all the stone that could have formed it. The tragic struggle, simplified and divested of accidentals, assumes even greater universality through having been placed in a timeless arena. Across the welter of interlacing figures, one human being and one lofty centaur gaze at each other in tragic and eternal hostility.

One wonders what the composition might have been like if Michelangelo had carried it to completion. Would he have smoothed the stone slab to form an inert background? What would have happened to the blank area above the row of heads? How would the ground have been treated? Perhaps these questions are as useless as they are unanswerable, for the vision of a muscular, heroic, passion-wracked humanity in an insoluble conflict, and springing from a formless, lapidary matrix, seems to us today an essential of Michelangelo's spiritual nature.

After the delicate, restrained, low relief of the *Madonna of the Stairs* the enormous projection of the *Battle of Lapiths and Centaurs* comes as a sharp surprise. This kind of relief has little or nothing to do with the high projection in the relief sculptures by Michelangelo's master at that time, the sculptor Bertoldo di Giovanni; modeling in wax for eventual casting in bronze, Bertoldo spaced his figures widely with a smooth background showing between them. Michelangelo's own ideas may even have changed as he worked. There are traces, especially at the right, of a continuous frame around the entire composition, which he seems to have cut away, possibly because it made the figures look as if they were enclosed in a box. Perhaps at the start he had not intended to undercut them so much. But with the frame removed, the figures in high relief assume the aspect of a group in the round. This appearance would have been further accentuated if the rest of the frame had been removed. As it is, the figures at the extreme left and two heads at the extreme right are entirely clear of the frame, which is thus

43

44

deprived of any value as an enclosure for a unified view of a single scene. The visual conception of relief has given way to a tactile one.

The photographs taken from angular views show that Michelangelo, at least in the principal foreground figures, had already arrived at a concept of freedom of action in space completely new to Renaissance sculpture, in fact unprecedented since ancient times. The supple figures already show an approach to the *contrapposto* (or twisting of the torso against the motion of the limbs) which was to be so characteristic of the artist's mature work. Although they have not received the final polish, and the marks of the toothed chisel are everywhere visible, the bodies palpitate with intense life. In spite of the lack of muscular definition, the inner rhythms of the figures are so strong and their surfaces so flexible that they are more than believable as real and active human beings. In the general composition and in his treatment of many individual figures Michelangelo has already arrived at conceptions he will repeat and amplify in later works, largely in painting—the cartoon for the *Battle of Cascina,* the background of the *Deluge* and the whole of the *Brazen Serpent* on the Sistine Ceiling, and major passages from the *Last Judgment*—as well as various whirlwind battle compositions which reappear again and again in his drawings throughout his life.

Especially beautiful are the standing figure at the left, identified by some as Theseus, and the central centaur, at whom Theseus seems about to hurl his missile. The centaur, towering above the others, lifts his arm above his head in a pose often to be repeated in the master's mature works. The mighty back of the fallen centaur below will also frequently reappear, notably in the *Giorno* of the Medici Chapel (colorplate 12; figs. 182, 184, 186). The Socrates-like head of the older man at the extreme left foreshadows the *Crepuscolo* of the Medici Chapel ◀ 42 (figs. 212, 213, 216). The medieval gesture of the seated Lapith in the lower left-hand corner,

45

46

holding his head, contrasts with the typically Michelangelesque, relaxed left arm with its hand hanging over the thigh.

Characteristically enough, the most finished portions are the torsos; the heads frequently remain mere masses of rough stone, and the feet are still enmired in the surrounding marble, from which rebellious humanity struggles vainly to escape.

47 ▶

3. CRUCIFIX

Wood, painted; height 53"
1492–93
Santo Spirito, Florence

Of all the vanished works by Michelangelo—the *Hercules*, the bronze *David*, the *St. John*, the *Sleeping Cupid*, the *Leda*, to name only a few—just one, the *River God* (figs. 252–55), had come to light until very recently. (The so-called Palestrina *Pietà*, now in the Accademia in Florence, is mentioned in no source or document and is far below the quality of Michelangelo's style.) In 1963 Dr. Margrit Lisner discovered the *Crucifix* that the young Michelangelo carved for the prior of the Augustinian monastery of Santo Spirito in Florence. As far as can be determined, this important early work never left the church for which Michelangelo made it; it had merely been displaced from the high altar, where its position was recorded in a drawing made at the end of the sixteenth century. In the eighteenth century it was mentioned as hanging in the sacristy, but "destined to be placed in the choir of the Church." There are no further records. When Dr. Lisner found the *Crucifix*, it was in a corridor leading to the kitchen.

If the account given by the artist himself to his friend Condivi two generations later is to be believed (and there seems no reason to doubt it), Michelangelo made the *Crucifix* for the prior in gratitude for aid in obtaining corpses for anatomical study, during his temporarily homeless period just after the death of Lorenzo the Magnificent in 1492. The *Crucifix* is Michelangelo's only known work in wood, and the artist was apparently unable to obtain a block large enough for his purpose. Not only the arms had to be pieced, which is quite general in wooden crucifixes, but also the inclined face and even portions of both legs.

48

49 ▶

Dr. Lisner's important discovery has been almost universally accepted by scholars, including some of the most noted specialists in Michelangelo's art. An attentive comparison of the accompanying illustrations and the reproductions of Michelangelo's other early works will show that these scholars are right. The personal idiosyncracies of the young artist's style are consistent throughout the entire group. For example, the characteristic twist of the legs so that the knees almost rub together is to be found in the attendant child in the upper left of the *Madonna of the Stairs* (figs. 36, 39), in the satyr in the *Bacchus* (fig. 72), and spectacularly in the *Pietà* (colorplate 4), in which the modeling of Christ's knees and calves is almost

51

52

identical to that of the Christ in the *Crucifix*. The face of the Christ, with its unrealistically thin nose and arching brows, is a curious simplification repeated in almost every head of the *Battle of Lapiths and Centaurs* (figs. 40–47), including even the slightly concave profile which recurs so often. This conception, greatly refined and amplified by experience, still underlies the construction of the face of the Bologna *Angel* (figs. 56–58), the *Pietà* (figs. 74–80), and even of the *Taddei Madonna* (figs. 82–84) and the *Bruges Madonna* (figs. 85, 88, 89, 97).

The anatomical construction of the figure has been unaccountably criticized in certain quarters. Michelangelo's understanding of anatomy was clearly improved by whatever work he was able to do at Santo Spirito, as can be demonstrated by a comparison between the sensitive analysis of the torso and limbs of the wooden figure and the more schematic reductions in the *Battle of Lapiths and Centaurs*. The Santo Spirito *Crucifix* yields in no anatomical respect

◄ 50
to the later, larger, and more elaborate *Rome Pietà*. The slender proportions of the relatively

53

soft and almost feminine figure should disturb no one. The Christ of the *Pietà* is even more delicate—after the full and heavy shapes of the *Bacchus*. There are innumerable examples of such relatively slender figures in Michelangelo's youthful drawings, and indeed the preference for such proportions recurs frequently throughout his mature works, including some of the figures for the Medici Chapel (figs. 172, 204, 219, 225); and it predominates in the figures of the late *Pietà* compositions (figs. 295, 306). The wooden Christ was completely covered with paint, generally limited to a soft ochre tone for the flesh, and brown for the long hair of the head and the occasional body hairs. This painted surface even accentuates the resemblance of the figure to the equally Hellenistic nudes in the background of the *Doni Madonna*, the only surviving panel painting entirely by Michelangelo's hand.

Startling, unprecedented, and especially characteristic of Michelangelo is the total nudity of the Christ, as in the *Christ Holding the Cross* (figs. 154–55) and some fourteen surviving drawings representing the Resurrection. As in the *Rome Pietà*, little or no attempt is made to show pain or grief. The graceful figure hangs there without suffering, as in a kind of reverie. From the back it seems almost to soar. Michelangelo is not, mercifully, always grandiose and violent. Like Beethoven in his gentler quartets and songs, the lyrical, dreamy side of Michelangelo's nature, especially evident in his drawings, remains perhaps too little understood. Dr. Lisner's discovery has added considerably to our knowledge of this intimate aspect of the artist's genius.

54 ▶

4. THREE STATUETTES ON THE TOMB OF ST. DOMINIC

ANGEL: *Marble; height (with base) 22¼", width of base 12", depth of base 6⅜"*
ST. PETRONIUS: *Marble; height (with base) 25⅛", width of base 4⅝", depth of base 4⅝"*
ST. PROCULUS: *Marble; height (with base) 23", width of base 3¾", depth of base 4⅛"*
1494–95
San Domenico, Bologna

For the first and last time in his life Michelangelo, in this commission, accepted the ungrateful task of supplying works of sculpture to complete a monumental composition entirely designed by others. In the chapel where the tomb now stands, however, the little statues by Michelangelo, however insignificant they may seem in bulk in comparison to the enormous mass of

55. The Tomb of St. Dominic, San Domenico, Bologna
upper frame: *St. Petronius*
lower frame: *Angel*
(*St. Proculus* not visible in photograph)

56 ▶

57   *58*

Gothic and Renaissance sculpture and decoration making up the Tomb, have the effect of hand grenades.

The Tomb (the so-called *Arca,* or shrine, of St. Dominic) is a strange hybrid (fig. 55). The sarcophagus, carved by the great Nicola Pisano and his pupil Fra Guglielmo da Pisa in 1265–67, was taken from its original position in the lower church of San Domenico early in the fifteenth century to a chapel on the south side of the church. In 1469 Niccolò dell' Arca, an accomplished south Italian sculptor, was called to Bologna to supply the sarcophagus with a towering lid surmounted by a huge ornamental construction composed of volutes enclosing the dead Christ standing in the tomb, and culminating in an urn flanked by garland-bearing *putti,* on which stands a statue of God the Father bearing the orb of the heavens. Statues of saints were to be placed around the lower edge of the sarcophagus lid. The whole structure was placed on an altar, and was to be flanked by two statues of kneeling angels bearing candlesticks. The reliefs below the sarcophagus were not executed until 1532–36, by the minor sculptor Alfonso Lombardi. In 1605 the whole composite work was transferred a second time, to the present chapel.

Although Niccolò dell' Arca's ornamental structure was placed on the sarcophagus in 1473, three statues were still lacking at the time of the sculptor's death in March, 1494. The commission for these was obtained for the nineteen-year-old Michelangelo, then a refugee in Bologna, by the learned Bolognese nobleman, Gian Francesco Aldovrandi. While the *Angel* is still in good condition, the two figures of saints have suffered badly. The head of *St. Petronius* was broken off and replaced rather crudely, patched with clay, the left cheek damaged, and a chip broken from the edge of the cope. The *St. Proculus,* knocked down by a careless monk in the late sixteenth century, had its head and right arm broken off, and its

64

legs and cloak shattered in two places. It also was badly mended, and the right foot is a complete restoration.

The *Angel* enjoys a curious distinction as Michelangelo's only known winged angelic figure. All his life the artist had an aversion to animal appendages, either classical or Christian, which could detract from the dominant humanity of a figure. But in this case he had no choice; the statue had to counterbalance the angel by Niccolò dell' Arca on the other side. This was the end of his submission, however. Niccolò's angel, charming as he is, looks like a portrait of an altarboy with goose-wings attached. Michelangelo's creation is a messenger from another sphere, announcing to the devout the mysteries of divinity. He holds the foot of the candlestick with his hand covered by a portion of his tunic, just as the priest holds the monstrance with his humeral veil at the Benediction of the Eucharist. The elaborate candlestick of Niccolò's angel has been replaced by a simpler and more classical baluster from the Florentine repertory of Luca della Robbia. The downy wings are firm, and seem almost to be still beating. The mouth is open as if chanting, and the eyes are so blurred in the final polishing that their gaze seems to be turned inward upon the soul, as if the angel were possessed by a vision. He is far more robust than the gracile counterpart by Niccolò, and the powerful muscular structure of his shoulders, chest, and thighs can be felt through the voluminous masses of soft drapery. Scaled to harmonize with the plumage of his wings, the locks of the angel's hair form a magnificent shaggy mass of interlacing curls, foretelling those of the *Bacchus*, the *David*, and the nude youths of the Sistine Ceiling. The Hellenic profile also suggests the *David* (figs. 100–8), as the rich, soft modeling does the *Bacchus* (figs. 65–73). Filled with a *furor divinus*, the little angel sings to us of the heavenly realm to which the saint whose shrine he attends has been translated. The unearthly feeling of dissolving mass and shimmering light and shade is increased by the systematic blurring of all detail, which seems to have been deliberately pumiced down by the sculptor. Not a line is clear, not an edge distinct. Despite his physical mass and power, the angel could soar away as easily and as lightly as he has appeared.

St. Petronius, the patron saint of Bologna, is shown in a manner recalling his appearance in the statue by Jacopo della Quercia over the central portal of the great church of San Petronio (fig. 11), still today by far the largest church of the city. Despite the fact that the young Michelangelo was deeply influenced by the great Sienese master of the early Renaissance, who had worked in Bologna two generations earlier, the resemblance between his statuette and Jacopo's more monumental figure is so close as to suggest that it was required by the clergy of San Domenico. But the external resemblance between the two figures only deepens the spiritual gap between them. Jacopo's saint holds out his city-model in an offhand way, without noticeable strain, as if the ascending drapery lines were doing the real work. Michelangelo's mournful figure balances the city on his hip, holds it firmly with his hands, and presses it against his body, in the manner of a standing Madonna holding her Child, conscious not only of its physical weight but of his own responsibility. His ravaged face betrays the depth of his concern. His lips are parted, as if in prayer. Although his wide-open eyes are directed slightly downward and to one side, they seem to see nothing external; like the angel, he looks within as he intercedes for the city. Both the tilt of St. Petronius' head and his detached and solemn gaze will reappear nearly sixty years later in the sad *Leah*, on the final version of the Tomb of Julius II (fig. 289).

Much more than with Jacopo della Quercia, the handling of St. Petronius' eyes and hair and the use of the drill in the locks of his beard suggest a familiarity with Early Christian sarcophagus sculpture—necessarily in Florence, Bologna, or Ravenna, as the young man had not yet visited Rome. This is the first finished, mature face by Michelangelo preserved to us; in it we can watch his exploration of the interrelations of the major and minor masses of bone, muscle, skin, and hair. The wrinkles around the eyes, the cavernous depressions of the cheeks, force the cheekbones into stronger relief. The eyelids are powerfully projected, the eyebrows undercut. A firm distinction is made between the texture of the eyebrows, of the locks issuing from under the mitre, and of the beard and moustache. In contrast to the soft treatment of the angel, all details of the saints are sharp and crisp.

The drapery masses show, in their turbulence, the influence of Jacopo della Quercia, but not so much as to trouble the compactness and density of the figure and its almost unbroken contour. Under the thick, pulpy folds, the principal divisions of the body and limbs are clearly felt. The contrast between the larger tubes and pouches of the tunic and the more delicate, small folds of the saint's linen undergarment will be exploited later in a spectacular way in the seated prophets and sibyls of the Sistine Ceiling. The back view of the statue is surprising in its simplicity. Once the work was in place, about seven feet above the altar steps, the back was presumably hidden forever. Michelangelo must have finished it, there-

60

61

fore, only for his own pleasure and that of his patron Aldovrandi, and possibly also to show to the clergy of San Domenico. If the front makes us think of Jacopo della Quercia, the broad masses of the cope at the back, descending unbroken from the shoulders to the base, recall the paintings of Masaccio which Michelangelo had so recently studied in the Brancacci Chapel and the cloister of the Carmine in Florence. A similar, startlingly simple back, with forms of the greatest abstract clarity and beauty, was provided for the *Bruges Madonna* (fig. 99), and is also now completely hidden from view. The eloquence and grandeur of these forms will reappear in the masses of the *Pietà* in Florence Cathedral (Frontispiece; figs. 294–98), which the artist intended for his own tomb.

In some ways the *St. Proculus* is the most arresting of the three little figures. Standing with his legs apart, this Bolognese martyr once held a lance at the ready. Three fingers of his left hand are clutched about the end of his cloak, which falls over his left shoulder and trails upon ◀ 59 the ground, its neck-band empty in the air behind him. The face, caught in a moment of

67

emotional turmoil, has reminded observers sharply of the *David* (figs. 105–7) and the *Moses* (figs. 146, 150). The dilated, rolling eyes and puckered brows—above all, the surge of indignation within the personality—point directly toward these later masterpieces. But if they are to be understood as spiritual self-portraits of the artist, this figure is in all probability a physical self-portrait as well. The big head denoting small stature, the contemporary costume, the close-knit figure, the broad cheekbones, the nose flattened by the vicious blow delivered by the jealous sculptor Torrigiani in the Brancacci Chapel, the extraordinary horizontal fold of flesh across the bridge of the nose—which reappears in the artist's death mask—all these create a convincing picture of the young sculptor, seething with ideas and emotions. The magnificent hand, the first of the tense, powerful hands so impressive in Michelangelo's sculpture, paintings, and drawings, should be compared with the slender, long-fingered hands of St. Petronius. In spite of the tiny scale in which the sculptor was forced to work, doubtless a disappointment after the freedom of his larger-than-lifesize *Hercules* (see page 249), he is able to project the tendons against the bones and knuckles in a manner truly monumental, in keeping with the muscularity of the legs, and the general stance and bearing of an angry young man.

All three statues witness a majesty of spirit alien not only to their scale, but to their surroundings. They are so grand that one forgets the delicate beauty of the work of Nicola Pisano and Niccolò dell' Arca, and so powerful that in photographs they seem many times their actual diminutive size.

63

64

5. BACCHUS

Marble; height (with base) 6' 7⅝", statue (without base) 6' ⅜"
Probably 1496–97
Museo Nazionale (Bargello), Florence

This, Michelangelo's first large-scale work preserved to us, was probably carved from the block of marble given him by Cardinal Riario, nephew of the late Pope Sixtus IV, a few days after the artist's arrival in Rome on June 24, 1496. It was bought by Jacopo Galli, a wealthy Roman banker in whose house the young sculptor worked, and was set up in Galli's garden. The hand holding the cup was broken off some time before 1532–35, within which years the Netherlandish artist Martin van Heemskerck made a drawing of the statue in its maimed condition; but before 1553, when Condivi published his biography of Michelangelo, what seems to be the original hand (the same marble and workmanship) was replaced, presumably by Michelangelo himself, or under his direction. Much of the original finish of the statue was roughened during its sojourn in the Galli gardens. In 1571–72 it was purchased by Francesco de' Medici, second Grand Duke of Tuscany, and it remained in the Florentine public collections. In July, 1944, when the Allies were nearing Florence, the Germans removed the *Bacchus* from its temporary refuge at the Villa Medici at Poggio a Caiano, and took it as far as the Alps, from which it was to be sent to Linz to form part of the museum Hitler was assembling to the memory of his mother. Along with over eight hundred works taken by the Germans, the Allies returned the statue to Florence on July 21, 1945.

What is extraordinary about Michelangelo's *Bacchus*, and unparalleled in ancient statues of the god of wine, is that he is shown as considerably affected by the consumption of his product. Boccaccio, more than a century earlier, had referred to drunkenness as the "sacrament of Bacchus," which, after it has passed, purifies the brain, so that the soul forgets all its troubles and becomes glad and tranquil. Vincenzo Cartari, the indefatigable late-sixteenth-century collector of Renaissance information regarding the gods, believed that Bacchus was often represented nude because wine and drunkenness often uncover that which has been hidden with much diligence: *"In vino veritas."*

Michelangelo may have had both these traditions in mind when he conceived his statue. He may also have remembered Noah, who in the Old Testament discovered wine and was displayed naked as a result, or Christ, who in the New Testament was prefigured by Noah, in that He was naked upon the Cross and daily reborn in the wine of the Eucharist. The parallel between the drunken Noah and the suffering Christ, vivid in Ghiberti's gates for the Baptistery of Florence, was to be repeated in 1509 by Michelangelo in his fresco on the Sistine Ceiling. Moralized, or Christianized, interpretations of the ancient gods and their myths were customary in the later fifteenth century. It is also perfectly possible that the twenty-one-year-old artist just wanted to make a beautiful statue of Bacchus, and was willing to leave all symbolic interpretations to the learned! Of one thing we can be certain—that the lovely fluid over which Bacchus presides was, in modest quantities, a delight to Michelangelo to the end of his days, and thus in the artist's private pantheon there could have been no more sympathetic divinity.

Whatever he may have thought or felt about the subject, he has left us an extraordinarily vivid statue of a potentially muscular youth whose forms have become soft and almost feminine through disuse, and who eyes the cup as if it were the source of all pleasures. It is one of the few statues in Michelangelo's career which were intended to be seen from all sides, and thus it has no "principal view" in the sense of Cellini's account of Michelangelo's sculptural procedure. In fact, the left side of the statue, rather than the front, most clearly betrays the practice of drawing directly on the surface of the block, for the arm and leg, and the little satyr gulping the grapes from the panther skin, and the tree-trunk on which the satyr sits,

colorplate 3

70

65

66

preserve the original plane of the block at all key points. Here the group is still largely a high relief. But in all other parts the artist has freed himself from the block. The right leg moves lightly in space, the toe only barely touching the rocky base. The right arm, also, is completely liberated, the original contours of the block being suggested only by the line of the right forearm and by the axis of the god's glance. Such openness, though limited indeed as compared to the sharp projections in the work of later fifteenth-century sculptors like Pol-

67

laiuolo and Verrocchio, was not to recur in the increasingly compact figural groups of Michel-angelo's maturity and old age.

In many ways the *Bacchus* seems ahead of its time. It looks already like a work of the High Renaissance, and in the amplitude of its forms and the richness of its surfaces, especially in the magnificent back, it may be considered a decisive step away from the more diffuse sculptur-al groups carved by Michelangelo's contemporaries in the last two decades of the fifteenth

70 ▶

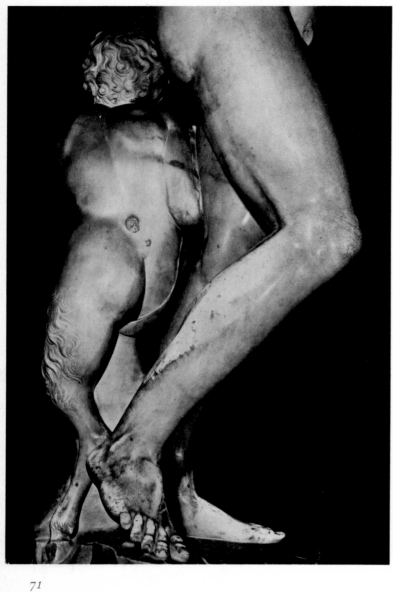

71

72

century. Perhaps influenced by ancient statues of Antinous, the young artist, rejoicing in his technical prowess, sought out the greatest subtleties of surface and line in the treatment of the soft flesh and the serpentine complexities of the hair entwined with vine leaves and clusters. After the earlier works, the six-foot *Bacchus* strides into our vision seemingly without introduction. But we should not forget that the artist had already prepared for such a triumph not only in the rich shapes of the newly rediscovered *Crucifix* (figs. 48–54) but, very probably, in the lost marble *Hercules*. And if the *Bacchus* may seem to lack something of the prophetic vision of the *Madonna of the Stairs* and the elemental fire of the *Battle of Lapiths and Centaurs*, it shows a new and more adult sympathy for the feelings of human beings. With his new technical gains the young man has lost none of his expressive depth or his power of form.

73 ▶

6. THE ROME PIETÀ

Marble; height 68½″, maximum width of base 76¾″, maximum depth 27⅛″
1498–1499/1500
St. Peter's, Rome

This renowned work, perhaps the most universally loved of Michelangelo's sculptures, is the first to have been commissioned by a French patron. This potentate, otherwise unremembered by history, was the elderly Bishop Jean Bilhères de Lagraulas, who had been made cardinal of Santa Sabina by Pope Alexander VI in 1493. The cardinal clearly contemplated commissioning the work as early as 1497, but not until late March, 1498, did Michelangelo arrive in Carrara to superintend the quarrying of the marble for the group. The contract was signed on August 27, 1498, under the supervision of Michelangelo's patron, Jacopo Galli. According to the contract the sculptor was to make a statue of the "Virgin clothed, with the dead Christ in her arms, as large as a man, for the price of 450 papal ducats in gold, in the space of a year from the day of the beginning of work." The group was to be "the most beautiful work in marble that exists today in Rome, and no master could do it better today" (a statement which few would dispute).

Alas, the old cardinal died on August 6, 1499, and we have no way of knowing whether or not he ever saw his *Pietà* finished. It was placed in one of the chapels of the church of Santa Petronilla, attached to the south side of the transept of Old St. Peter's. When Santa Petronilla was destroyed to make way for Bramante's new building, the group was moved to the Chapel of the Virgin of the Fever, on the south side of Old St. Peter's. It was moved twice again, once to the choir of Sixtus IV, and finally, in 1749, to its present position in the first chapel on the north side of the new St. Peter's—a setting of Baroque splendor incompatible with Michelangelo's taste. In one of the moves, four fingers of the Virgin's left hand were broken off; these were restored in 1736, it is still not certain how accurately. It has been recently shown that in one of its locations, possibly when the group was placed on its too-high pedestal in the eighteenth century, it was wedged up with mortar to lean forward. If the wedge, easily visible in the photograph, were removed, the present-day observer could look more directly into the face of the Virgin, and the whole fluid rhythm of Christ's body would also be more impressive.

The image of the Virgin seated and holding her dead Son on her lap was familiar to the late Middle Ages and Renaissance; mystics wrote that as she did so she thought of the time when, as a child, He played there; also, in describing the Nativity, they credited the Virgin with foreknowledge of her Son's Passion and death. In most fifteenth-century Italian representations of the Pietà (a word which means both "piety" and "pity") the Virgin is shown as middle-aged, but Perugino, earlier than Michelangelo's work, had painted in Florence a meditative and quiet *Pietà* without any apparent difference of age between mother and Son. Michelangelo has gone even farther, and shown the Virgin as a very young woman. Apparently there was some discussion about this discrepancy in the mid-sixteenth century on the part of those whom Vasari characterizes as "more clumsy than not," but Michelangelo's reply as recorded by both Condivi and Vasari does not help matters: he is reported to have explained that virgins maintain their appearance for a long time without any spot, while the afflicted, like Christ, do the opposite. This elucidation, offered by the artist more than half a century after he created the statue, impressed Condivi as "worthy of any theologian." Today it almost reminds one of the old story about the man who asked a foolish question and thereby got back a foolish answer.

Michelangelo's art is invariably symbolic and timeless, and cannot be pinned to literal meanings or specific, transitory circumstances. Perhaps he was thinking of Dante's celebrated invocation to the Virgin, *"Vergine madre, figlia del tuo Figlio"* (Virgin mother, daughter of

colorplate 4

74, 75, and 76 ▶

77

thy Son), which Botticelli had inscribed on the throne of the great altarpiece painted for the church of San Barnaba and now in the Uffizi. Giovanni Battista Strozzi the Elder recalled this very passage when he composed his poem for the copy of Michelangelo's *Pietà* set up in the church of Santo Spirito in Florence:

> *He is also, in spite of Himself,*
> *Our Lord and thy*
> *Spouse, son and father,*
> *O His only spouse, daughter and mother.*

The twenty-five-year-old sculptor has shown us the Mother of God in her eternal reality beyond age and time—virgin mother, mystic bride, mortal vessel for the divine purpose realized in the Incarnation and the Atonement. What have such truths to do with wrinkles? These appear no more than do tears or blood, or the nails, the crown of thorns, the sponge, the lance, or any trace of the scourges. Even the wounds in hands and feet and side, which had to be represented, are shown as unobtrusively as possible so as not to shatter the observer's meditation on the beauty of the blessed Mother and the incalculably precious, innumerably repeated, omnipresent eucharistic sacrifice of her Son. She does not weep over her dead Son— her hand covered by her mantle (again like the humeral veil with which the priest holds the monstrance for the Benediction of the Eucharist), she presents Him to us for adoration:

> *Ave verum corpus natum*
> *De Maria Virgine,*
> *Vere passum, immolatum,*
> *In cruce pro homine:*

78

Cuius latus perforatum
Unda fluxit sanguine,
Esto nobis praegustatum
In mortis examine.

Not maternal grief, but grateful reverence in the presence of a mystery in which Mary participates is the theme of Michelangelo's first *Pietà*.

Despite its enormous popularity, this work has puzzled scholars. It is not "Michelangel-esque." It does not seem to fit preconceptions of the artist's grandiosity. Nor can it be easily inserted into our notion of his development. Disconcertingly enough, it must be dated after the *Bacchus*, which looks in so many ways more "advanced." On the threshold of the High Renaissance—later than Leonardo's *Last Supper*, in fact—the complexity of elements and the attenuated proportions look Gothic. Luckily, Michelangelo is the last artist to succumb to principles superimposed by posterity. The elaborate linearity of the work, which suggests late Gothic art, had already been revived in Florence in the styles of Botticelli and Filippino Lippi. Michelangelo shows a certain kinship with this "medievalistic" tendency in his newly rediscovered *Crucifix* for Santo Spirito. He was to return to it again and again in later life, usually when meditating on Christ. Only in the *Christ Holding the Cross* (figs. 153–58), the Almighty Judge of the *Last Judgment,* and a single *Resurrection* drawing in Windsor Castle does he confer on Christ the athletic power generally associated with the art of Michelangelo. As we have already seen (page 60), the artist often shows us a slender, delicate figure, utterly remote from the Hellenic ideal. Only purity of thought and single-minded unity of purpose mark the composition as a Renaissance conception.

At this moment in Michelangelo's development, the richness and complexity of the drapery folds comes as a surprise. The mantle of the Virgin symbolizes heaven; in paintings it is almost

always blue. Frequently, in representations of the Madonna of Mercy, she extends it in protection over mortals. Michelangelo's Virgin has taken the mantle from her shoulders and spread it over her knees to receive the body of her Son, so that the folds stretch out upon the ground. The toe of her left shoe barely peeps forth under the edge of the gigantic mantle. Two fingers of Christ's right hand have converged about one of its folds; another supports His left. The broad sweep of the outlines of the cloak encloses a host of broken rhythms, still more minute when the eye rises to the loincloth of Christ and the tunic of His mother. Against this welter of discordant, generally angular folds, suggesting the intricacy of the drapery treatment in Donatello's latest works, the slender torso and limbs appear even purer and more perfect. Particularly striking are the concentration of criss-cross folds over the Virgin's bosom (through which the shape of her firm breasts can be clearly seen), and in the tumbled masses of her veil, which seem to embody in abstract forms the intensity of the emotion restrained in her quiet countenance. These folds are, as if symbolically, held in check by the strap of her mantle which crosses her breast.

The soft and slender anatomical forms recall those of the wooden *Crucifix* (figs. 48–54), especially in the modeling of the knees and the long, slender feet. As in the *Crucifix*, the toes of one foot are slightly bent. But the torso is even thinner. It hangs so limply in the Virgin's arms that the head falls back as if asleep, and the rib-cage rises to show through the delicate outer muscular layer of the chest and abdomen, strongly suggestive of the modeling of the torso in one of the artist's later *Pietà* drawings, which he gave to his friend Sebastiano del Piombo. The facial type of the Christ has been compared with His appearance in the engravings of the great German master Martin Schongauer, one of whose prints the youthful artist is known to have copied exactly. The little curls of the moustache and beard are alien to Italian representations of Christ, but the long tresses suggest the treatment of hair in some

85

of Botticelli's paintings. Something of the rich and gracious beauty of the Madonna types of Antonio Rossellino is still apparent in the features of Michelangelo's Virgin, a trifle more astringent, however, in the shapes of the slightly tilted nose and firmly held lips.

The artist's delight in his tools is everywhere apparent. Not only has he achieved a higher degree of surface polish than in any of his other works, earlier or later, but he has set this taut surface in active conflict with brilliantly incisive line. The wrinkles around the eyelids, the edge of the transparent veil over the Virgin's forehead, the sharp contours of her lips, above all the curls of Christ's short moustache and beard, cut into the surrounding flesh, sometimes to a measurable degree. This conflict between surface and line, between mass and contour, will be maintained in the artist's work until line is fused with mass in the *Moses* and the Louvre *Slaves* (colorplates 8, 9, 10; figs. 134–52). According to the story preserved by Vasari, Michelangelo was watching a group of Lombards in St. Peter's after the statue had been set up, and heard them say that this wonderful work must have been done by their compatriot Cristoforo Solari, the Hunchback. Thereafter the artist hid in the basilica by night, and with the aid of lamplight carved his name on the Virgin's mantle-strap. There it stands, "MICHAEL·AGELVS·BONAROTVS·FLORENT·FACIEBAT," the handsome Renaissance forms of the letters cut a little roughly, as if in a hurry. The position of this, the only signature on any of Michelangelo's works, pressed against the Virgin's marble breast, recalls the artist's own remark that he drank in his love for his hammer and chisel with the milk of the stonecutter's wife. As the young man crouched there in the night, he must have been able to gaze down into the features of the dead Christ, illuminated by the tiny lamp. The observer was never intended to see fully the almost unbearable beauty of this face. The modern camera admits us into a hidden aspect of the artist's spiritual life.

80

7. THE TADDEI MADONNA

Marble; diameter 42⁷/₈"
Probably 1500–1502
Royal Academy, London

In fifteenth-century altarpieces the Madonna and Child, often accompanied by other members of the Holy Family and with a varying attendance from the court of Heaven, were customarily represented on a splendid throne. In other works, the Virgin was usually seated on a chair in a luxurious interior, with or without a view of a landscape through the window, or else presented as a celestial vision surrounded by clouds and angels. But beginning with Luca Signorelli's circular *Madonna and Child* in the Uffizi, possibly painted as early as 1490, a new type appears, which became increasingly popular in Florence in the first decade of the sixteenth century, especially in the Florentine Madonnas of Raphael from 1504–8. The Madonna and Child, again frequently attended by relatives, are shown out of doors in a landscape setting. The Virgin is usually seated on a convenient rock, and she either plays with the Child (often also with His infant cousin, St. John the Baptist), or instructs Him from a little book she holds in her hand. It is perhaps no accident that this new type of Madonna and Holy Family image arose and found wide acceptance in Florence, so desperately concerned with the liberation of its surrounding territory from invading armies in the closing years of the fifteenth century. Interestingly enough, after the return of the Medici to power in 1512, the type to all intents and purposes died out. For this new conception, which might be called the "Madonna of the Land," recalls the ancient custom of the Rogations, the blessing of the land; and the Introit of the Mass for Rogation Sunday, the fifth Sunday after Easter, reads:

> *Announce with a voice of joy, and be heard, announce to the ends of the earth: the Lord will liberate his people.*

Michelangelo's four Madonnas done in Florence during these years—the *Taddei Madonna*, the *Bruges Madonna* (colorplate 5; figs. 85–99), the *Pitti Madonna* (colorplate 7; figs. 121–25), and the painted *Doni Madonna*—all belong to this new type. Three of these four are *tondi* (from the Italian word for round); this form is unsuitable for altarpieces, but it is related to the favorite shape of a number of precious objects associated with the domestic life of wealthy Florentine citizens, especially the painted salvers customarily given to new mothers, and to circular mirrors, with their symbolism of the Blessed Virgin as the unspotted mirror of divinity. The *Taddei Madonna*, according to Vasari, was made for Taddeo Taddei (born 1470) whose father, Francesco Taddei, was Gonfaloniere ("Flagbearer," or leader of the Republic) in 1502, and led the armies of Florence in a campaign to regain the territories lost by rebellion or through the depredations of invaders—chiefly Cesare Borgia, son of the wicked Pope Alexander VI. These lands were finally restored to the Republic in July of that very year, through the intervention of King Louis XII of France, whose armies held the balance of power in Italy. According to one document, Taddeo was married to Gostanza Strozzi in 1499, but another, giving the wedding-date after 1500, seems more accurate, as Taddeo's first child was born in 1503. Michelangelo's *Doni Madonna* was painted for the wedding of another young woman of the Strozzi family.

The *Taddei Madonna* is usually dated about 1504. The date 1500–1502 suggested here is based on strong ties with the open composition and the complex forms of the *Pietà*. The Virgin, with her tilted nose, daintily pursed lips, and long neck, closely resembles her counterpart in the Roman work (figs. 75–77). Despite the unfinished condition of the *Taddei Madonna*, it is clear that she would have had the same sharp wrinkle under her eye visible in the Virgin of the *Pietà*—the last time this particular detail appears in any of Michelangelo's Madonnas. The same softness of shape is also evident in her face, soon to be replaced in the *David* (figs.

82 ▶

100–112) and the *Bruges Madonna* (figs. 85–99) by the blocky, squared treatment of the facial masses so powerful in the considerably later *Pitti Madonna* (figs. 121–25). Even the cloak, falling diagonally across the bosom and puckered into a host of little, jagged shapes, recalls the mantle in which the Virgin of the *Pietà* holds the body of her dead Son. This motive, too, will not recur in Michelangelo's later work. If the Taddei *tondo* had been completed in every elegant detail, it would undoubtedly have resembled the *Pietà* very strongly. Certainly the almost-finished modeling of the Child's body, with all its dimples and hollows, suggests the same concern with minute surface detail—to vanish from Michelangelo's art after the *Doni Madonna* in 1503.

It is impossible to make out from the rough masses of marble surrounding the figures how Michelangelo intended to treat the background. He may have wished to show rocks, like those of the *Pietà* and the *Bruges Madonna*. He might have desired to clean off the raw stone completely and silhouette the figures against a smooth disk, but so large an inert area is hard to parallel in his compositions. Surely, however, the scene was intended to be set outdoors. Mary's crouching position could hardly be justified for an interior, and St. John's travel pouch forms a prominent element in the composition. Most important of all, the drama over the bird must have taken place in the open air.

For the Baptist has captured a bird and is presenting the little creature, his wings still beating, to the terrified Christ Child, Who takes refuge in His mother's lap. The bird may be a goldfinch, which was believed to subsist largely on a diet of thorns, and therefore to signify mystically the Passion of Christ and the crown of thorns. There are many examples in earlier Italian art of the Christ Child holding a goldfinch, and some even show Him in similar terror before this symbol of His suffering and death. This would seem to be the first

83

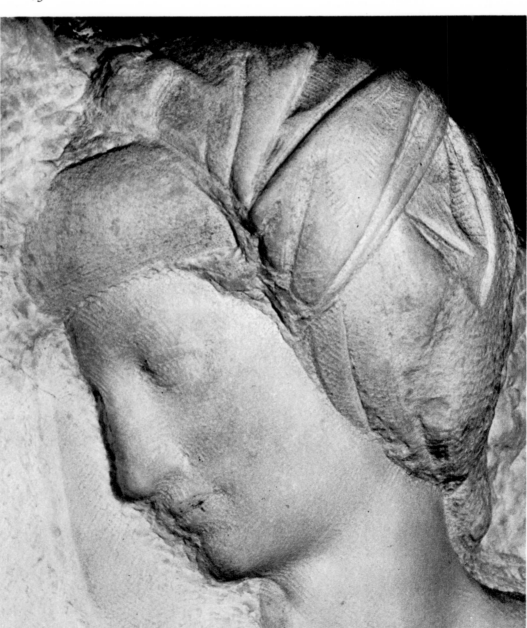

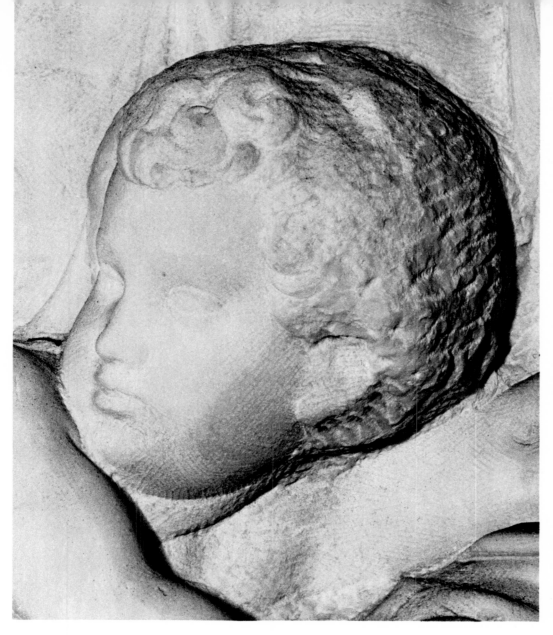

84

time that the bird was presented to the Child by the infant St. John the Baptist who, it should be remembered, is the patron saint of Florence. It is as if the Baptist were appealing to Mary and Christ, through the Passion itself, to liberate the city he protects.

A further allusion to the Passion, characteristically enough in this era of classicism, appears in a motive borrowed from ancient art. It has been shown that the pose of the Christ Child was derived literally from representations of the legend of Medea on Roman sarcophagi well known in Michelangelo's youth. In these Medea's children seek refuge in her lap, just before the dreadful moment when she will murder them and take off in her fiery chariot. Strange as it may seem today, the parallel between the slaughtered children of the savage princess of Colchis, and the sacrificed Christ, appeared quite reasonable to the Renaissance; to Francesco Taddei it perhaps seemed even timely, reinforcing his invocation to the Virgin to liberate the people of the Florentine countryside from their not dissimilar sufferings at the hands of the rapacious armies of Cesare Borgia and Vitello Vitellozzi.

No later sculptural group by Michelangelo will have either so open and complex a composition, or so immediate and episodic a content; even here, however, the drama is eternal, for the sacrifice to which Taddeo Taddei appeals is never ending.

8. THE BRUGES MADONNA

Marble; height (with base) 48", statue (without base) 36⅞"
About 1503–4
Onze Lieve Vrouwkerk (Church of Our Lady), Bruges

This little group of the Madonna and Child, lifesize if we consider that the average Italian woman in Renaissance times was probably not much over five feet tall, was probably carved in Florence at about the same time that Michelangelo was painting the circular *Madonna* for Francesco Doni. The face of the Christ Child is so similar in both as to make any appreciable difference in time most unlikely. There are, however, no documentary records which might pertain to the work before January 31, 1506, when Michelangelo wrote to his father from Rome, asking to have a certain marble Madonna brought from his Florentine studio to the family home, and not to show it to anyone. (This might, of course, refer to any of the three other early marble Madonnas.) But on August 13 of the same year arrangements were under way to send a work of sculpture to Viareggio, where it could be put on board a ship bound for Bruges. This surely refers to our Madonna, which had been purchased by a prosperous Flemish merchant with extensive Italian business, Alexander Mouschron, who had ordered a new altar for the statue in the Church of Our Lady in Bruges. Oddly enough both Condivi and Vasari, neither of whom ever saw the work, refer to it as a relief in bronze, and Michelangelo never bothered to correct them.

During World War II the group was removed from its altar by the Germans and taken to Altaussee in Austria, whence it was returned to Belgium in 1945 by the Allies. At some time prior to this journey, the edge of the veil was damaged in two places and the left armhole of the mantle chipped.

colorplate 5

85   86

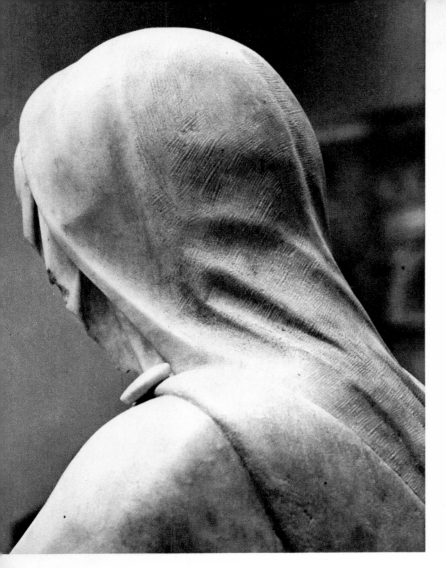

As in all of Michelangelo's early Madonnas, overtones of the Passion can be sensed in the *Bruges Madonna*, seated on her rock—another example of the Madonna of the Land. Mary's expression is pensive, as she gazes downward and past her Son. She holds His right hand firmly with her left as, from His unprecedented refuge between her knees, He seems about to try a step forward with one chubby foot, steadying Himself with the other hand against her knee. The book lies idle on the Virgin's lap, supported lightly by her right hand.

A considerable change has come over Michelangelo's style since the *Taddei Madonna* (figs. 82–84). Although the *Bruges Madonna* is much smaller than the *Pietà* (fig. 74), it looks larger in photographs, due to a sense of balance and integration—absent from the earlier work —that recalls aspects of the *Madonna of the Stairs* (figs. 36–39), especially in profile. All the diffuse and complex drapery rhythms, so loosely held within the Virgin's mantle in the *Pietà* and the *Taddei Madonna*, are now densely massed in one compact group. All forms are fuller, stronger, less slender. The Virgin's gravely beautiful face has none of the pinched quality so visible in the *Pietà*, and although the head veil is arranged in much the same manner, both this and the features are at once more blocky and less pointed. A strong interplay of planes builds up the principal shapes, but the planes are rounded at their intersections. The conflict between line and form continues, but both are strengthened. No longer does the line have the engraving-like character it showed in the *Pietà*; it is broader, more supple, and more deeply undercut, especially around the eyes, nose, and mouth. The Virgin's lips are fuller, even slightly tremulous. No longer do her eyebrows appear groomed and polished. Soft hairs grow naturally and in profusion on the broad, straight brows, set at a somewhat greater height above the fuller, larger eyes. The forehead, like that of a Roman matron, is less than half the height of that of the Virgin in the *Pietà*, and is now bordered by masses of hair combed back on either side from a central part. Fifteenth-century elegance, even in dress, has given way

89 ▶

91

92

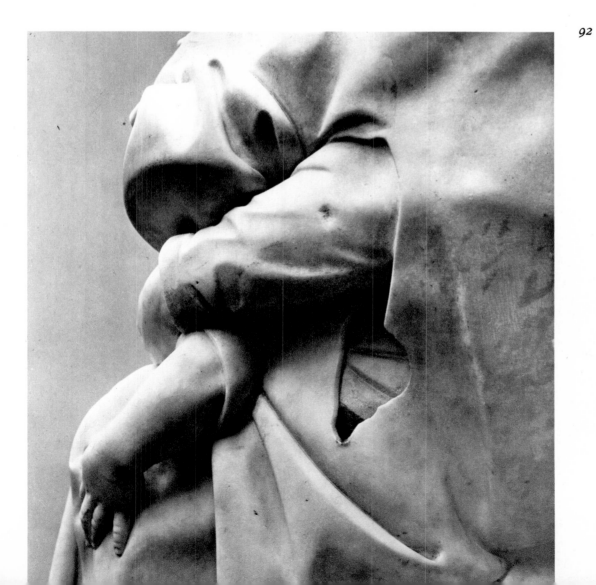

◀ 90

to the sober classicism of the High Renaissance. It is remarkable that this new composure of style and taste arises in Florence and not in Rome. There was, doubtless, little incentive for it in the Rome of Alexander VI, but in the Florence of Piero Soderini (elected Gonfaloniere for life), which felt itself the worthy successor to the ancient Roman republic, the new ideas found fertile soil. In the work of Leonardo, Michelangelo, Raphael, and Fra Bartolommeo, these ideas expanded rapidly. The *Madonna of the Land* not only blessed the Florentine countryside, which the Republic was dedicated to maintaining in freedom, but presided over a new ideal of human conduct, of stoic womanhood, of intellectual clarity and power. That ideal infuses every line and fold of the *Bruges Madonna* with a new conviction and beauty.

The sweet, grave Christ Child is one of the artist's most winning creations, partly, perhaps because he never makes the least concession to the whimsicality, charm, even cuteness so frequent in fifteenth-century representations of the Christ Child. The boy seems aware of the grandeur of His mission, even of its perils, and His tentative step toward the world is accompanied by a certain solemnity. The soft, round cheeks are those of a child, but the mouth is full of resolve and the eyes of sadness, echoing the downcast gaze of Mary. Strong muscles move under the skin of the childish limbs. The arm crossing the body, with its rich alternation of rounded swellings and sharp, straight depressions, is a motive later to recur in the blacksmith arms of the *Cumaean Sibyl* on the Sistine Ceiling and of *Moses* on the Tomb of Julius II (figs. 144, 145, 151, 152), both overwhelming witnesses to the power of divine revelation embodied in mortals. All the full, broad rhythms of the early figures, notably of the children in the background of the *Madonna of the Stairs,* are revived here, reinforced by a knowledge of the structure of the body which builds up a succession of volumes and contours even richer in plasticity and more accomplished technically than the forms of the *Bacchus* (figs. 65–67).

After the exquisite interplay of flesh and drapery masses in the front or principal view, the restraint of the side and back views comes as a surprise. We have, of course, no notion of the circumstances under which Michelangelo created this work. Doubtless it was a commission, but perhaps the original patron may have defaulted, died, or been expelled from Florence;

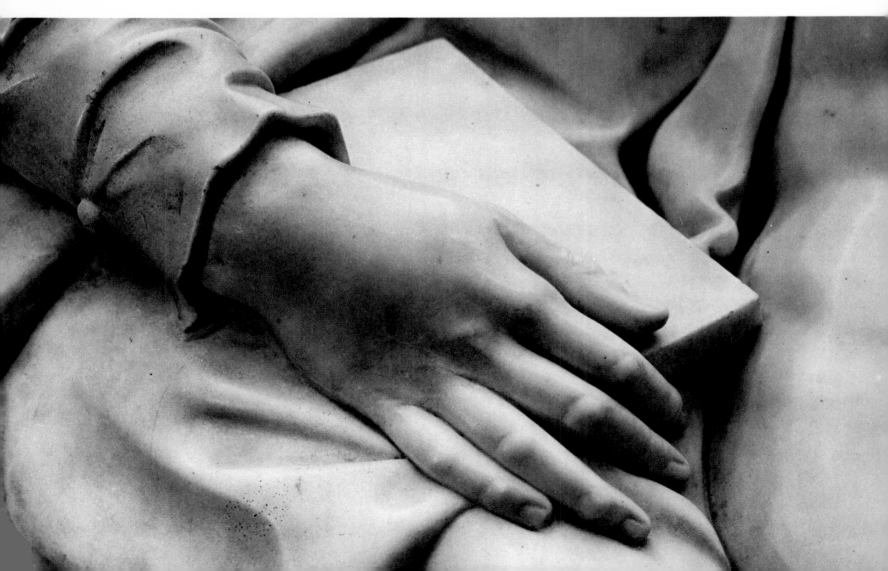

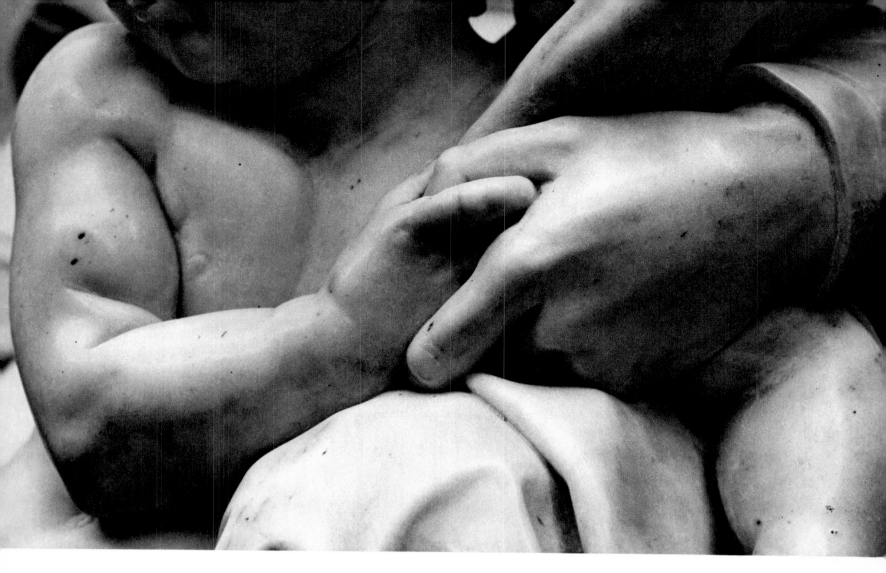

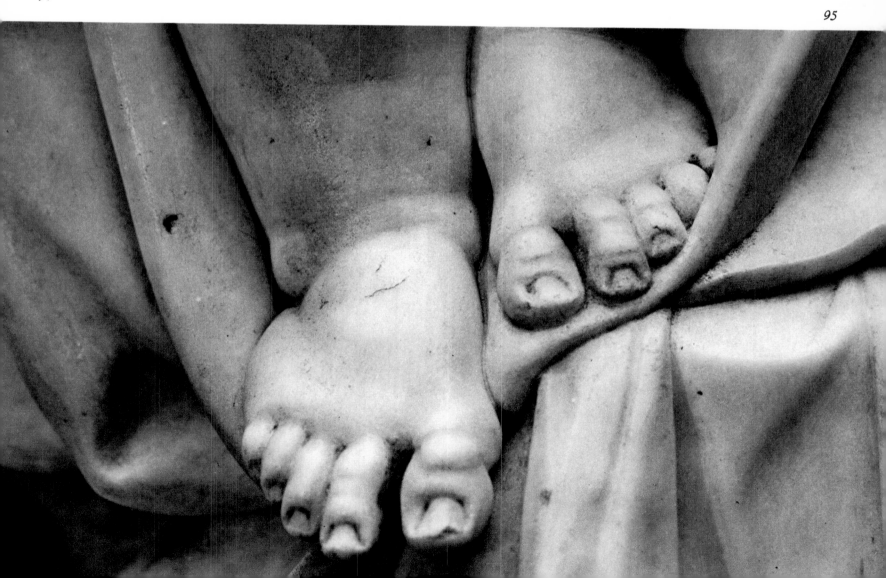

Michelangelo may not have wished to lower the value of the statue by over-exhibiting it while he was negotiating with Mouschron. In any case, he could not have intended that it be seen from the back, because, although every portion of the work is finished in all essentials, he never troubled to polish off the chisel marks on the veil or the mantle at the back of the group. The austere shapes of the back were made, therefore, for his own enjoyment. To modern eyes they comprise some of the greatest beauties of the work. The purity of the forms, the simple flow of contour and mass, the detachment from all the accidents of existence, are very pleasing to the century of Lehmbruck and Brancusi.

Not only did Michelangelo achieve, in the back and side views, a classical repose suggestive of Greek funerary sculpture; he showed himself master of surprising nuances of form and surface, as in the breathless poise of the button on Mary's left shoulder, or the soft pulsation of the mantle where the underlying arm approaches the armhole. Even the rocks have their own character, as abstract and undescriptive as the planes in a Cubist painting. All these quiet masses, closed and strong, are there, of course, to provide a kind of shell around the final revelation of beauty in the faces and forms of the Virgin and her Son. They constitute the calix from which flowers the mystic Rose.

9. DAVID

Marble; height (without base) 13' 5⅜, width of base 1' 5¼", depth of base 1' 2⅞"
1501–4
Accademia di Belle Arti, Florence

To those who have seen the original in its present setting, its actual dimensions may prove surprising; it looks much larger. The *David* is the first specimen of the new race of supermen with whom the Italian High Renaissance was to populate its fantasy world. The statue was originally intended for one of the buttresses of the apse of the Cathedral of Florence in a series begun by Donatello (whose *Joshua* is lost) and Ghiberti (whose *Hercules* was never executed), and had been commissioned from Agostino di Duccio in 1464. He went to Carrara, brought back the marble in one piece, but never completed the work. Recent research suggests that Agostino di Duccio was in reality carrying out a design by the aged Donatello, and that work ceased on the latter's death in 1466. In 1476 Antonio Rossellino was given the assignment of finishing the statue; but little or nothing seems to have been done. For the next twenty-five years the badly cut block, generally considered to have been ruined, lay around the Cathedral workshop, and collected the nickname of "the giant."

On August 16, 1501, Michelangelo signed a contract with the Cathedral *Operai* (Board of Works) to carve a David in the space of two years at a monthly salary of 6 gold florins, which was raised to a total of 400 gold florins in February, 1502, when the statue was half done. In January, 1504, doubts seem to have arisen as to the wisdom of placing so impressive a work high on the Cathedral where it could never be properly seen. The *Operai*, with Michelangelo's approval, summoned a group of thirty-five artists, artisans, and city officials to decide on a proper spot. Their deliberations are preserved, and make amusing reading as they were interrogated one by one, publicly, and many (especially artisans or elderly artists) tried to state their views in a way that would offend no one. A woodworker said that he, frankly, thought the statue ought to be placed where it had been originally intended to go, and could not see why it had to be moved. Messer Francesco, Herald of the Republic, wanted the *David* set up on the terrace outside the Palazzo Vecchio, where Donatello's *Judith* then stood; his opinion was shared by only one other person. Francesco also thought it might go very well in the courtyard of the palace; a goldsmith and the father of Benvenuto Cellini both agreed with him. A tapestry worker and the painter David Ghirlandaio favored a spot toward the extreme left of the terrace, in place of Donatello's *Marzocco*; while two more painters, Cosimo Rosselli and Sandro Botticelli, thought the giant would look particularly well at the far right, near the steps to the church of San Piero Scheraggio (now swallowed up by the Uffizi). It is noteworthy that the painters preferred a site from which the statue could be seen by passers-by, and said so. They were opposed by a goldsmith, Andrea il Riccio, who maintained that passers-by ought to go into the courtyard and see the statue, rather than have the statue come out and see them.

But by far the largest number of recorded opinions agreed with the architects Giuliano and Antonio da Sangallo. They were worried about the softness of the marble, which they maintained could not withstand prolonged exposure to the elements. For this reason they insisted that it be placed in a covered position under the Loggia dei Lanzi, preferably under the central arch. Another Herald objected to this spot, which would obstruct various public celebrations, but the proponents pointed out that a niche (Giuliano wanted a black niche, for better contrast) could be erected for the statue, at the back. Leonardo da Vinci, who probably could hardly have cared less where his younger rival's masterpiece went as long as the place was dark enough, agreed. Filippino Lippi and Piero di Cosimo said everybody had spoken very well, but maybe they ought to ask Michelangelo himself. There is no record that they ever did, and no one really knows where he wanted the statue to go. In spite of recent contrary

colorplate 6

100

proposals, the wording of Piero's testimony permits no other conclusion. It is highly unlikely that Michelangelo would have suggested the Loggia dei Lanzi, which would have
dwarfed the statue and kept its back in permanent shadow.

As is the way with the reports of commissions, this one was practically disregarded, and in
May, 1504, the authorities went ahead and set up the statue where they had probably intended
to all along—in place of Donatello's *Judith*, which was shifted to another spot on the terrace.
The move of the colossal *David*, facilitated by an ingenious rolling scaffold devised by Giuliano
da Sangallo, was not accomplished without adventure, for on the night of May 14 a band of
mischievous youths, perhaps supporters of the exiled Medici, stoned the statue; eight of them
were rounded up and cast into the prison of the Stinche. In 1873, the *David* was moved to its
present location at the end of the long gallery of the Accademia: time had proved that
Giuliano da Sangallo was right—the marble was too soft to resist rain, sun, and ice. As a con-

101

sequence of long exposure the top and back of the head, with all their splendid locks of hair, and the surface of the shoulders, may be regarded as destroyed. Other portions of the great work, notably the hands and arms and certain passages of the torso, have lost much of their original finish. Only the face, sheltered by the immense mass of hair, is perfectly preserved. In addition to the damage inflicted by weather, the left arm was hit by a bench thrown out of the window of the Palazzo Vecchio during the riots attending the expulsion of the Medici in 1527. The arm fell to the terrace and was smashed in three pieces. These were reverently gathered up by Vasari and his friend, the painter Francesco Salviati, both then small boys, who dragged the heavy pieces of marble into the church of San Piero Scheraggio, and later transported them to safety in the house of Salviati's father. The breaks in the arm and hand may still be seen.

If it was simply a matter of placing the statue in a more easily visible spot, why did this

102

have to be the civic center of the Florentine Republic? We can only surmise that, in everyone's imagination, including conceivably that of Michelangelo himself, it had already come to symbolize the ideals of manly strength and heroic vigor required of the citizenry—now that the Republic itself, so precariously resuscitated, was in constant danger of invasion and subjection. It has been shown that David, whose name was translated as *manu fortis* ("strong hand"), was equated with Hercules during the Middle Ages and Renaissance, and Hercules was a favorite hero and symbol of the Florentine Republic. Only four years after the *David* was set up the Republic commissioned Michelangelo to carve a Hercules for the other side of the entrance to the Palazzo Vecchio, but this work was repeatedly taken away from him after the return of the Medici to power, and was finally given to his chief enemy, Baccio Bandinelli (see page 249). Also, the Palazzo Vecchio already held Donatello's marble *David*, requisitioned from the Cathedral under similar conditions of crisis in 1416, and Verrocchio's

103 ▶

104 106 105 107 108 ▶

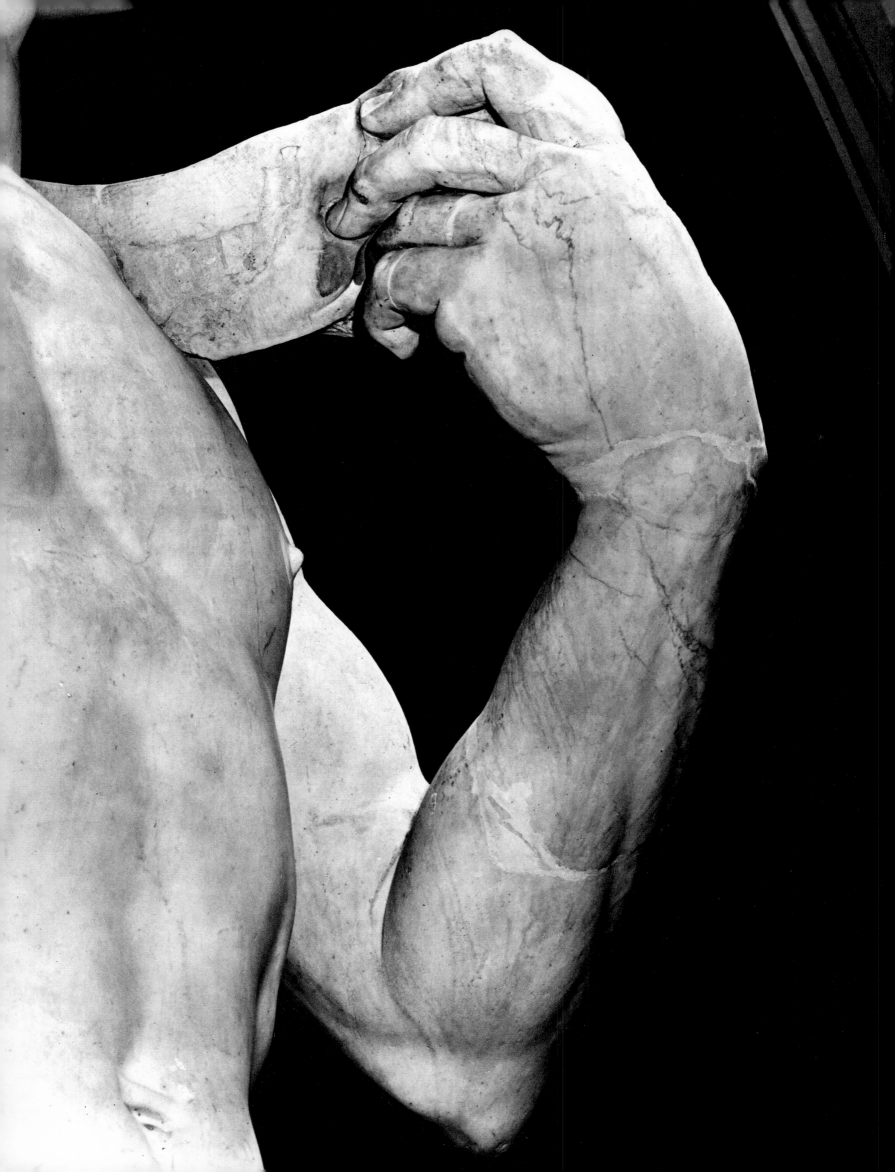

110

David, which stood in the courtyard. This last was removed after the Medici principate had been established.

Michelangelo's new conception of the *David* is incommensurable with any of the numerous fifteenth-century treatments of the subject. Instead of showing a slender, delicate child, as did Donatello and Verrocchio, Michelangelo portrays an adolescent hero, in the manner of the painters Castagno and Pollaiuolo; but David is now completely nude, glorying in his physical strength without the slightest reference to the major enemy, Goliath, whose severed head he was usually shown standing over, or even pushing about with his foot. He holds the slingshot in such a way that he could not use it quickly; it is no more than an attribute, a symbol of the slender material resources available to the hero who, in the last analysis, must rely on his own body and his own courage. As always, Michelangelo carefully avoided depicting a passing moment, and concentrated on the timeless and the universal. To the Florentines this courageous youth may well have typified the qualities demanded of them in their crisis; to the visitors who sit or stand before him today he seems an ideal for all humanity.

Despite echoes of classical antiquity, it is not the tension and restlessness of the statue that separate it from classical norms; the proportions are those of a youth who has not yet finished growing up to the size of his head, hands, and feet. And the powerful muscles, without an ounce of surplus tissue, denote a boy of the people rather than the soft and pampered child shown by earlier sculptors. Both the pose and the expression, with dilated eyes and knitted brows, are a grand fulfillment of the early promise of the little *St. Proculus* in Bologna (figs. 62–64); but there is no longer any hint of a self-portrait. In profile at least, the features seem strongly Hellenized, but in full face they are far from regular. The flaring lips are asymmetrical, ◀ *109* the left eye slightly higher than the right, the nose unevenly pinched below the bridge. The hairy eyebrows are full and shaggy, and the forehead, already lined by anxiety, unevenly compressed. Perhaps these very deviations from cold canons of perfection play a part in rendering the colossal statue accessible to observers of ordinary size.

Throughout the statue, but especially in the head, the conflict between line and form which began in the *Rome Pietà* is intensified and deepened. The features are more sharply undercut than in any of the earlier works, possibly because of the height from which the statue was originally intended to be seen. A measurable space separates the eyeball from its enclosing lids. The enormous eyes are made especially expressive by delineating the cornea and hollowing out the pupil, in the manner of the two saints in Bologna (figs. 59–64); in consequence they seem at once liquid and fiery, in contrast to the limitless reserve of the blank, half-hidden eyeballs of the *Pietà* (figs. 74, 78) and of the *Bruges Madonna* (fig. 89). The flat planes joining at determined angles, visible for the first time in the *Bruges Madonna*, underlie all the construction of the *David*, not only in the squared-off masses of the features but throughout the knotty, bony, sinewy, half-developed, and unprecedentedly beautiful torso and legs. For the first time Michelangelo, now nearing thirty, is able to embody in the quality of a single human body all the passionate drama of man's inner nature. The sinews of the neck seem to tense and relax, the veins of the neck, hands, and wrists to fill, the nostrils to pinch, the belly muscles to contract and the chest to lift with the intake of breath, the nipples to shrink and erect, the whole proud being to quiver like a war horse that smells the battle. But of the nature of the battle there is no indication whatever; it is eternal and in every man.

If, as is claimed, Michelangelo really had difficulty with the shallow fifteenth-century block, one would never know it today. From all sides, including the wonderful back, the statue seems perfect. There was even room to reinforce the leg bearing the weight with the usual device of a treetrunk, sharply and exactly carved, and to allow the free foot to play easily over the edge of the rock. This is still just the beginning for Michelangelo's nude heroes; the full development of the figure in conflict is yet to come.

112 ▶

111

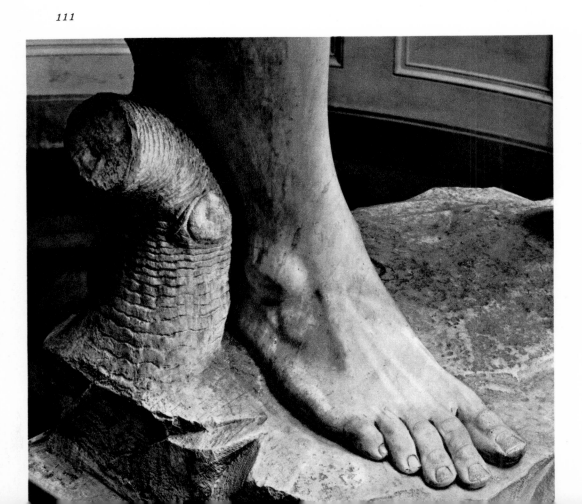

IO. THE TOMB OF JULIUS II (1505)

Project never carried out

In March, 1505, in the second year of his pontificate, Julius II called Michelangelo to Rome to design a tomb which was, according to Vasari, to surpass "in beauty and pride and in ornament and in richness of statues . . . every ancient and imperial sepulcher." It was also to become a source of torment to the artist for the next forty years.

Standing before the hybrid structure (now in San Pietro in Vincoli, fig. 113) concocted from statues and architectural elements of widely varying dates, it is difficult to imagine the magnificence of the original project, which was designed for an as yet undetermined spot in the old Constantinian basilica of St. Peter's, extensively restored in the fifteenth century under Pope Nicholas V. We do not even possess sufficient evidence to reconstruct the Tomb's probable arrangement with accuracy above the lowest story. In consequence, a number of sharply different solutions have been proposed by scholars. The design given here (fig. 114) is one more hypothetical attempt, but it corresponds to the literary accounts in certain features which have previously been discounted or even overlooked.

Vasari tells us that Michelangelo "passed many months" in Rome before the Pope allowed him to start work (actually it seems that the time was less than two months), and Vasari as well as Michelangelo's own letters state that the artist made many drawings for the Tomb before the Pope finally selected a satisfactory design. The original contract, if there was one, has disappeared along with Michelangelo's model, his plans, and all his drawings for the Tomb, save for an occasional figure sketch. We know from the sculptor's own letters only that the work was to have been completed in five years, for the sum of 10,000 ducats. He never described the appearance of the project, and no other contemporary descriptions survive. The first accounts of the plan are those published by Vasari in 1550, by Condivi in 1553, and by Vasari again, greatly amplified, in 1568—the first two during Michelangelo's extreme old age and the third after his death. No one knows what evidence was available either to Condivi or to Vasari, and both are frequently in error when recounting facts that can be verified. For instance, Condivi says Michelangelo's *Moses* (which he must have seen many times) supports his chin on his right hand; Vasari got the dimensions of Michelangelo's group for the Piazza della Signoria seriously wrong; and both biographers refer to the *Bruges Madonna* as a relief in bronze.

Their statements, therefore, must be examined with caution: the trouble comes in deciding which to accept and which to reject. Condivi and Vasari's second account agree that the Tomb was to be freestanding, twelve cubits wide by eighteen in length: a proportion of two to three, or roughly 25 feet 3 inches by 37 feet 10 inches. Yet the Tomb now in San Pietro in Vincoli measures only eleven cubits in width, or 22 feet 7 inches, and these are the dimensions to be found in Michelangelo's own notes and sketches for later contracts. Since the most economical and sensible solution obviously was to use in later projects any elements already cut out of marble, it is assumed here that the proportions given by the biographers are only approximate, and cannot be trusted in detail. The width of eleven cubits was probably that adopted at the start. In this case the depth of the whole structure—which from the second contract of 1513 (see page 138) seems to have been about 26 feet 10 inches, only 19 inches greater than its width—may also have been the measurement established in 1505, and retained in 1513 because the blocks had already been cut.

The lower story of the 1505 project was to contain niches flanked by herms, whose heads upheld the cornice. To each of these herms, Vasari says, "with strange and bizarre attitude was attached a nude prisoner, whose feet rested upon a projecting base." Although Vasari does not mention them, Condivi states that the niches were to contain statues. So far the

113. Tomb of Julius II
San Pietro in Vincoli, Rome

accounts agree with a ruined drawing now in Berlin (which shows winged, draped female victories standing over nude, recumbent male figures in the niches), and with a well-preserved and apparently careful copy of that drawing made by a pupil of Michelangelo (fig. 15). This much-discussed drawing has been variously dated by scholars, but the beardless representation of the Pope (he grew his famous beard only during the winter of 1510–11) leaves no room for doubt. The drawing certainly embodies one of the many alternative projects Michelangelo made for the Pope, according to Vasari, from which Julius chose one.

According to both Condivi and Vasari, the lower story was to contain a burial chamber, which Vasari says was entered from both ends of the structure, between the niches (Condivi mentions only one entrance). There is no suggestion of solid doors. "It was arranged so that one entered and left at the ends of the rectangle of the work between the niches," says Vasari in 1568, "and inside it was, walking about in the custom of a temple, in oval form, in which it had the chest, where was to be placed the dead body of that pope. . . ." Vasari's syntax is elusive, but not his meaning. Clearly the visitor could walk in and out at will, as in a chapel. The openings would have had the further advantage of providing the necessary illumination for the oval interior. One is reminded of characteristic Italian Gothic tombs of the fourteenth century, which frequently placed the sarcophagus in an open space, surrounded by a complex structure of combined architecture and sculpture, and of the freestanding chantries so common in northern Europe.

On the second story of the Tomb, both Condivi and Vasari tell us, four statues were to be

114. Tomb of Julius II
Author's reconstruction
of 1505 project

placed at the four corners, and Vasari identifies these as the *Active Life,* the *Contemplative Life,* *Moses,* and *St. Paul.* These, too, appear in the Berlin drawing, but the resemblance stops at this point. Now comes the most difficult passage in Vasari's description: "The work rose above the cornice in diminishing steps with a frieze of scenes in bronze, and with other figures and *putti* and ornaments in turn; and above there were finally two figures, of which one was the Heavens, who smiling held on his shoulders a bier together with Cybele, goddess of the earth, who seemed that she was grieving, that she must remain in a world deprived of every virtue by the death of this man; and the Heavens appeared to be smiling that his soul had passed to celestial glory."

There is *no mention* of a statue of the Pope, and this omission has excited considerable speculation. True, a blocked-in statue of Julius II was reported in a letter from Michelangelo's stone-cutter in Carrara in 1508, when as far as we know no work was being done on the Tomb by the artist, then wholly absorbed in designs for the Sistine Ceiling. This statue was being sent to Rome by the stonecutter along with a large quantity of "very beautiful marble." The statue, together with the specially beautiful marble which accompanied it, can only have been intended for the interior of the monument, just the place where we would expect it—on the sarcophagus within which the body of the Pope was to be laid to rest. It is hard to believe that anything as conspicuous in the design as a colossal statue of the Pope at the apex of the monument could have been ignored by both biographers, who describe with such eloquence the bronze statue of the Pope Michelangelo actually made for Bologna in 1506–7. And it is impossible to accept the famous, but wholly unsupported, guess that the block ordered in 1505 and delivered in 1508 was the same one found, still unfinished, in Michelangelo's studio after his death nearly sixty years later. The "St. Peter dressed like a Pope" was, much more likely, a statue roughed in for the never-executed tombs of the Medici Popes. It could even have been a St. Peter intended for the second story of the 1513 version (see page 138). The 1505–8 statue is certainly the same recumbent figure which, in the alternative version represented by the Berlin drawing (fig. 15), appears on the second story of the Tomb and, in the 1513 project and all subsequent ones, was actually moved to that position. Moreover, it is there right now, merely recarved, as the artist so frequently did with important figures (see pages 235, 294), so that Julius is leaning on his right elbow and facing outward, instead of being lifted up by angels with his head bent down. We can hardly imagine that every time the plans for the Tomb changed Michelangelo abandoned all the blocks, quarried at such vast labor and expense, and rushed off to get new ones—and in fact he never did. Common sense alone should tell us that he reused each block insofar as possible for its new position, adding a minimum of new material. This hypothesis is supported by all the surviving documents, as well as by the scrupulous incorporation into the final version in 1542–45 of surviving ornamented stones from 1505, 1513, 1516, and 1532, no matter how discordant.

Condivi's *arca* (coffin) and Vasari's *bara* (coffin, bier, or litter) would turn out to be the same thing, a symbolic marble chest upheld by the two figures, as sarcophagi so frequently are in Italian Gothic tombs. A *sella gestatoria*—the portable throne still used today for ceremonial papal appearances—cannot be extracted from the word *bara* by any amount of torture; for even a litter, whose occupant is recumbent, cannot be compared to the monumental *sella,* always called a *sedia* by Vasari. Moreover, the *sella gestatoria* with its slender handles would be wholly unsuitable for marble sculpture, as well as aesthetically intolerable at such a height, and ideologically absurd. Since the sarcophagus was to be upheld by only two caryatid figures, these would in all likelihood have been represented kneeling, possibly winged in order to bridge the gap between them and the mass of the sarcophagus.

On what kind of pedestal would the caryatids have rested? Vasari is explicit on this point—diminishing steps, with a frieze. Since the interiors and exteriors of Michelangelo's buildings are, whenever possible, sensitively interrelated, we must imagine that the oval inner chamber, doubtless vaulted by a cupola, found its expression in the plan of these diminishing steps. The most harmonious solution is that of a flattened octagon, which would adapt the oval interior plan to the rectangular exterior and leave convenient corner spaces for the statues. Such a flattened octagon can be encountered often in Michelangelo's architectural sketches. In one of his early drawings for the Sistine Ceiling, a work closely related to the Tomb of Julius II and containing many elements Michelangelo had first devised for the Tomb (fig. 18), the large central scenes are given this very shape. Finally, in a drawing made in 1559 or 1560 for an equestrian statue of King Henry II of France (fig. 115), Michelangelo used the same shape—herms, niches, diminishing octagonal steps, and all—and roughly the same proportions as in the reconstruction given here (fig. 114). The volutes bridging the profiles of the steps are derived from this drawing, as is also the number of steps. Similar volutes also appear in preliminary drawings for the Sistine Ceiling, and eventually turned up on the Tomb in place of the captives.

Positions are suggested here for the bronze reliefs and for the *putti* Vasari describes, clearly visible in the Berlin drawing. The statues have been so arranged as to produce the compact, dense effect Michelangelo always desired in his interrelations between architecture and sculpture, and to avoid any projecting architectural elements which, from eye level, would cut off the lower portions of the statues. The poses of two of these, *Moses* and the *Contemplative Life*, are derived from the Berlin drawing. The other two, *St. Paul* and the *Active Life*, are based on two mysterious and much-discussed drawings. One of these, badly damaged, is now in the British Museum (fig. 16). Although generally considered a prophet, it certainly represents a female figure. The top and back of the head are largely destroyed, but enough remains to show a headdress composed of intermingled veil and tresses. The mantle-strap running diagonally across the bosom recalls those of the *Pietà* (figs. 74–78) and the *Taddei Madonna* (fig. 82–84). The curious slope of the knees and the extreme length of the twisted torso are understandable only if the figure were designed to be seen from below, and set in a

115. Drawing for equestrian monument of Henry II
1559. Black chalk, 5⅛ × 4¾″
Rijksmuseum, Amsterdam

116

117

corner position. The *putto* upholding the pedestal corresponds both to the Berlin drawing and to Vasari's description of the frieze. Vigorous in its pose and intense in its gaze, the figure would do well as the *Active Life*, for which it is here suggested.

The other drawing, now in the Musée Condé at Chantilly (fig. 17), is much better preserved, but was extensively touched up at the extremities and in the torso by a very feeble hand, on the basis of an underlying drawing in black chalk by Michelangelo. In the corners there are two studies for the *Pitti Madonna* (colorplate 7; fig. 125). Tense and rawboned, the figure would make an admirable *St. Paul*, and, like the *Active Life*, is so placed and proportioned as to counteract optical distortion when seen from below. The position of the outstretched right hand suggests what would also seem likely, that the heads of the statues came well above the second and probably final step of the superstructure—and the gaze, like the pointing finger, seems turned toward the sarcophagus.

In the present reconstruction only thirty-nine figures are accounted for, although Vasari speaks of forty and Condivi of over forty. Perhaps the discrepancy, if significant, could be explained by the presence of the customary angelic figures in the interior guarding the sarcophagus. If the two attendant angels and two *putti* of the Berlin drawing were merely transferred to the outside of the tomb in 1513, when the idea of a burial chamber was renounced, the number comes to forty-three. In all respects except the elusive dimensions the descriptions of the biographers have been followed as closely as possible, and nothing has been added that cannot be found in relevant drawings by Michelangelo himself.

Previous interpretations of the meaning of the pyramidal structure present it as a kind of ascension from a life of misery and struggle on earth through a severely abridged succession of Neoplatonic realms to the ultimate perfection of the Pope's translation to a heavenly existence at the summit. This view would seem to suffer if the statue were not to have been placed at the top, but, as we have seen, there is not a scrap of evidence that it was intended for any such position. Perhaps interpretation should take a different tack, one based more realistically on the character and ambitions of a pontiff who, as far as we know, never showed himself particularly attracted to Neoplatonism or its advocates, but took a lively interest in his own tomb.

One might begin with the fact that for thirty-two years Julius II had been known as "San Pietro in Vincoli" (St. Peter in Bonds), the name of the church of which he was cardinal until his election to the papacy in 1503. This fact was not forgotten in the vast contemporary literature about him, both panegyric and satiric, nor was it forgotten by Julius himself. In the Stanza d'Eliodoro, painted to commemorate the Pope's greatest victories in 1512, Raphael made of his St. Peter liberated from prison a recognizable portrait of Julius II. The unprecedented appearance of the papal effigy in our only surviving evidence—the Berlin drawing (fig. 15) and Michelangelo's own description in the second contract—as upheld by angels, suggests inevitably the pose of Raphael's St. Peter in prison. Apparently the intention of the artist and his papal patron was to suggest that the Pope, instead of being laid to rest in his tomb, was actually being lifted out of it, freed from the chains and the prison of this mortal life, by angelic figures, like his apostolic predecessor whose church he was rebuilding and whose work he was emulating, and in a way, challenging.

Incidentally, whether in its burial chamber in 1505 or elevated to a platform in 1513, the effigy would have presented itself to the observer feet first. This position has distressed one scholar to the point of supplying the dead Pope with a thoughtful but unnecessary blanket to cover his feet, in spite of the Berlin drawing. The Renaissance, however, was less fussy. Frequently the funeral of the Virgin, or even the dead Christ himself, was represented feet foremost, both as a test of prowess in foreshortening, and as a means of bringing home the fact of death more forcibly to the observer. That such a tradition has by no means been lost in the Catholic Church may be shown by the fact that the mortal remains of the late Pope John XXIII were exhibited in St. Peter's in much this position, elevated on a slanting bier, feet toward the observers.

The first sentence of the Introit for the Mass of the Feast of St. Peter in Bonds, which Julius must have known by heart, is taken from the account of the Saint's liberation in the Acts of the Apostles:

> *Now I know in very deed that the Lord hath sent his angel, and hath delivered me out of the hand of Herod . . .*

The second sentence comes from the 138th Psalm (137th in the King James version):

> *Lord, thou hast proved me, and known me:*
> *Thou hast known my sitting down and my rising up.*

But instead of "rising up," the Latin sentence says "resurrection," and this is what we were intended to see dimly through the chamber door as in the prison cell of Peter—the resurrection of the Pope, like Peter, to eternal life.

What, then, was to be the meaning of the bound prisoners and the groups in the niches between them? The latter are invariably characterized as "victories" in modern literature. Vasari does not mention them at all, and Condivi refers to them only as "statues." No other evidence of their identity has yet been produced. The prisoners are called by Vasari, in his first edition, the provinces captured by the Pope; Condivi refers to them as the liberal arts, made prisoners by the Pope's death. (In his second edition Vasari uncomfortably combines both ideas.) As has often been pointed out, in 1505 both Julius' captive provinces and his patronage of the liberal arts were still in the future. He was having a hard enough time pacifying Rome itself, and had as yet commissioned no major work of art except for this very Tomb.

It has been sensibly suggested that by the second half of the sixteenth century, the original content of the Tomb had simply been forgotten. As for the herms, the biographers do not refer to them as such but rather as *termini*. Their significance has possibly been somewhat underrated.

Actually the same Mass of St. Peter in Bonds provides a reasonable explanation for all these figures. The first prayer for the day reads:

> *O God, Who made the blessed Apostle Peter to go from his bonds absolutely unharmed, absolve us, we pray, from the bonds of our sins and graciously keep all evil from us.*

The prisoners, then, twisting and writhing in their bonds, are held by sin, and by the example of St. Peter can appeal for deliverance. That deliverance takes place in the niches, in which winged figures, although clearly female and thus derived from ancient representations of Victories, raise their hands in exultation as they perform the angelic function described in the Introit and entreated in the prayer—the delivery of the quiet captives at their feet from the bonds of sin.

The termini (to which the standing prisoners are bound) have been described as symbols of death, and this they certainly are. A famous letter written by Erasmus in 1528 describes and justifies the great humanist's choice of this very emblem, which he derived from a ring that was given him in Rome in 1509, while Michelangelo was at work on the Sistine Ceiling, by Prince Alexander of Scotland, Archbishop of St. Andrew's. The ring contained an intaglio gem representing Terminus, whose significance as the god of ends and boundaries, the least movable of which was death, was explained to Erasmus at the time by an Italian friend in Rome. The gentle scholar adopted Terminus as his personal emblem, a kind of *memento mori*, with the motto, "I yield to none."

It would scarcely seem accidental that the only Christian saint included on the Tomb is St. Paul, to whom the second prayer of the Mass of St. Peter in Bonds is dedicated, as well as one of the secret prayers and one of the post-Communion prayers. Paul, like Peter, was delivered from bonds, to which he repeatedly refers in his Epistles. And in the First Epistle to the Corinthians he gives the unforgettable account of the final victory:

> *Behold, I tell you a mystery. We shall all indeed rise again: but we shall not all be changed . . .*
> *And when this mortal hath put on immortality, then shall come to pass the saying that is written: Death shall be swallowed up in victory.*
> *O death, where is thy sting? O grave, where is thy victory?*
> *Now the sting of death is sin: and the power of sin is the law.*
> *But thanks be to God, who hath given us the victory through our Lord Jesus Christ.*

Pointing to the coffin that surmounts the tomb, Paul prophesies both the Christian victory over the bonds of sin that bind the struggling soul to death, and the consequent incorruptible resurrection of the Pope in his dim chamber.

It is especially striking that both in the Berlin drawing and its derivatives, and in the only two prisoners to be actually finished (colorplates 8, 9; figs. 134–43), the powerful captives are bound only by narrow bands of cloth, clearly insufficient for their purpose unless endowed with supernal powers. Now the Latin word *vincula*, which is used throughout the Vulgate, was translated in the Douai version of the Bible not as "bonds" but as "bands." There would seem to be no other explanation for this extraordinary feature, which excites so much wonderment among the visitors to the Louvre. In Roman triumphal art, clothed captives are usually led by their captors, not represented as struggling against their bonds. But in Antonio Federighi's holy water stoup for the Cathedral of Siena (fig. 10), often adduced as a prototype for Michelangelo's captives, the nude prisoners do indeed struggle (against ropes, this time), and their meaning is clear enough: they are souls bound by the venial sins that holy water washes away. No termini appear as symbols of death, since holy water is powerless against

mortal sin. The meaning of the captives in connection with the effigy of the released successor of St. Peter (Julius' family name, Rovere, means "oak") was admirably summarized in an epitaph by Antonio Flaminio after the Pope's death:

> *There shall at last be none whom the bonds of sin make captive;*
> *The Julian oak shall feed the heavenly sheep.*

The appearance of Moses with St. Paul on the upper story of the Tomb has a manifold justification. First of all, he liberated the Chosen People from bondage in the land of Egypt, as Paul and Peter were liberated from their bonds. Then, Paul tells us in the Epistle to the Romans that "death reigned from Adam unto Moses." Moses is important, then, as prophet of the resurrection of all mankind through the Law, whose Tables he brandishes so airily in the Berlin drawing. Moses and St. Paul, as related figures, have been connected by the Neoplatonists. One can only say that they had the best Christian authority on their side.

The relevance of the *Active Life* and *Contemplative Life* to this scheme, even the identification of the two female figures as the *Active Life* and *Contemplative Life* (which rests upon the unsupported word of Vasari), is far from clear. It has been suggested that they may have been sibyls, forerunners of the Sibyls of the Sistine Ceiling. In the absence of any sure evidence this question can hardly be pursued further. We know even less about the bronze reliefs on the upper story. The Liberation of St. Peter and the Conversion of St. Paul would make convenient subjects, but we have no slightest evidence. Whatever may have been the meaning of these mysterious elements, that of the surviving stones, which seem to have been carved for the 1505 project, is clear enough, and most helpful. One, a pedestal for a captive, shows two leering masks in profile and a third in full face. Masks, as symbols of lying dreams, were characteristically used in Michelangelo's funerary decoration to denote the falsity of death. The spandrels above the niches that were to contain the victory groups have on one side fantastic floral ornaments terminating in winged horses and phoenixes, symbols of resurrection, and on the other fantastic animals, burning lamps, phoenixes again, and cornucopias

119. Tomb of Julius II
Detail: spandrels above niche of
Active Life

120. Tomb of Julius II
Detail: spandrels above niche of
Contemplative Life

overflowing with flowers and the fruit of the Julian oak. In the keystones of these arches demonic masks howl in apparent rage and frustration above the victors over sin and death.

The complicated fabric was to have been an unprecedented combination of architecture and sculpture, rich in its surfaces, powerful in its vertical motives made of struggling figures, imposing in its presentation of apostle and prophet, compelling in its many suggestions of the torment of earthly existence and the heavenly release, and transparently simple in its message. It remained a dream. Before the end of April, 1505, Michelangelo's plans for the Tomb had reached such a point of precision that he was able to go again to Carrara to superintend the quarrying of the blocks from his measured drawings. He was careful, incidentally, to stipulate marble of the highest quality, freshly quarried, white, free from veins or other flaws. Contracts with the shipowners for the transportation of the marble to Rome—some ninety-four wagon-loads in all—began in November. But even before the marble started to arrive in Rome the artist was in serious trouble. In January, 1506, the shipments were held up by bad weather, and one whole boatload of marble was sunk in the Tiber. The blocks had to be fished out with great labor. Meanwhile Michelangelo had been given a house off the Piazza San Pietro, behind the now-vanished church of Santa Caterina. Clearly the house was not nearly large enough for his work as, according to the sculptor's own subsequent account, the immense mass of marble blocks covered half the Piazza, and a considerable quantity were still at the port on the Tiber awaiting transportation.

At the start the Pope took great interest in the project, to the point of ordering a draw-bridge built from the Vatican to the improvised studio, so that he could easily watch the sculptor and his assistants at work. So vast was the undertaking that at the very least a new chapel in St. Peter's would be required to house it, and Michelangelo was asked to examine the ancient building to determine a suitable spot. On Holy Saturday, April 11, Michelangelo overheard the Pope (who was inspecting gems offered to him for sale) say that he did not want to pay for any more stones, large or small. On Easter Monday, and again every day that week, the worried artist tried unsuccessfully to gain admittance to the papal presence to plead for money to transport the remaining marble. On April 17, as he claimed in a letter to his friend, the architect Giuliano da Sangallo, he was "chased from the palace."

What had happened? We will probably never know exactly, but in any case Michelangelo left Rome immediately. His own story of the trip grew more adventurous every time he told it. He always blamed Bramante for the fiasco of the first Tomb project, and it is true that the cornerstone of Bramante's completely rebuilt St. Peter's was laid on April 18. But Michelangelo could scarcely have been unaware of such extensive plans, requiring lengthy and visible advance preparations, until the very eve of the laying of the cornerstone. It has recently been suggested that essential modifications of Bramante's first plan for St. Peter's, in which a chapel had been actually designed for the Tomb, made its location there impossible. But, for all we know, someone at the papal court may have succeeded in convincing Julius that it was bad luck to complete his tomb during his lifetime. In the same letter to Giuliano da Sangallo Michelangelo refers mysteriously to another reason for his departure, "which I do not want to write; enough that it made me think that if I stayed in Rome, that my tomb would be made before that of the Pope." Apparently he thought he was in a jam so serious that not even the Pope could get him out.

The stones remained in the Piazza San Pietro or in the port on the Tiber for years, and many of them "went bad" (Michelangelo's expression). The banker Agostino Chigi, builder of the delightful Farnesina Palace, was not above appropriating some of these marbles for his own purposes.

We have, of course, no idea how much work Michelangelo had been able to complete during the three months or so that he was actually carving. Possibly some of the present statues were roughed in by that time. Mr. Richard J. Betts has made the persuasive suggestion that the *Dying Slave* was one of these. At least two of the extant early drawings of the right arm and hand of this figure show that his judgment was correct. Some of the carved ornamental details look as if they were completed in 1506, especially the arches over the two niches in which *Rachel* and *Leah* now stand, and the base at the extreme right, intended for one of the captives. But we should certainly bear in mind that the blocks had been cut to the sculptor's specifications in Carrara, and that any major alterations in the plan would have had to utilize these blocks or waste large sums of money. So in all probability the dimensions and disposition of all the elements of the ground story of the Tomb were fixed.

II. THE PITTI MADONNA

Marble; 33⅜ × 32½"
Probably 1506
Museo Nazionale (Bargello), Florence

According to Vasari, this imposing Madonna was commissioned by Bartolommeo Pitti, whose son gave it to a member of the Guicciardini family. In 1823 the work was bought for the public collections of Florence.

Although many scholars consider the *Pitti Madonna* to be earlier than the *Taddei Madonna* (figs. 82–84), a later date is suggested here for several reasons. The last trace of the open composition, complex rhythms, and pointed shapes of the *Pietà* (colorplate 4; figs. 74–81) has vanished. The squared forms, so evident in the features of the *David* (colorplate 6; figs. 100–112) and throughout the *Bruges Madonna* (colorplate 5; figs. 85–99) apply to the entire figure of the *Pitti Madonna*. The shoulder, the elbow, the knee, as well as the head, the hand, and the drapery masses, show the new ideal of mass. This is particularly striking when we compare the features of this Virgin with the more refined and delicate features of her predecessor in Bruges. A fresh phase of Michelangelo's art is well under way—a phase of tremendous vigor and intensity. The artist is impatient with the *tondo* form. He does not even shape it accurately, and refuses to compose within it. The Virgin's head protrudes from the frame at the top, as her blocklike bench (reminiscent of the block on which the Madonna of the Stairs is seated), and even her garments, break the border at the bottom. There are no more gymnastics with the circular form and its possible permutations and combinations. The artist has built up a monumental group with a new grandeur and sense of scale; the group is compact and vertical, and the *tondo* frame lingers on as an echo.

These facts point to the assumption that the experience with the first project for the Tomb of Julius II in 1505–6, including the seven months spent in Carrara quarrying the blocks, had revolutionized the artist's style. The new phase of his art—accustomed to grandeur, impatient of enclosures—is evident in the *Pitti Madonna*. If we wish to picture the probable appearance of the seated *Active Life* and *Contemplative Life* for the Tomb of Julius II, the *Pitti Madonna* is our most reliable source. It was, in fact, first sketched out in the margin of the drawing suggested as *St. Paul* for the Tomb (fig. 17). It was surely contemporary with the fierce *St. Matthew* for the Cathedral of Florence (figs. 126–28); the handling of the chisel and the method of blocking out the shapes are almost identical in both. And, as has often been remarked, the pose and the facial type of the Virgin are close indeed to those of the *Delphic Sibyl* on the Sistine Ceiling, painted in 1509. Very probably they are close in date also.

As in the *Bruges Madonna*, the Virgin holds a book upon her lap; as in the *Taddei Madonna*, the infant St. John the Baptist appears. What is new is the wide-eyed gaze of Mary into the distance, her lips parted as if in a prayer or chant, while the Christ Child, pressed against her knee and protected by her mantle, contemplates the meaning of the open pages. The Baptist remains only a voice crying in the wilderness. One of the few remaining concessions to charm is the way the Child props the book open with one chubby arm, but even this is quickly overcome by the passionate intensity of His face under the windblown curls.

The cubic delineation of Mary's features results in strong angles even in the formation of the eyelids and eyebrows, and the same process flattens the masses of her headdress. The band across her forehead is supplied with a cherub's head and wings, in relief. Her hair falls on either side of her face in weighty shapes. But even though the mantle now runs squarely across Mary's shoulders, some curves are permitted, notably in the hem of her tunic and the rounded forms of the Christ Child's body. These curves unite what remains of the *tondo* shape to the masses of the emergent, almost statuesque central group.

Certain portions, notably the lower sections of the background, are only rudely blocked

colorplate 7

in, others are carried much farther: the face, bosom, and knee of the Virgin and the body of the Christ Child are complete in all essentials, their masses fully shaped with a toothed chisel. They lack only the final smoothing and polishing. As is often the case, we have no means of guessing what induced Michelangelo to abandon this majestic and solemn work. Perhaps it was the Pope's peremptory summons to Bologna in November, 1506. Whatever may have been the reason, the *Pitti Madonna*, even in its present condition, gives us a precious insight into an otherwise little-known period of the artist's sculptural imagination.

12. ST. MATTHEW

Marble; height 7' 2¾", width of base 2' 6", depth of base 1' 10¾"
Probably after 1506
Accademia di Belle Arti, Florence

This single statue, of shattering emotional and plastic intensity, is all that remains of Michelangelo's first cyclical commission on a grand scale—the twelve Apostles for the Cathedral of Florence. On April 24, 1503, he signed a contract to deliver one Apostle each year for twelve years, for a salary of two gold florins monthly. They were to be placed either in the chapels of the cathedral, to replace the paintings by Bicci di Lorenzo, or elsewhere, at the final discretion of the Consuls of the Wool Guild and the Cathedral *Operai* (board of works). A house was built for Michelangelo by the architect Simone del Pollaiuolo called Il Cronaca, and in 1504 the quarrying of the marble for the statues began at Carrara. But on December 18, 1505, Michelangelo, absorbed for the foreseeable future in the first project for the Tomb of Julius II, obtained his release from the contract.

How much had actually been done? In 1523 Michelangelo wrote that he had already begun one of the Apostles when he was called to Rome in 1505. Never a model of accuracy in his chronological statements, he may simply have confused the facts after so great a lapse of time. On the other hand, he really might have started the *St. Matthew* by the time of his departure for Rome. In any case, he can have done little or nothing on it during the period when he was occupied with the *David*, and immediately thereafter the lost cartoon for the great mural painting of the *Battle of Cascina* must have taken most of his time. We are informed by a letter from Piero Soderini, Gonfaloniere of the Florentine Republic for life, that in November, 1506, Michelangelo really was working on the Apostles again, so apparently the old contract had been resuscitated. The present appearance of the *St. Matthew* makes more sense if we date it after the fiasco of 1505–6; like the *Pitti Madonna*, it seems to breathe a new grandeur, a new monumentality, a new control by the twisted figure of the space outside it—not to mention a new authority and a new prophetic vision.

A great deal of romantic nonsense has been written about the unfinished state of the *St. Matthew*, as well as of other statues by Michelangelo. We have no reasonable evidence that he consciously intended to leave it in any such condition. We must imagine the *St. Matthew* as brought to the stage of completion represented by such other early works as the *David* or the *Bruges Madonna*. The masses of unfinished stone, to eyes trained in the tradition of Rodin, look wonderfully suggestive and mysterious. At first sight, indeed, the *St. Matthew* can easily be confused with the four *Slaves* from the 1532 version of the Tomb of Julius II (figs. 265–76), among which he is placed in the Accademia. Surely, however, all the marble would have been cut away, there would have been a space between the lower legs, the right arm would have hung free from the body, and the head would have been seen in the kind of jutting profile later to be so brilliantly exploited in the *Ezekiel* of the Sistine Ceiling. Undoubtedly the figure would have had a back as well as a front, and was intended from the start to be very nearly freestanding.

The violence of the pose and expression confers upon the figure a resemblance to the Louvre *Slaves* as adventitious as that established with the Accademia *Slaves* by its unfinished condition. The figure is not struggling against any sort of bonds. Rather, St. Matthew seems to be represented, as he should be, in a moment of inspiration, in the tradition of the great evangelist portraits of the Middle Ages, with some of which Michelangelo must have been familiar, as he must have been with the inspired sibyls of Giovanni Pisano's pulpit at Sant'Andrea in Pistoia, dating from the opening years of the fourteenth century. St. Matthew's symbol was the angel, although Michelangelo surely had no intention of representing one. There is no room for an angel in the block, and in a series of twelve Apostles it would have been improb-

126

able to add the eagle of St. John, and to deprive the other Apostles of attendants. Only the book, which Matthew clutches in his left hand and presses to his heart, attests to his evangelical mission—the book and his arresting pose of rapt listening to a voice beyond all worlds. As the soul of the saint is filled with the voice he hears, his eyes look upward to the source of his inspiration, his mouth is open as if singing, and his right hand holds the forgotten money-bag of his profession as tax-collector and publican. It is not the calling of St. Matthew that is represented here, or the book would scarcely have been shown. In keeping with the lifelong interests of Michelangelo, it is the timeless message, in this case the soul in ecstatic communion with the very source of revelation.

The *Pitti Madonna* and the *St. Matthew* remain our most reliable evidence for the mental reconstruction of the poses and feeling of the never-executed statues for the Tomb of Julius II in 1505–6. In the *St. Matthew*, as has often been noted, something of the convulsive wildness of the Hellenistic *Laocoön* group (discovered while Michelangelo was in Rome at work on the Tomb) is also evident. But the figure would have been tall and slender, still in the tradition of the *David*. The abbreviated garments, clinging to the pulsating abdominal muscles, would have revealed a spare, lithe body, taut and strong, very different from either the languorous softness of the *Dying Slave*, or the gigantic power of the *Rebellious Slave* (figs. 134–43). The use of the toothed chisel in broad curves to define the masses of the neck and head may be compared closely to the technique of the unfinished portions of the *Pitti Madonna*.

127

During the unhappy episode of the short-lived colossal statue of Pope Julius II for Bologna (see page 29), and during the four years Michelangelo was engaged in painting the Sistine Ceiling, the Pope seems not to have wanted to hear of the Tomb again. The only new event we know about is the shipment of the "beautiful marble" and of the probably recumbent, blocked-in statue of the Pope in 1508. Even after the completion of the Sistine Ceiling, and in spite of his desperate and seemingly fatal illnesses, there is no definite indication that Julius wanted Michelangelo to start work again. In fact, during this brief period the artist twice complained in his letters that the Pope had no work for him.

But after the old pontiff's death on February 21, 1513, his executors, Cardinal Leonardo Grosso della Rovere (the so-called "Cardinal Aginensis") and Lorenzo Pucci, the papal Datary (later Cardinal of Santi Quattro Coronati), contracted with Michelangelo for a new kind of tomb. The elaborate agreement, in Latin but with an Italian translation for Michelangelo, was signed on May 6. Apparently because Bramante's new designs for St. Peter's excluded it, the structure was temporarily homeless, and possibly for this reason the idea of a free-standing temple was abandoned. The Tomb was designed to be attached along one of its short sides to the wall of whatever church could be found to receive it. We can only presume as usual that, for obvious reasons of economy, as much as possible of the already quarried marble, blocked-in statues, and ornamented stones would be utilized in the new design.

Vasari refers to the new project as a reduction. True, there were now to be two fewer niches with sculptural groups, and four fewer captives. But, *en revanche*, two more seated figures were to be added to the second story, above which was to tower a lofty *cappelletta* of marble containing five more statues, larger than all the others because they would be further from the eye. The contract raised the total price of the work to 16,500 ducats, and obligated Michelangelo to finish the Tomb in seven years. Since the whole idea of a burial chamber had been renounced, probably because access and illumination from both ends was no longer likely, there was no more need for the diminishing steps devised to cover the cupola. The alternative design of 1505, represented by the Berlin drawing (fig. 15), doubtless promised to fulfill in general the new requirements, and was revived for the purpose. The effigy of the Pope, supported on its sarcophagus by two angels, was therefore transferred, probably without major changes, to the position indicated in the Berlin drawing—on the second story of the monument. It must be admitted that, at this height above the ground, the group would have presented a strange appearance. A few simple calculations demonstrate that within thirty-six feet, except from the sides, a spectator could have seen nothing of the departed Pope save the soles of his shoes. Beyond that range, the Pope's visage would have appeared to be supported on his hands and framed by his feet—sufficient reason for the tilting of the whole group forward in the 1516 project and the eventual arrangement reclining on one elbow, parallel to the surface plane of the monument, in the final disastrous version of 1542.

The description, appended to the contract, was in Michelangelo's own hand and referred to a wooden model. In general the elements correspond remarkably well to the Berlin drawing (fig. 15), which shows a beautiful, soaring niche, with a Madonna and Child in the center, and standing saints on either side. However, the two saints of the Berlin drawing become four in the contract. Also, the saints in the drawing were the height of the standing captives, and only the Madonna was given the colossal size later required by the contract. In any case, neither the statues planned nor the *cappelletta* was ever executed. There are discrepancies between the dimensions given in the contract and those recorded by the subcontract of July 9, in which Michelangelo agreed on much of the actual carving of the architectural and ornamental elements with a Florentine stonecutter, Antonio da Pontassieve. In every case the figures in the subcontract correspond to those in later notations and to the actual dimensions of the portions of the work executed in the years following 1513. So one can only conclude that Michelangelo did not bring the dimensions with him when he presented himself at the Vatican to sign the contract, and therefore made mistakes in translating his familiar Florentine cubits into Roman palms.

Some mysteries about the 1513 arrangement will probably never be solved. On the second story in the Berlin drawing, *Moses* is recognizable enough with the Tables of the Law, and the veiled female figure, clasping her hands on her breast and looking heavenward, is a natural for the *Contemplative Life*. But then where would *St. Paul* and the *Active Life* have been placed? And what would be the identity of the other two figures? St. Peter would probably have been selected to go with St. Paul. Who would be the four standing figures—saints, or personifications, or what? And was the Madonna, so strikingly close in pose and character to the *Sistine Madonna* of Raphael (also associated with the death of Julius II), intended to be a freestanding figure? If so, how was she to be supported, floating through the air so lightly in her mandorla?

129. Tomb of Julius II Author's reconstruction of 1513 project

It is not inconceivable that she was planned as a statue without a base, to be attached to the back of the niche. Similar visionary appearances of the Virgin were customary in the second decade of the sixteenth century in Roman art. Of the exactly forty statues destined for the 1513 project, only three were executed by Michelangelo's own hand, but these are among the grandest works of his entire career. In majesty of conception, in force and vitality, even in sheer volume, they far surpass anything which might have been expected from the relatively brittle design preserved in the Berlin drawing. The *Moses* and the two Louvre *Slaves* constitute the great artist's challenge to eternity.

130

131

132

Michelangelo set to work on this second project with such fury that in July, 1513, he wrote that he did not have time to eat. If we are to believe his own account, written under great stress nearly a generation later, in 1542, many of the marbles he had in the Piazza San Pietro, especially the little pieces, had in the meantime been stolen. It seems amazing that the materials for a Pope's tomb could have been filched from under the windows of the Vatican, but perhaps life was like that in sixteenth-century Rome. At any rate, the pieces that were left, as well as the rough blocks still remaining at the port on the Tiber and the pieces already carved or in progress in the inadequate workshop behind Santa Caterina, were moved to a more commodious house on the Macello dei Corvi. This property, which Michelangelo retained until his death, must have been fairly extensive as it bordered Santa Maria di Loreto on the Forum of Trajan on one side, and on the other it went as far as Piazza San Marco behind the Palazzo Venezia. According to the documents, the house possessed gardens, orchards, and wells. All this was levelled for the Victor Emmanuel monument now disfiguring the center of Rome.

In this pleasant house Michelangelo worked until the beginning of 1516 on the *Slaves* and the *Moses*. From one of his letters we know he was carving a figure which corresponds to the *Dying Slave* in 1513, when Luca Signorelli came to the house to borrow money, and that when Michelangelo complained of not feeling well enough to work, Signorelli assured the sculptor that an angel would come from heaven to guide his hand. In the summer of 1514 Michelangelo took a few months off to spend with his family in Florence. In June of the following year he bought a large quantity of copper for the bronze reliefs, and throughout the summer made models for figures, in order, as he hoped, to finish the whole work in two or three years, with the help of his pupils. A number of small wax, clay, and terracotta models still exist, five of which seem genuine (figs. 1–6) and probably belonged to this group. We have no idea how many statues were actually begun. In April, 1516, the now-deposed Duchess of Urbino visited

PUPILS OF MICHELANGELO
Tomb of Julius II
(see figs. 113, 118)
130. statue base, left of center
131. statue base,
right of center
132. statue base, extreme right

133. Tomb of Julius II
Author's reconstruction
of 1516 project

Michelangelo's studio to see how the work was progressing, but by that time the sculptor was already deep in the negotiations with Pope Leo X which were to deal the great project its death blow.

Late in 1515, apparently, the artist had become fascinated with the enormous design for a façade for the church of San Lorenzo in Florence, whose building and decoration had constituted a major undertaking of the Medici family off and on for nearly two hundred years—from the days of Cosimo the Elder in the early fifteenth century to those of the grand dukes of Tuscany in the late sixteenth. The façade, "a mirror of architecture and sculpture for Italy," eventually resulted in an artistic tragedy far worse than that of the Tomb; it was to waste three years of Michelangelo's life and energies. By the summer of 1516 a new contract was necessary for the Tomb, and this was signed on July 8. The heirs of Julius II, who had in the meantime incurred the enmity of Pope Leo X and consequently had lost the duchy of Urbino, were not in the most favorable position to enforce their rights. The time limit was extended from seven to nine years (to date from the second contract of 1513). Michelangelo was given the house in the Macello dei Corvi rent-free, and permitted to work on the Tomb wherever he wished—Rome, Florence, Carrara, or Pisa. Profiting by this clause, he may very well have taken with him the wax models for the Academy *Slaves* and the *Victory*. Many elements of the Tomb—as far as one can judge from the correspondence, those most nearly finished—remained in Rome, where they did not have the best of care. Michelangelo's friend, Leonardo the Saddler, complained to him that the roof of the house in the Macello dei Corvi leaked badly and was collapsing, and that some of the pieces were being damaged. Perhaps the *Moses* acquired at that time the unfortunate crack across the right knee (the guides, of course, tell the helpless tourist that Michelangelo hit the statue a blow with his hammer, and said, "Now, speak!").

According to the new contract, however, the mass of the monument itself was greatly reduced, although it was probably improved esthetically (at least in harmony with Michelangelo's known preferences), as compared to the somewhat discordant 1513 version (fig. 129). Upper and lower stories were to be united in a single, overwhelming composition. Two more niches with victories and captives, as well as the reliefs on the sides of the structure, were to be eliminated, leaving on the front of the lower story the same two niches, containing victories and flanked by termini and captives, that appear at every stage of the project except the last. At the sides were to be returns, each with a niche, a victory, termini, and captives. The second story was to be divided by columns above each terminus, and above each of the four niches, on the front and the returns, was to be placed a seated figure—probably a revival of the four figures of the 1505 scheme.

In the center of the lower story, and above the heads of the four seated figures, were to be reliefs in bronze. The central section of the upper story was to contain a niche, with the Madonna and Child, and in front of it the Pope upheld by two angels. A drawing by Michelangelo, probably for this effigy (fig. 19), shows him seated across the sarcophagus rather than recumbent upon it. Surely this was to be the selfsame effigy blocked out in 1508 for the burial chamber of the 1505 version, and destined for the upper story in 1513, now merely reworked so as to be tilted almost upright. It was to be recarved again in 1542–45. Although the contract does not say so clearly, the whole structure could not have been crowned by a single, unbroken cornice, for this would have provided deep, shadowy boxes for the figures. The upper edge must have been relieved by alternating impost blocks above the columns, and recessed bays of entablature above the seated figures and reliefs, much as in the final version, surmounted by the candlesticks carved for the 1513 project and still in place today. The bases of the columns, unlike the present plain ones, would have been ornamented.

A further dilemma presents itself in the central section. The *Madonna and Child* group in its niche must still have soared above the effigy of the dead Pope, for which otherwise there would be no space; so we must preserve the lofty niche and freestanding statue of the 1513 contract, modified and reabsorbed, like all other protrusions, into the total mass.

Apparently little or nothing was ever done to make this third contract a reality, since Michelangelo's time was almost completely taken up in work on the façade of San Lorenzo until 1520, and from that year until 1527 on the Medici Chapel. In 1523, shortly after the election of Clement VII to the papacy, the heirs of Julius II protested vigorously; prolonged negotiations ensued, during which the artist at one time even offered to sell all he had in order to return the money and let the Tomb be completed by someone else. Eventually, in 1525, Michelangelo proposed to reduce the monument to a simple wall tomb like those of preceding Popes in St. Peter's. We have no idea what this project was actually like, for the heirs never accepted it and, in the ensuing state of total disorder in central Italy from 1527 to 1530, no new contract was possible. The next acts of the tragedy belong to other chapters of this book (29 and 32).

What was the state of the monument when Michelangelo abandoned it for the second time, in 1516? Aside from the three finished, or almost finished, statues, there must at the very least have been blocks for many more. We know the block for the papal effigy already existed. The *Madonna and Child* now on the Tomb may have been carved from the block designed for the 1513 project. Most likely the *Prophet* and *Sibyl* were roughed out at this time also, but of a size to harmonize with the *Moses*. (The present *Rachel* and *Leah* were probably carved in 1542–45 from blocks intended for two saints in the uppermost story of the 1513 project, flanking the *Madonna and Child*.) Among the ornamental elements, three more bases had been completed, doubtless by pupils, in a somewhat more orderly and compact style than the first one, and the four candlesticks which now crown the structure seem also to date from 1513–16. The now headless wax models must have been done at this time. One (fig. 1) was used later for one of the four Florence *Slaves* (figs. 265–67), and another (figs. 2, 3) may have been also, but its condition is too fragmentary for us to be certain. A brilliant little model (fig. 6), now wrongly exhibited on its side, is clearly for the second captive from the right in the Berlin drawing (fig. 15); its leg-crossed pose was taken directly from ancient sarcophagus figures. The most beautiful figure of all, a supple and sinuous athlete (fig. 5), was intended for the last captive on the right in the same drawing. Something, of course, must have been done about the Victories. A nude female figure, whose anatomical peculiarities (especially the breasts so sharply distinguished from the underlying pectoral muscles) make it difficult to give to anyone other than Michelangelo (fig. 4), is posed in a position similar to that of the Victories of the Berlin drawing. Michelangelo may have decided on nudity for the Victories also, by this time, or he may merely have chosen to sketch the figure nude and add the drapery later according to the customary method (see pages 15–16). There are imitations of his Victories in Florence which show both possibilities.

A final opportunity for speculation presents itself. The wonderful drawing for a *Resurrection* preserved in the British Museum (fig. 22) has usually been dated in the 1520. The pose of the Christ was, however, utilized by Sebastiano del Piombo line for line as the principal figure in his *Raising of Lazarus*, begun in 1516, not only in the finished painting but in one of the preparatory drawings. Therefore Michelangelo's study must date from 1516 or before. Moreover, the shape of the drawing fits quite well the proportions of the space allotted for the relief. The *Resurrection* would make a perfect subject for the central relief of the projects of 151 and 1516, in conformity with the text from the Mass of St. Peter in Bonds (see page 122) and as a replacement of the view into the interior of the monument which, in the 1505 project, was to have disclosed Julius II lifted, like Peter, from the earthly prison.

14. THE DYING SLAVE

Marble; height 7' 6⅛"

THE REBELLIOUS SLAVE

Marble; height 7' ⅝"
Date: see discussion below
The Louvre, Paris

Although the names of these statues cannot be traced back earlier than the nineteenth century, they are generally accepted; and it is useless to try to rechristen the figures more accurately. In all likelihood they were finished (insofar as they *are* finished) for the 1513 project, although the poses were almost certainly determined for the 1505 project, as original drawings by Michelangelo for both Slaves date clearly from that period. The *Dying Slave*, in particular, retains some of the verticality of Michelangelo's earlier figures, notably the *David*, and even the *Bacchus*. There is no clear evidence that Michelangelo intended to use them in any of the later projects. Possibly he discarded them because of their incompatibility with the four much later Captives still in Florence (figs. 265–76). When the Tomb was completed in 1546 neither the Louvre nor the Florence Caprives was included. The Paris statues were given by Michelangelo in 1546 to his friend Ruberto Strozzi, in whose house he had twice recovered from severe illnesses. Strozzi, then an exile in Lyon, gave them to King Francis I, who in turn made a present of them to the Connétable de Montmorency. For some time they were shown in niches of the Connétable's château at Ecouen. In 1642 they were given to the Cardinal de Richelieu, and for a while adorned the portal of his château. By the eighteenth century they had found their way to Paris, and had been housed in a stable when they were bought for the Louvre in 1794.

Since the two figures correspond only in a few elements to any of the Captives appearing in the Berlin drawing (fig. 15), we can have no clear idea of the positions intended for them on the Tomb. They may well have been intended for the front, and they may have been designed as counterparts on either side of the same niche, but there is no conclusive evidence.

While no one places much belief in Vasari's assertion that the Captives were intended to symbolize provinces conquered by Julius II, Condivi's characterization of the whole series as the liberal arts fettered at the Pope's death has either been accepted or refuted at face value. It is, of course, not easy to reconcile such an interpretation with the fluctuating number of the Captives (sixteen in 1505, twelve in 1513, eight in 1516, four in 1532). Discussion has chiefly revolved around the fact that, in the unfinished masses of marble behind the Captives in the Louvre, apes are to be seen—only lightly roughed in behind the *Rebellious Slave*, but clearly visible and holding a small object of some sort alongside the left knee of the *Dying Slave*. The proponents of a Neoplatonic interpretation of the Tomb find the meaning of these little creatures in traditional medieval and Renaissance symbolism, according to which the ape represented all the subhuman tendencies in mankind; these apes thus could easily characterize the agonized figures as exemplifications of the Neoplatonic doctrine of the Lower Soul, fettered irrevocably to matter. On the other hand, with Condivi's assertion in mind, others have pointed to the long tradition in which apes indicate the figurative arts ("Art the ape of Nature"), and have insisted that the two figures are really personifications of painting and sculpture.

If the Christian interpretation of the Captives, according to the Mass of St. Peter in Bonds, is correct, it would by no means be incompatible with the Neoplatonic concept of the Lower Soul. Certainly mere allegories of the arts are foreign to Michelangelo's taste and preferences, and repugnant to the expressive depth and power of his figures. Moreover, subsequent representations of the arts, including those on Michelangelo's own dreary tomb in Santa Croce, are invariably depicted as partly or entirely draped female figures. Yet if each of the Captives

colorplate 8

was to be accompanied by an ape indicating that he personified the Lower Soul, how much monkey business was the observer expected to tolerate, even on the 1513 project, with twelve Captives and thus, presumably, twelve apes?

The answer to the dilemma may be quite simple. Where there is so much smoke there is always some fire. When Condivi makes a mistake, it is usually on the basis of some actual fact. The two monkeys, one of which seems really to be holding a mirror up to nature, may have been Michelangelo's own personal addition to the two figures, to indicate that the visual arts, also, were now fettered, but without any intention of turning these splendid statues into mere personifications. This proposal is in keeping with the grim humor Michelangelo frequently shows in unobtrusive portions of his vast compositions (the caricature of the

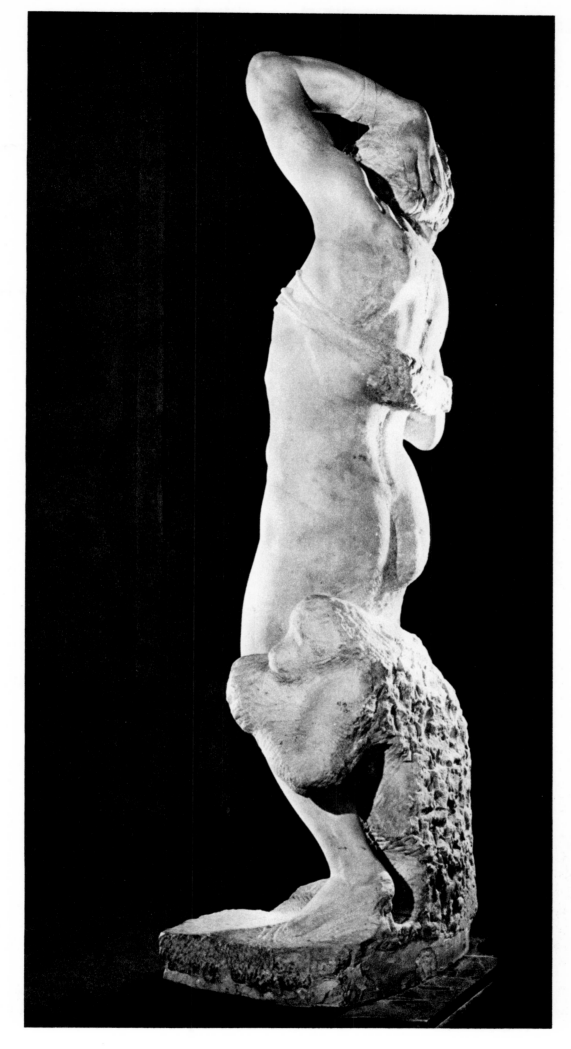

136

137

138

bearded Pope, in the staff held by Boaz in a lunette of the Sistine Ceiling, for example; or the mouse Condivi says he wanted to put in the Medici Chapel to indicate Time that gnaws all things away). For all we know, these whimsical beasts may have been intended to disappear along with the rest of the yet-uncarved stone, as there is no indication of them in any of the surviving studies, including the Berlin drawing. But, whether or not the monkeys were expected to be permanent, their suggestion that painting and sculpture had died with Julius II may well have been a hint to his successor, who at the time the Louvre *Slaves* were carved had given the great Vatican commissions only to Raphael and his school. Such impudence reminds us of Michelangelo's frequent sarcastic references to the Medici popes, in letters and poems.

The statues themselves, despite all their vicissitudes (both physical and intellectual), and despite their unfortunate placing in a low cross-light, are tremendously effective. Their polished surfaces have taken little harm from exposure to the elements at various noble residences. A severe crack runs across the nose and face of the *Rebellious Slave*, and down across both shoulders. Presumably the crack developed in the course of Michelangelo's work

colorplate 9

148

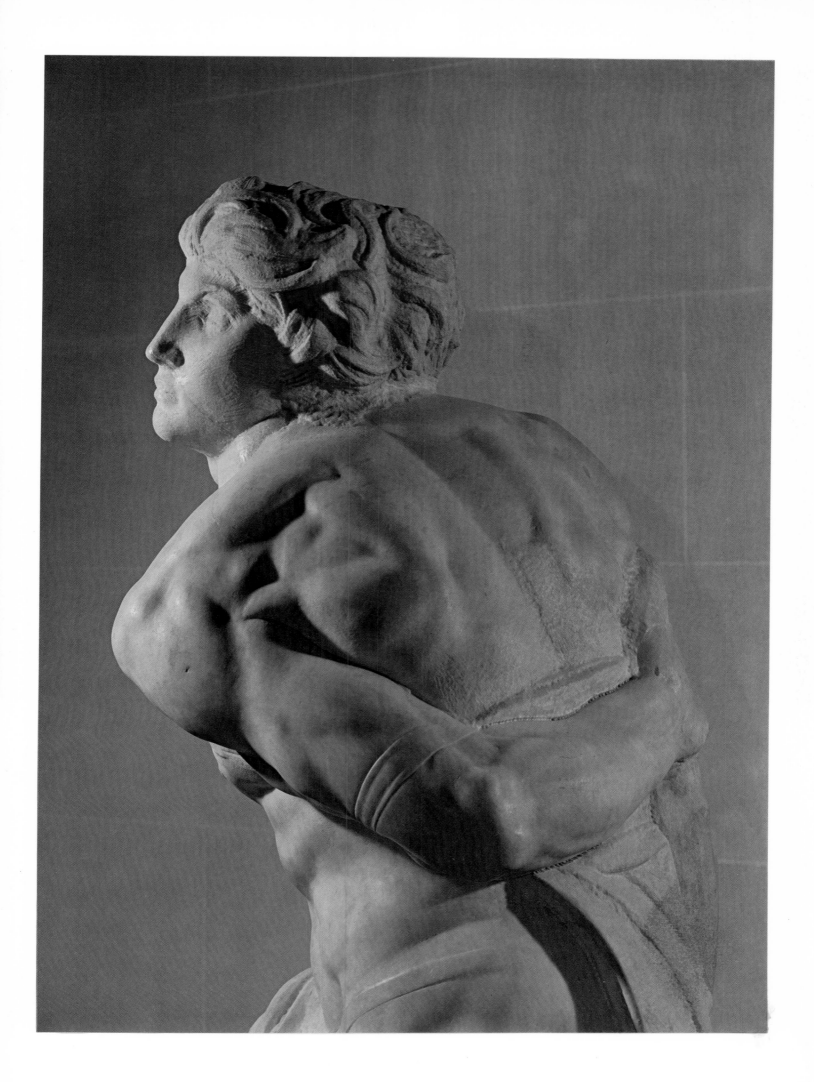

139

(or it might conceivably have been the result of mishandling during the statue's many moves), but it is not sufficient to mar the general effect. There is also no clear indication of the places the two statues were intended to occupy on the Tomb. The shapes of the bases make it clear that both figures were designed to back up to the termini, but since the left side view of the *Rebellious Slave* is the most dramatic, it was probably conceived for a right corner position, from which standpoint it could be especially well seen.

Seething with hopeless rage, the mighty figure struggles against the slender bands tying back the immense torso, the powerful arm, the waist, the heaving masses of muscle and bone that comprise the back. Although in a sense prefigured by some of the most massive nudes in the latest section of the Sistine Ceiling, this being comes from another race than do those

graceful youths. He is crushed, tormented, anguished, and also much older, so that his forms have lost the freshness and resiliency of youth. The face seems to have held less interest for the artist than the body. With its backward twist and rolling eyes it suggests the agonized *Laocoön*, but the mouth is closed. Some of the drill marks are still visible at the roots of the hair and among the locks. The toothed chisel moves with great rapidity and violence across the surface, suggesting the knowledge of pictorial technique and resources that Michelangelo gained while painting the Sistine Ceiling. The free, crisscrossing sweeps of the chisel are worlds apart from the neat, engraver-like circular hatching of the *Taddei Madonna* (figs. 82–84) and even the *St. Matthew* (figs. 126–28).

But the face has not received its final treatment, despite the three years the sculptor devoted almost entirely to the 1513 project for the Tomb. The body, on the other hand, except for a few passages in the middle of the back, and the rough marble of the right arm, is finished and polished. Michelangelo's conception of the character of musculature and the way it should be treated has changed in its essence since the days of the *David* (colorplate 6; figs. 100–112), completed only nine or ten years before. This change again is doubtless due to the experience of the Sistine Ceiling. The muscles are no longer individually defined and separated, but flow together in a tide which even obliterates the boundaries between leg and torso, or torso and arm. It is as if the figure were formed from some primal anthroplasm, pulsating with life but not yet functionally differentiated. Such a treatment is visible here and there in Michelangelo's early work, especially in background figures, such as those in the *Doni Madonna* and the *Deluge* scene in the Sistine Ceiling. Only in the latest sections of the Ceiling does it take over altogether, replacing the system of sharp linear definition which had prevailed, till then, in all foreground figures.

During the period when the *Dying Slave* must have been done, and during the ensuing decade or so, Michelangelo frequently drew the human figure almost or even entirely without contours, resorting only to shading in leadpoint to indicate the beautiful swelling and subsidence of this ocean of turbulent physical life. Here, throughout the back and left arm, in the belly and the brilliantly rendered flank, this kind of pulsation reaches a completely new peak of plastic intensity. Not that Michelangelo had forgotten contours—the composite profile of the figure itself, probably constituting at that point the very corner of the monument, is eloquent enough. But the new muscular flow has little to do with the relatively static contours of the earlier statues, composed of isolable units.

The legs and feet are lovingly handled, down to the last silken passage of skin around a thigh or calf, and the faintest change in the pressure of toes and the tension of ligaments. Again the contour sweeps along them, uniting with the roll of the intervening volumes. One is led to wonder, in view of the seemingly deliberate contrast between the absolute finish of the legs and the rough stone next to them, what was the conscious intent of the artist with regard to the accessory portions. Would he have carved jagged rocks, as in the *Bruges Madonna* and the *David?*

Perhaps because they are the only Captives from the 1513 project ever to be completed, and are both in the Louvre (and both have monkeys), the two *Slaves* have always been considered counterparts, for either side of the same niche. There is no evidence for this assumption, and it is perfectly possible that they were originally destined for widely separated portions of the monument. On the other hand, they might equally well have appeared almost back to back, on either side of the same corner. The one figure so powerful, the other so weak, the one bending forward, the other leaning back, would have complemented each other's natures and shapes in a manner thoroughly typical of the artist who, in the last section of the Sistine Ceiling, characteristically worked out such angular relationships among the attendant nudes. Back to back, at right angles, they would have combined to produce a closely integrated sculptural corner.

The *Dying Slave* is, of course, not dying but simply overpowered by the bonds against which he plucks idly. It is as if he were drowsy, overcome by the stupefying effects of a potion. His tall figure seems ready to collapse, or rather to sink slowly downward. Related more strongly

to the front plane than is the *Rebellious Slave*, the statue was very probably blocked out for the 1505 project. Certainly it is full of reminiscences of the artist's earlier works. The knees move together much like those of the Santo Spirito *Crucifix* (figs. 48, 51, 52); the head falls over like the Christ of the *Rome Pietà* (figs. 76–79); the soft abdomen, buttocks, and thighs recall the *Bacchus* (figs. 65–67); the left arm is lifted like that of one of the last nudes on the Sistine Ceiling. But at the very least the surfaces, as we see them finished everywhere save for portions of the back and the hair, show all the fluidity of Michelangelo's mature style. Nowhere do the lines cut into the mass as they do in all the finished early sculpture. Line and mass have fused. And if here and there, as in the detail of the right hand and the treatment of the nipple, some vestiges of the earlier linear manner persist, they are swept away in the flood-tide of moving surfaces through the arms and legs.

Whatever may be the specific literary meaning of these figures—allegorical, Neoplatonic, or, as would seem appropriate to a papal tomb, Christian—their meaning to Michelangelo himself and to the modern observer as ideally projected images of a universal human dilemma may not be far apart.

15. MOSES

Marble; height 7' 8½", width of base at front 3' 1½", depth of base 3' 3¾"
c. 1515
San Pietro in Vincoli, Rome

Brought down from its destined height to a spot only a few feet above the ground, wedged between reveals originally meant to flank a relief, and bases and termini designed to receive the *Captives*, the *Moses* cannot today exert anything like the effect for which it was intended. Yet nothing that has ever happened to this masterpiece can be worse than its daily fate in San Pietro in Vincoli, where the serious student is shoved aside by guides who, every fifteen minutes, lead in a new herd of camera-flashing tourists, telling them in four languages that Moses is shown just back from Sinai, ready to rise from his seat and smash the Tables of the Law in anger against the Israelites, who are adoring the golden calf. This although he has a close grip on the Tables and a firm seat on his block, and, if the Israelites were supposed to be there, Michelangelo would have represented them.

This kind of legend, dating in the present instance only from the eighteenth century, is typical of the episodic interpretations that falsify the timeless and universal concerns of Michelangelo's genius. (See pages 83 and 107 for similar instances of symbolic presentations.) The giant prophet was intended for the front of the Tomb on the second level, seated as a guardian of the sarcophagus. "Death reigned from the first Adam until Moses," said St. Paul, whose statue was probably to have appeared on the right side, toward the back; Moses would have sat at the left of the Pope and the sacred figures, as befits his prophetic position in the Christian scheme of revelation. From an ecclesiastical standpoint, then, he fits into his place in the massive structure of salvation from sin and death which the Tomb was meant to epitomize. His "closed" right side, often analyzed by scholars in general terms, can be accounted for both symbolically and visually by this position. The Tables of the Law are held near the sarcophagus of the departed Pope, and unite with the vertical of Moses' right leg and the vertical of the terminus behind it, as essential elements in the composition of the central aspect of the Tomb. The "open" left side, with its jagged profiles of jutting knee, elbow, and beard, continues the movement of freely ascending elements to form the outer corner of the monument.

The figure has, of course, changed enormously in Michelangelo's mind since the Berlin drawing (fig. 15), which shows the prophet brandishing one of the Tables in each hand. The masses have been more densely grouped in order to suppress or at least minimize all openings, in keeping with the general direction of Michelangelo's development as a sculptor. The turn of the head and the lowering of the left knee reinforce the statue's function as a corner figure, and carry the eye around to the next statue, either the *Active Life* or a sibyl. As has frequently been observed, the torso is unnaturally prolonged in order to appear correct when seen from below. A recent effort to study exactly what this effect would have been (by photographing a cast of the *Moses* from the proper angles) has resulted in some important observations. First, the statue would have presented, from below, an array of violent zigzags, translating into major compositional movements the jagged contours of the smaller elements. The drapery over the left leg was almost certainly much longer, coming down almost to the left foot when the statue was originally carved, around 1515. It was apparently cut off by Michelangelo himself in order to make the foot visible from the front when the statue was reworked for its present position in 1542–45. Finally, the projecting blocks with their decorative *putti*, seen flanking the thrones in the Berlin drawing, would have had so disastrous an effect upon the statues, especially the *Moses*, when seen from below, that it is hard to imagine that Michelangelo did not eliminate them in his general tightening-up and simplification of the composition.

A number of peculiarities call for comment. The horns on Moses' brow are, of course, the

colorplate 10

horns generally shown there in Christian art, through a possibly deliberate mistranslation of the original Hebrew word *qaran* ("shine") used in Exodus to describe Moses' radiant face the second time he came down from Sinai. In the Vulgate, probably to avoid confusion with the Christian halo or nimbus, Moses' face is described as *cornutus* ("horned") at this juncture, which strange translation survives in the Douai version ("shone" in the King James), providing the best of reasons for the dismay with which Moses' companions regarded him. In any case, and this would seem to be final, Moses' face displayed neither horns nor light at the time of the golden calf episode.

Over his left shoulder appears the characteristic mantle-strap, so often utilized by Michelangelo for varying effects, as if to hint at the bonds of the captives below. And Moses' legs are clothed in gartered breeches suggesting those of the barbarians, usually oriental, represented on Roman triumphal arches. Such leggings are often given to Renaissance and Baroque representations of Hebrew priests.

The mighty figure is closely related to some of the most powerful prophets and sibyls on the Sistine Ceiling. The sharply turned head and jutting beard suggest *Ezekiel*, and the incredible left arm, of superhuman muscular force, repeats almost exactly the left arm of the

144

Cumaean Sibyl. But the overwhelming face, disturbed by the divine vision, shaken by the fire and thunder of the mountain-top revelation, is derived directly from Michelangelo's own face-to-face colloquies with the Almighty, especially the *Creation of Sun and Moon*. The immense vitality of the Hebrew prophet and precursor of Christ, lawgiver and leader of the Chosen People, is expressed in the increase in the volume of drapery, as in the mantle boiling over the right knee, and in what is probably the most astonishing beard in the history of human imagination. This cataract tumbles in irresistible waves, billows, and freshets from the prophet's cheeks and chin down over his deep chest. While the bulk of the locks are pulled aside by the index finger and second finger of the right hand, they almost join the loose lock, to arrive in the gigantic lap, hidden behind the left hand.

Both the *Moses* and the Louvre *Slaves* are mentioned in a letter from Michelangelo in 1542 as "almost finished." We should therefore imagine the *Moses* as still possessing, at that late date, a certain quantity of uncut marble. It is far from certain to what pitch the statue had actually been carried. At any rate, the upper portions of the hair and the right side of the neck are still not entirely finished; indeed they show marks of a toothed chisel. It could very well be that the troubled face and the great left arm (so similar to corresponding elements in

145

the sad frescoes of the Pauline Chapel, on which Michelangelo was engaged while finishing the Tomb) received their final surface treatment at this moment. The left hand, for all its beauty, is polished only above the middle finger.

When the statue was finally placed on the Tomb there began an extraordinary custom, which persisted for many years. The Jews of Rome came solemnly every Saturday to venerate the statue of their great leader and liberator, despite the Mosaic prohibition of making or worshiping graven images. As one moves around the divine face, full of anger and beauty, of inspiration and awe, one can understand their feelings.

152 ▶

151

16. CHRIST HOLDING THE CROSS

Marble; height 6' 8¾", depth of base 2' 1"
1519–20; see discussion below
Santa Maria sopra Minerva, Rome

The over-lifesize statue of the resurrected Christ that stands in the dim interior of Santa Maria sopra Minerva is scarcely one of Michelangelo's best-loved works. For one thing, it is very difficult to see the figure in the bad light of that much-restored church. Again, in the seventeenth century ecclesiastical prudery supplied the statue with a ghastly metal loincloth, considered unnecessary in the brave days of the High Renaissance. Also, once the excrescence is removed, modern eyes find a totally nude statue of Christ hard to accept. Finally,

153

it was not finished in its entirety by Michelangelo himself, and in places its quality is disconcertingly bad.

Such drawbacks should not blind us to the statue's many virtues, chiefly its calm and contained presentation of a theme, the Man of Sorrows, which had always been shown as tragic, and was designed to appeal to the emotions of the pious observer. Michelangelo has shown us the resurrected God-man, triumphant over death and exhibiting none of its sufferings or terrors. He holds the Cross, the reed, the sponge, and the scourge very quietly, having passed beyond their sway. Yet there is no hint of classical stoicism, no false heroics. He merely stands there, "noble and nude and antique," yet radiant with the beauty of spiritual as well as physical perfection.

The statue was ordered in 1514 by Bernardo Cencio (canon of St. Peter's), Maria Scapucci, and Metello Vari Porcari, the latter from an old Roman family, noble despite its name ("swine-

154

155

herds"). When Michelangelo left Rome for Florence in 1516 the statue was unfinished, because of a black vein which had turned up in the face. In this condition the artist made a present of it to Porcari. This first version has since disappeared. But Porcari insisted on a completed statue, which Michelangelo carved anew, save for the finish, in Florence in 1519 and 1520. It was not shipped to Rome until 1521, and was finished there by Michelangelo's pupil, Pietro Urbano, who made some bad mistakes in the face and hands. The sculptor hired a new workman, and eventually retouched some portions of the work himself, but he seems always to have been dissatisfied, since in 1522 he offered to make a third statue.

Under the conditions prevailing in Santa Maria sopra Minerva, it is next to impossible to separate the portions done by Michelangelo from those finished by pupils, but it is clear enough that the face, with its insipid expression and softly curling beard, is largely assistants' work. The quality of the surface, particularly of the beautiful left arm, the hands, and the torso, with the exquisite movement across the abdominal muscles, is unexpectedly high. Little is left of the original surface of the feet, largely worn away by the hands of the faithful, who, unfortunately, can reach just that high.

The arms of the Cross are obviously far too short to hold a human being. Michelangelo must have shortened them to avoid the technical difficulties of handling so great a projection, as well as esthetic objections. As a result the Cross appears as a symbol of the Crucifixion rather than as an exact representation of its instrument, in keeping with the essentially symbolic nature of Michelangelo's art.

158 ▶

17. THE MEDICI CHAPEL

1519–34
San Lorenzo, Florence

After the first and second acts of the tragedy of the Tomb of Julius II, and the even more humiliating fiasco of the San Lorenzo façade, Michelangelo was given yet another opportunity to embody his new ideas on the interrelation of architecture, sculpture, and perhaps even of painting, in a vast, monumental complex—the last of his great architectural-sculptural fantasies, and the only one to be realized in anything approaching entirety. And, although even this time the work was never finished in all details, it has been recognized ever since as a resounding triumph. Certainly no one suspected in the summer of 1519, when Michelangelo accepted the commission to construct the New Sacristy of San Lorenzo and furnish it with tombs for various members of the Medici family, how noble the result would be. But much of the energy and ambition, and some of the frustration expended in the designs for the façade of San Lorenzo clearly was absorbed in the originally modest project for the Medici Chapel, just as many of the ideas for the 1505 design of the Tomb of Julius II eventually found their way into the Sistine Ceiling.

Under the pontificate of his cousin, Leo X, Cardinal Giulio de' Medici (later Pope Clement VII) commissioned Michelangelo to build a chapel at San Lorenzo, to enshrine the tombs of Leo's father, Lorenzo the Magnificent, Lorenzo's brother Giuliano (the Cardinal's father), the younger Giuliano, Duke of Nemours (Leo's brother), and the younger Lorenzo, Duke of Urbino (Leo's nephew). Lorenzo, the last surviving scion of the legitimate male line of the Medici family, died in May, 1519. According to a recently discovered document, plans for the funerary chapel were divulged in great secrecy by Cardinal Giulio de' Medici to Giovan Battista Figiovanni, canon of San Lorenzo, in June of the same year. Plans must have been elaborated rapidly, because construction began on November 4, 1519, and Michelangelo was the architect from the start. He was apparently under the obligation to build on a plan which would be a twin to Brunelleschi's Old Sacristy, a masterpiece of the early fifteenth century. It is remarkable that the windows on the exterior of the New Sacristy do not always correspond with those on the interior. Michelangelo arranged the lighting very carefully to produce the subdued, all-over illumination essential for the prevailing mood of his architectural and sculptural compositions.

The work progressed irregularly, and may not have been entirely finished even as late as 1533. The cupola, however, was already terminated in 1524, and the following year its golden ball was set in place. The tombs and their sculptures, meanwhile, must have been designed very rapidly indeed, because from Michelangelo's letters and memoranda we know that by April, 1521, he was in Carrara with all the measurements, on the basis of clay models and preparatory drawings, ready to order the blocks.

At first the Cardinal wanted a freestanding monument in the center of the Sacristy. Each of the four sides of this structure would have contained the tomb of one of the four departed Medici. Michelangelo seems to have been able to talk the Cardinal out of this proposal fairly soon. An unusually large number of sketches are preserved, showing various stages in the evolution of the freestanding monument, alternative schemes for a kind of four-sided triumphal arch on the principle of the Arch of Janus in Rome, and proposals for wall tombs, all of which may have been studied simultaneously. The final arrangement placed the two younger members of the family—the Dukes—in their present wall tombs, and relegated the two *Magnifici* to a place under the statues of the Madonna and the patron saints of the Medici, Cosmas and Damian, on a third wall, between the entrances and facing the altar. The third wall was not completed at the time Michelangelo abandoned the entire project, and no one can be really sure which of the several drawings represents his latest ideas on the subject (figs. 20-21).

159. Medici Chapel
View from altar

Leo X died on December 5, 1521. His successor, the Dutch Pope Adrian VI, did not arrive in Rome for many months—and then only to paralyze all artistic undertakings at the Vatican. Cardinal Giulio de' Medici, nonetheless, did not drop the great project for the tombs at San Lorenzo. Recently discovered documents show that the quarrying continued at Carrara, although the marble was not shipped to Florence. In September, 1523, after the universally welcomed demise of Adrian VI, Giulio was elected Pope as Clement VII. Early in 1524 the marble blocks began to arrive in Florence, possibly including those for the nude figures; and by June so much work had been done on one of the ducal tombs that neither the design nor the location could any longer be changed. The carving of the statues from the rough-cut blocks began in Florence that year, and by March, 1526, four were almost finished.

Michelangelo began two more by June, 1526, at which time he wrote that in two weeks he would start on the last ducal statue, and that, of the important figures, only the four River Gods remained. Nothing would seem, then, to stand between the great artist and the completion of his work—except history. By June, 1526, hostilities had broken out between the new Pope and Emperor Charles V. In September the Vatican itself and St. Peter's were attacked and plundered by the Colonna party, and in January the Pope ordered the fortification of Rome against the imperial forces. Early in the morning of May 7, 1527, began the terrible sack which put an end to the High Renaissance, or what was left of it, in Rome. After months of unspeakable horror the Pope, a prisoner in Castel Sant'Angelo since June, escaped and fled to Orvieto on December 7. Not until October, 1528, was he able to return, poverty-stricken, to his burnt-out and half-depopulated capital. Florence, meanwhile, had thrown off the Medici yoke for the third time, and reestablished the republic. All work on the Chapel had stopped.

Only after the siege and capture of Florence by papal and imperial forces in August, 1530, in that unexpected alliance which was to pin despotism on most of Italy, was it possible to recommence the great Medici project. Michelangelo, in hiding until November because of his assistance to the republican government in organizing the defenses of the city against the Medici, began work again, but in so feverish a manner that by September, 1531, his friends thought he was endangering his life. The work on the interior architecture, the tombs, and the statues went on until August, 1532, when Michelangelo went to Rome for nearly a year. In 1533 he spent only four months in Florence, and returned there for another four months or so in 1534, when, in spite of the unfinished Medici Chapel, he was called to Rome by Clement VII to paint the *Last Judgment*. He never saw Florence or the Chapel again. The statues, except for those of the Dukes, were apparently left in the greatest disorder, and not until 1545 were they placed on the tombs by the sculptors Niccolò Tribolo and Raffaello da Montelupo. In 1559 a sort of sarcophagus was concocted for the *Magnifici* from slabs left in Michelangelo's studio. Out of the whole ambitious complex of statuary, only the Dukes were completed down to the penultimate details. The two female figures, *Aurora* and *Notte*, still show passages of rough marble around their legs and feet, which were to be finished heaven knows how, and the male allegorical figures, *Crepuscolo* and *Giorno*, show, in addition to unfinished lower portions, heads that are scarcely more than blocked in.

The River Gods were never done, and only a few sketches and the model for one figure survive. *Cosmas* and *Damian* (figs. 24, 25), were carved, after a fashion, by Raffaello da Montelupo and Giovannangelo Montorsoli respectively. Various *disjecta membra* have come to light: roughed-in trophies probably intended for positions above the two dukes but eventually abandoned, and a crouching nude boy, now in Leningrad (figs. 248–51), possibly designed as one of a series for an attic or similar high placement. The mystery of the other statues has never been resolved. In his life of Michelangelo, Vasari mentions none, but in the chapter he devotes to Tribolo ("trouble"), he justifies the nickname of this unfortunate by recounting how he was to have done two ill-fated nude statues for Michelangelo, representing Heaven and Earth, to be placed in niches flanking Giuliano. True, Michelangelo (see below, page 173) does mention Heaven and Earth in connection with Giuliano, but the descriptions of the never-executed statues sound anything but Michelangelesque. And the worst of it is that no one has been

160. Medici Chapel
Tomb of Lorenzo

able to come up with reasonable suggestions for the corresponding statues to flank Lorenzo, since Heaven and Earth seem already fairly inclusive. The frescoes, if there were to have been any, were never started. But despite every fault and failure, enough survives to render the Medici Chapel one of the most impressive artistic and spiritual experiences available to man on this planet.

The supposition that every major monumental complex of imagery by Michelangelo is to be interpreted as a synopsis of the Neoplatonic cosmogony has become to its proponents an article of faith. Seldom in humanistic scholarship has so imposing a fabric been constructed upon such treacherous foundations. Few would deny, to be sure, that Michelangelo's contact with Neoplatonism in Medici circles during his extreme youth played an important part in determining aspects of his content and even of his style. But to extend this principle to the point of ruling off each of Michelangelo's plastic structures into superimposed zones, corresponding to hierarchical divisions of the Neoplatonic universe, and to identify each element accordingly, strains our credulity. No later texts are adduced than some from the first Neoplatonic movement of an earlier generation, and it has not yet been shown that these texts apply. In fact, to make them even seem to fit, they have to be drastically simplified, edited, shuffled, recombined, or otherwise altered.

Neoplatonic interpretations receive little or no comfort from Michelangelo's highly personal and always unsystematic writings, unless these are sharply distorted. Most embarrassing of all, those Neoplatonists who survived into the sixteenth century (including Benedetto Varchi, who lectured before the Florentine Academy on Michelangelo's poems, which he considered full of "Socratic love and Platonic concepts") say not one word about Neoplatonic structures in any of his sculptures or paintings. Such a "discovery" had to await the late nineteenth century.

So rigidly is Neoplatonic dogma held in certain circles that any attempt to question it is met with disbelief and even mockery. It has become heretical to suspect that the visual imagery

Medici Chapel
161. Tomb of Lorenzo
View from entrance
162. Tomb of Giuliano
View from altar

161

162

of papal chapels intended for the celebration of Mass might have a Christian content! Yet in all other fields of artistic interpretation the meanings of such programs are customarily sought in the nature and purpose of the individual monument; in the personalities, ambitions, beliefs, and pronouncements of the patron and his advisers; and above all (when available) in the words of the artist himself. Why should Michelangelo studies alone be exempt from so reasonable a procedure? The extent of our present impasse may be measured by the fact that one of the most ambitious recent Neoplatonic interpretations of the content of the Medici Chapel fails even to identify the original patron, Pope Leo X; and that another has found Neoplatonism equal to the task of accounting for the presence of candlesticks on the altar, and also divides the Chapel in such a manner as to consign the Virgin and Child to Hades.

For three centuries, tradition, starting in Michelangelo's own circle, understood the Chapel to be a grandiose allegory of princely and papal power, both temporal and spiritual. That all the earliest sources, from the sixteenth, seventeenth, and eighteenth centuries, should have been totally off the track passes belief, especially when they agree with traditions current in Michelangelo's studio (see below), with the accounts of Michelangelo's own words, and with fragments preserved in Michelangelo's handwriting. One of these is written above and below sketches for architectural elements in the Chapel:

> *The heavens and the earth... Night and Day are speaking and saying, We have with our swift course brought to death the Duke Giuliano; it is just that he take revenge upon us as he does, and the revenge is this: that we having slain him, he thus dead has taken the light from us and with closed eyes has fastened ours so that they may shine forth no more upon the earth. What would he have done with us then while he lived?*

No less solemn is the briefer phrase which appears under a sketch for the tombs of the two *Magnifici*:

> *Fame holds the epitaphs in position; it goes neither forward nor backward for they are dead and their working is finished.*

Disjointed and, in the original, unpunctuated, these jottings were apparently intended to crystallize in the artist's mind portions of the allegorical structure to which he was giving plastic embodiment. Presumably there were still other such notes which have not been preserved. Would that we possessed anything at all in the artist's hand to throw a similar light on the enigmas of the *Sistine Ceiling* and the *Tomb of Julius II*!

What the late, beloved Bernard Berenson called the "sovereign grandeur" of these lines is adequate, in spite of their roughness, to convey Michelangelo's awe as he summons up the struggle between the mighty dead and devouring Time. (Condivi recognized this symbolism, and related that the artist wanted to include a gnawing mouse, to indicate the destructive power of Time, like the owl and the poppies given to the *Notte*; see page 207.) The superhuman dukes have conquered even the remorseless cycle of the days and nights and deprived them of their light, and Fame holds epitaphs forever above the dead *Magnifici*. Vasari, who worked in Michelangelo's studio for a brief period in 1525 while these statues were being carved, recognizes in his descriptions the defeat of the Times of Day.

That the beautiful ducal statues were never intended to be recognizable portraits of the bearded Medici has been generally recognized. Again Michelangelo's words, recorded in 1544 by Niccolò Martelli, come to our aid:

> *When Michelangelo had to carve the illustrious Lords of the most happy house of Medici, he did not take from the Duke Lorenzo nor from the Lord Giuliano the model just as nature had drawn and composed them, but he gave them a greatness, a proportion, a dignity . . . which seemed to him would have brought them more praise, saying that a thousand years hence no one would be able to know that they were otherwise . . .*

From these words, from the idealized appearance of the Dukes, and from their Roman armor, the proponents of a Neoplatonic interpretation have concluded that the statues represent the immortal souls of the Dukes, although Roman armor is hardly the customary attire for departed souls. It is appropriate for military leaders, however, and as such adorns innumerable Renaissance statues of commanders, including those of several other members of the Medici family, which were publicly exhibited in Florence and its dependencies.

Roman armor was even more appropriate to Captains of the Roman Church. It has been noted that Giuliano holds in his hand the baton of a *capitano della chiesa*, and that the gaze of both Captains is turned toward the Virgin. That only Giuliano holds the baton of his office should trouble no one. The artist's letters refer to *both* figures as *capitani*, as does Vasari's account. Six months after his coronation, Pope Leo X caused the Roman patriciate to be conferred upon both Giuliano and Lorenzo at a splendid ceremony on the Capitoline Hill, among Roman triumphal trophies and Medici symbols, while Mass was said at an altar. This famous event may well have been the nucleus for the program of the Medici Chapel.

The gaze of the two Captains in the direction of the Virgin acquires a special meaning, deepened by the fact that Michelangelo has represented her as the *Virgo lactans* ("nursing Virgin"), a representation infrequent in the sixteenth century and unparalleled on such a scale. In a movement of passionate intensity, whose significance was recognized by the Neoplatonist Benedetto Varchi, the Child turns toward her breast to derive His sustenance. Now in innumerable instances, both literary and artistic, the Virgin Mother of Christ is interchangeable with Holy Mother Church, from which, during the lean years of their second exile from 1494 to 1512, the Medici had derived *their* sustenance. Michelangelo's *Medici Madonna* is closely related to the type known as the Madonna of Humility, one of whose great shrines, the Umiltà, was being built in nearby Pistoia while the Medici Chapel was in its planning stage. In the *Iconologia* of Cesare Ripa, the great late-sixteenth-century compendium of existing tradition relating how allegorical qualities should be represented, the figure symbolizing Humility presses to her breast a ball, for the reason that a ball bounces higher into the air the more it is struck upon the ground, and Christ said, "Whoso humbleth himself shall be exalted." The ball, of course, is the device on the Medici arms, and was the battle cry of their party. Only in this veiled (and humble) allusion to the quality it symbolizes does the Medici device, so proudly emblazoned in the spandrels of the Old Sacristy, make any appearance at all in the New.

After Leo's coronation Medici rule was maintained in Florence first by Giuliano, who died in 1515, then by Lorenzo. At the latter's death in 1519 (he was the last legitimate male descendant of Cosimo the Elder), Leo was inconsolable, less for personal reasons than because the dynasty was threatened. In the spirit immortalized in Michelangelo's *Medici Madonna*, he is reported to have exclaimed, "Henceforth we belong no more to the House of Medici but to the House of God!"

The Captains gaze toward the lifegiving Mother, one in peace, the other in dark meditation. St. Cosmas strikes his breast in longing, St. Damian holds his physician's cup as if to catch the flow of milk, as a divine medicine. (Medici, of course, means "doctors.") Strange as such symbolism may seem to modern eyes, it should disturb no one sensitive to Christian tradition. During the Middle Ages Mary frequently appeared to her worshipers, St. Bernard of Clairvaux among them, and favored them with drops of milk from her breast. Representations of St. Bernard's lactation (as this miracle was called) are familiar to students of early Netherlandish art, but were by no means limited to northern Europe. The Blessed Paula of Florence, precursor of Pope Leo's grandmother, Lucrezia Tornabuoni (in that she lived in a cell at Camaldoli, a monastery long under Medici patronage), had a similar experience as a result of long contemplation of an image of the *Virgo lactans*.

Giorno and *Crepuscolo*, both male, face the Madonna and her Son, while *Notte* and *Aurora* turn away from her. *Aurora*, with her high, firm breasts under which runs her zone, is characterized as a virgin; *Notte*, whose abdomen and breasts are distorted by childbirth and lactation, as a mother. In Mary the two states are miraculously united. Thus, while the Times of Day grieve in childless defeat, Mary, with a look of unutterable love, presses her divine Child to

163

164

her breast. In fact, Michelangelo has purposely compared the maternal satisfaction of lactation in the *Madonna* to the frustration of *Aurora*, who has never given suck, and the distress of *Notte*, with her distended bosom.

It has been shown that the only point of view from which all the elements of the Chapel and their interrelationships are visible is that of the priest behind the altar. The celebration of the Mass for the Dead becomes, therefore, the central energizing principle of the Chapel. Even the unearthly light—that pearly radiance so carefully contrived by Michelangelo him-

Medici Chapel
163. Epistle Candlestick
164. Gospel Candlestick

175

self through his narrowed windows and his lofty lantern, as compared to the harsher light of the Old Sacristy—suggests the universally known sentence of the Introit and the Gradual of the Requiem Mass:

> *Requiem aeternam dona eis Domine: et lux perpetua luceat eis.*

When Cinelli amplified Bocchi's guide to Florence, in 1677, two priests were still praying in the Chapel without stop, at all hours of the day and night, for the departed Medici, and every morning at least four Masses were still said, to fulfill orders left in 1532 by Cardinal Giulio de' Medici as Pope Clement VII. The celebrant stood, as he must, between two candlesticks. On the Gospel side was represented the pelican, age-old symbol of Christ's sacrifice providing from His own breast nourishment for His children like the milk the Virgin gave to Him, a comparison often drawn by theologians. On the Epistle side was the phoenix, which Michelangelo had already represented in the ornamentation of the Tomb of Julius II as a symbol of Christ's resurrection, and therefore of that of the true believer.

Between the symbolic candlesticks, then, and over the crucifix in the center of the altar, the celebrant would probably have looked up from the *Virgo lactans* to a fresco of the Resurrection in the lunette. This is pure speculation, but the drawing at Windsor (fig. 23) does correspond to the shape of the lunette, and can be connected with no other commission. After the darkness of His Passion and death, Christ leaps gloriously from the tomb. From the Epistle on the Mass for the Dead comes the great passage on the universal Resurrection, from Thessalonians (I, 4: 14–16), which includes the verses:

> *For if we believe that Jesus died and rose again, even so them also which sleep in Jesus will God bring with him. . . .*

> *For the Lord himself shall descend from heaven with a shout, with the voice of the archangel and with the trump of God: and the dead in Christ shall rise first.*

If recent reconstructions are correct, the celebrant would also have seen over the tomb of Lorenzo the attack of the fiery serpents, and over that of Giuliano the delivery of the Israelites from the serpents, as shown in another wonderful drawing at Oxford (fig. 26), but never the Brazen Serpent by whom the miracle is performed. The apparent mystery is easily solved. The Brazen Serpent is, by His own words, the crucified Christ.

> *As the brazen serpent was lifted up by Moses in the wilderness so shall the Son of man be lifted up.*

The liturgically indispensable crucifix on the altar unites the two lunettes, and there is a possibility that Michelangelo had designed the cross for this spot.

The connection of the three proposed frescoes with one another and with the defenders of the Church, and especially with the motive of nourishment, is strikingly elucidated by the Bull dated June 15, 1520, a few months before the commission of the Medici Chapel, and founded on the Resurrection and the fiery serpents. Significantly enough this Bull, launched by Leo X against the Lutheran heretics in a moment of deadly peril for the Catholic Church, was entitled "Exsurge, Deus" (Psalm 74: 22):

> *Arise O Lord and judge Thine own cause . . . incline Thine ear to our prayers, since there have risen the foxes who seek to destroy Thy vineyard (Song of Songs 2: 15), of which Thou alone dost tread the winepress . . . Rise up, O Peter . . . defend the cause of the Holy Roman Church, mother of all Churches . . . which thou at God's command hast consecrated with thy blood . . . There rise up lying teachers introducing sects of perdition, . . . whose tongue is fire, restless evil, full of deadly venom . . . they begin with the tongue to spread the poison of serpents.*

The visual suggestion that the milk of Mary and the wine of the Church could heal the effects of the poison of the fiery serpents may also be understood in terms of the very name,

Medici. Michelangelo himself, during the time when he was working on the Chapel, sarcastically referred to Clement VII as "major medic of our ills," and, after the Sack of Rome, Erasmus addressed a famous letter to the humanist Sadoleto, declaring that the ills of mankind deserved a famous *medicus* and that the Pope would fill the bill.

The appeal to the Resurrection in Pope Leo's Bull was clearly personal, for he was crowned on Easter Saturday. The connection of the Resurrection with Mary was possibly reinforced in this instance by the festival of the *Scoppio del Carro* (explosion of the car), the triumphal event of every Easter Saturday in Florence since the Middle Ages. At noon a towering car, drawn by oxen with garlanded necks and gilded horns, appears outside the open doors of Santa Maria del Fiore, and a dove flies from the car through the doors to the high altar, bearing the sacred fire from the Holy Sepulcher, from which during the morning had been rekindled, one by one, the altars of the other churches of Florence, dark since Holy Thursday. When the Paschal candle is lighted and the other lights spring into flame, the dove returns to the car, which at once bursts out in fireworks, to the mingled jubilation and terror of the crowd, recoiling before the shower of explosives. The bells ring in the tower, the archbishop intones the Gloria, and at that moment Christ is, in Florence, officially resurrected. This ceremony, on the successful completion of which the safety of the harvest is predicated, may even account for the explosive type of Resurrection in Michelangelo's drawing and the unprecedented fright of the surrounding figures. The Medici Chapel is dedicated to the Resurrection, and Santa Maria del Fiore was the cathedral of which Cardinal Giulio was Archbishop.

The River Gods have been identified as the Four Rivers of Hades by the defenders of a Neoplatonic interpretation, regardless of the fact that there were five named rivers in Hades, not four, and that one of these, Styx, was a swamp and was customarily represented by a female figure, according to Cesare Ripa. Oddly enough, the only other river god ever designed by Michelangelo (at the bottom of all three drawings of the *Fall of Phaeton* which he made for Tommaso Cavalieri) refers to a specific earthly river, the Po. All of the innumerable imitations of Michelangelo's River Gods, including those on tombs, represent geographically identifiable rivers. His own catafalque, in fact, was adorned with personifications of the Tiber and the Arno copied from the River Gods of the Medici Chapel.

165. Medici Chapel
Tomb of Giuliano
Detail: pilaster capitals

166. Medici Chapel
Detail: corner pilaster capital

That the implications were ludicrous, of surrounding Christians (or for that matter anyone else to be honored) by the Rivers of Hades could have escaped only a desperate rearguard, bent—dare one say hell-bent?—on consigning Giuliano and Lorenzo to the Styx. In fact, the only time Michelangelo ever represented a mortal in connection with one of these infernal streams (the papal chamberlain Biagio da Cesena next to the Styx, in the *Last Judgment*)— and this without any river god—it was considered so much the reverse of a compliment that the injured party appealed desperately to the Pope to extricate him. And among the innumer- able references to death and the hereafter in Michelangelo's letters and poems, neither Hades nor its rivers can be found. If these statues were not to personify earthly rivers, the least we might expect in a Christian chapel is that they be the Four Rivers of Paradise, a realm to which Popes Leo and Clement were at some pains to insure safe passage for their departed relatives. And even if, in defiance of all tradition, the Medici Chapel were to constitute a hybrid of Christian and pagan beliefs, the customary region for people one liked, among Renaissance humanists, was Olympus—to which, in some astonishing orations delivered at the court of Leo X, his departed friends and ultimately the Pope himself were playfully imagined as going.

Like the rest of the supposed Neoplatonic content of the Chapel, the identification of the statues as the Rivers of Hades eluded all the people who ought to have known. Vasari, for example, who was there at the time, although he did not mention the River Gods specifically among the "infinite other statues" planned for the Chapel, remembered the geographical content quite clearly when he said: "considering the making of the tombs of the Duke Giuliano and the Duke Lorenzo de' Medici, [Michelangelo] thought that not only the earth was sufficient for their greatness to give them honorable burial, but wished that all the parts of the world were there . . ." The River Gods are even mentioned in a poem by one Gandolfo Porrini, quoted in 1546 by Michelangelo's admirer, the Neoplatonist Benedetto Varchi, in his two lectures on Michelangelo delivered before the Florentine Academy. The wording of the poem,

> The magnanimous kings of Tiber and Arno
> The great sepulchers will await in vain.

would seem to leave little room for doubt. Porrini was evidently referring to the models of the two River Gods which in the mid-sixteenth century stood below the tomb of Giuliano. Nonetheless one is presently advised (E. Panofsky, *Tomb Sculpture*, New York, 1964, p. 92) that the best thing to do about this passage is to forget it, on the grounds that the magnanimous kings of Tiber and Arno are undoubtedly Julius II and Lorenzo and Giuliano de' Medici, still awaiting their tombs. What a delightful picture—the vicar of Christ on earth sharing with two private citizens in an ostensible republic the joys of being river kings! The Tiber, incidentally, was called by Virgil "king of rivers" in a passage frequently quoted in the Renaissance, and river gods were generally crowned, and not always just with garlands. When Varchi gave the lecture, and probably when Porrini wrote the poem, it was perfectly clear that the Pope would never be "laid to rest" in San Pietro in Vincoli, for the 1542–45 version of the Tomb of Julius II is no more than a cenotaph (see above, page 271). This well-known fact could, in any case, hardly be blamed on Michelangelo.

What rivers do the statues represent, then? The Tiber and the Arno have already been named, and were personified at the ceremony honoring Giuliano and Lorenzo in 1513 (see page 174). There were many other rivers in the Medici dominions, and although small Italian streams—torrents in winter and sandlots the rest of the year—cannot compare with self-respecting rivers elsewhere, even the Mugnone (which flanks Florence on the west) was personified as a superb, water-spouting deity by Niccolò Tribolo (who worked in the Chapel) in a fountain in the gardens of the villa at Petraia (for the Medici family, who had commissioned the Chapel). It may even be that Michelangelo was as careless, and as universal, about exact identifications as about other iconographic niceties (see, for example, his treatment of the legend of the Battle of Lapiths and Centaurs, pages 49–50), and that Vasari was correct in remembering only that Michelangelo "wished that all the parts of the world were there."

Exactly what elements were to have been placed above the ducal tombs is not entirely clear. The trophies which turn up in the London drawing (fig. 20) have been recently rediscovered; they were carved by Silvio Cosini, and are at present on view in the entrance corridor to the Chapel. Possibly they were not finished and mounted in position because they could not be flanked by the eight crouching figures, also visible in the London drawing, of which only one was ever completed (figs. 248–51). The four structures surmounting the coupled pilasters of the ducal tombs have been generally interpreted as empty thrones, "the oldest symbols

for the invisible presence of an immortal." That they were really intended to be thrones, however, is by no means certain, and this becomes even less probable when one notes that their missing backs would in the London drawing have been constituted by shells (such shells were intended for the center of the broken lid of each sarcophagus, from which spot Michelangelo mercifully and eloquently eliminated them). The backless blocks are made to look like the actual altar of the Chapel, flanked by garlands of laurel leaves and decorated by more laurel garlands, shells, and trophies. So, far from being unborn souls or mourning genii, as has been variously suggested, the youths were undoubtedly military captives, in combination with the other symbols—laurel leaves of victors, trophies of vanquished, altars—suggestive of the ceremony of 1513 at which the Roman patriciate was conferred upon the two Dukes, now re-enacted in celebration of their final triumph over death. For the dolphins in the spandrels (those on the tomb of Giuliano were never executed) are among the oldest Christian symbols of the Church and of resurrection; and shells here, as in the Sistine Chapel, indicate eternal life. In the sense of the Mass for the Dead performed here for centuries four times daily, the Dukes are resurrected through the Resurrection of Christ, and light perpetual shines upon them.

167. Medici Chapel
Detail: molding above sarcophagi

180

The Chapel abounds in nightmarish suggestions of the terrors of death. The masks we saw in the Tomb of Julius II have proliferated to such an extent that they leer from the pillow of *Notte*, from the capitals of the pilasters flanking the ducal effigies, from the armor of the Dukes themselves; they even whicker and snarl from the ornamental band running behind the Times of Day—a band entirely composed of masks. They are, however, frequently counteracted by shells, for example, in the capitals and at the top of each fluting of the pilasters, as if in fulfillment of the offertory of the Mass for the Dead:

> *Lord Jesus Christ, King of glory, liberate the souls of all the faithful departed from the pains of hell, and from the deep lake: liberate them from the lion's mouth, let not Tartarus swallow them, neither let them fall into darkness.*

The imagery of the Chapel is also, of course, connected with the growing appeal to princely and papal absolutism on the part of many Italians in the sixteenth century, as the sole release from the chaos to which centuries of republican civil warfare had brought them. In his masterpiece, *The Prince*, Machiavelli had vainly appealed to Duke Lorenzo to liberate and unify Italy. The statue of Fame, indicated in the drawing below the *Medici Madonna* (fig. 21) but never executed (although the idea eventually reappeared in other drawings by Michelangelo and was used above his catafalque), is central to the structure of the Chapel. For the idea of the magically charged and supernaturally justified Prince was the great collective fantasy with which Renaissance Italy tried to assuage its sense of its own inadequacy to unite before the multiple threats from the North. Like all such fantasies, this one fiercely resisted reality. That the princes themselves were so openly recognized as worthless could, under such circumstances, only lend the legend stronger wings.

A great art historian, in private conversation in the Medici Chapel, once characterized its works of art as "disturbing." They are indeed—deeply disturbing—chiefly because they are so convincing. The silent and unreal war waged by Michelangelo's creatures corresponds to a profound and very real battle within himself. In the gathering Italian crisis of the 1520s which was to end in disaster and eventual tyranny, the inner battle took a frightening turn, manifested in periods of bitter depression and seeming helplessness on the part of the artist. His mood doubtless reached a climax of despair in 1530 when he learned that the Medici governor of the defeated Republic had marked him for assassination. What could, in the hands of a lesser master, have become an empty eulogy derives its intensity from a great artist's at once tragic and heroic view of human destiny.

Although the two finished tombs were widely separated in time of execution, they correspond minutely in all details of ornamentation and articulation, save only in the omission of the dolphins from the spandrels over the tabernacles flanking Giuliano. It is impossible to determine which was executed first. But the two compositions are also opposites, in subtle and significant ways. It has often been noted that while Giuliano is characterized as open, cheerful (to use the ghastly modern phrase, "outgoing"), Lorenzo is described as closed, moody, self-contained, and deserving of his nickname, *Il Pensieroso*. This deliberate contrast, of ideal types rather than actual persons, may well have suggested the opposition in Milton's poems. Giuliano idly holds several coins, as if in intended largesse; Lorenzo's elbow is planted on a closed money-box, decorated with a nasty mask, variously identified as belonging to a bat or a lynx. The light which plays freely on the beautiful countenance of Giuliano is prevented from reaching the blank face of Lorenzo, enshadowed by his immense helmet and half hidden by his left hand. *Notte* and *Giorno*, arranged in angles counter to the shapes of the volutes, toe sharply out; *Aurora* and *Crepuscolo*, weighed down by the prevailing gloom, conform to the volutes, and toe downward. In the attic story, the lustral pitchers above *Giuliano* pour outward, those above *Lorenzo* pour in. There is, to be sure, an old and oddly persistent superstition that *Giorno* and *Notte* were not intended for their present positions, but for the tombs of the *Magnifici*, in spite of Michelangelo's own words and the absence of any evidence for reclining statues on those tombs.

The old conflict between line and mass, softened during the artist's second Roman period, seems now to have been revived and moved to a higher sphere. For line has become a property of the embracing architecture in the traditional Florentine *pietra serena* (clear stone)—the gray sandy limestone used for trim by Brunelleschi and his followers—relieved by white stuccoed wall surfaces, within which the tombs and flanking tabernacles, of a smooth, polished white marble incommensurate with the *pietra serena,* not only live an independent life of their own but even project. In the tombs themselves, the linear detail and crisp execution contrast sharply with the succulence of the ornamental carving on the Tomb of Julius II. The small heads, hands, and feet of the figures, and their mannered postures and gestures, suggest a new concern with linear elegance, visible even more strongly in the ornamentalization of the features—those that are finished. But the bony and muscular masses of the figures seethe with an energy which refuses to be confined by linear structure. Seen from the sides the statues seem almost to spill from their enclosures, in a muscular wave which would have been completed by the River Gods poised on their marble plinth. These would also have had, in elevation, the function of completing the circle of time and space from which the Captains have escaped. Tension and struggle, evident to all in the "uncomfortable" poses of the Times of Day, would have been more oppressive than ever. But such tension is implicit in every form and line of the entire Chapel.

The sarcophagi themselves, shapes of strange and bitter beauty, were derived from an ancient Roman sarcophagus well known during the Renaissance for the simple reason that it stood in front of the Pantheon. But the forms of this structure, almost exactly imitated by Antonio Rossellino in the fifteenth century in his tomb of the Cardinal of Portugal at San Miniato in Florence, have now become angular and broken, harsh and biting, although executed with a wonderful clarity. The brilliant notion of the two volutes which do not meet suggests the breaking of the bonds of death and of the tyranny of time.

168. Medici Chapel
Detail: corner

I8. GIULIANO DE' MEDICI

Marble; height 72⅛″, width 22¼″, depth 29⅞″
See discussion of date on pages 168–70
The Medici Chapel (Tomb of Giuliano), San Lorenzo, Florence

From the present extent of our documentary knowledge, it appears that all seven extant statues by Michelangelo for the Medici Chapel were designed by 1521, that they were reaching completion in 1526, and that the finer carving on all of them was mostly done from 1530 to 1534. It would appear futile, therefore, to indulge in refined speculation as to which statue was finished first. They belong together, and were meant to go together from the start. The harmony of the Medici Chapel (and it is a successful harmony, including its system of dis-

colorplate 11

169

sonances) depends largely on this fact. For all we know, Michelangelo may have moved from statue to statue, keeping them all at about the same level of completion at the same time. He did not, however, do every bit of carving himself. We know from the artist's correspondence with the painter Sebastiano del Piombo, who acted as go-between in negotiations with Clement VII, that Giovannangelo Montorsoli assisted him with the *Giuliano*, probably in the decorative details of the armor. The quality of the face, the muscular torso showing through its leather cuirass, the knees, and the overpoweringly beautiful hands, can hardly be attributed to anyone save Michelangelo.

170

The remarkable photographs indicate above all how close a relationship exists between the architecture and the figures. *Giuliano*, for example (see fig. 162), was intended to be seen partly emerging from the niche in which Michelangelo placed him before departing finally for Rome in 1534. The figure loses something of its quality when the tension with the surrounding masses is removed. From the left side it becomes almost grotesque, with its head poked forward at the end of a long, twisted neck, its shoulders consequently humped, and worst of all, its left leg rather awkwardly bent. All these unpleasant features not only are hidden in the niche, but are a direct result of calculating the masses of the figure for their effect when seen from below. The twisted neck and rounded shoulders are characteristic of marble statues looking out of niches from above eye level, at least as early as the statues designed by Giovanni Pisano for the Cathedral of Siena in the late thirteenth century. The surprising fact is that the back, which the artist assumed would be forever hidden, was beautifully constructed and carried to an almost final state—only the polishing remaining to do. Even more astonishing, therefore, is that while the left ear, invisible from the floor, is completely finished, the right ear, turned toward the observer, vanishes into shapeless marble where the lobe should be. Possibly the artist was called away too suddenly to complete this crucial feature.

186

171   172

The middle-aged Duke, whom Michelangelo had known as a boy, is shown as a young man of ideal grace and beauty, and immense latent strength, yet seized by a strange paralysis of the will, as if too enchanted by his own physical magnificence ever to be able to act or to exert command. His baton lies in his lap, one superb hand hanging heavily over it without grasping it; the other lets the coins slip from its fingers. A heavy richness fills the modeling of the flesh, the curling hair, and the swollen veins of the hands, in keeping with the structure of the languid eyes, the relaxed nostrils, the full lips, the slightly receding chin. At once sunny and somnolent, the figure completely lacks the energy that could turn the noble frame into a formidable thing. The same lassitude, the same easy rhythm, runs through all the surfaces and all the lines of every mass and every detail. It is interesting to contrast the torpor of the *Giuliano* with the pride and courage of the *David*, filled with the spirit of a more optimistic moment. In spite of the Captain's intent gaze toward the saving vision of the blessed Mother and her divine Son, he seems lost in a kind of dreamy euphoria.

174 ◀ 173   176   175   177

178

179

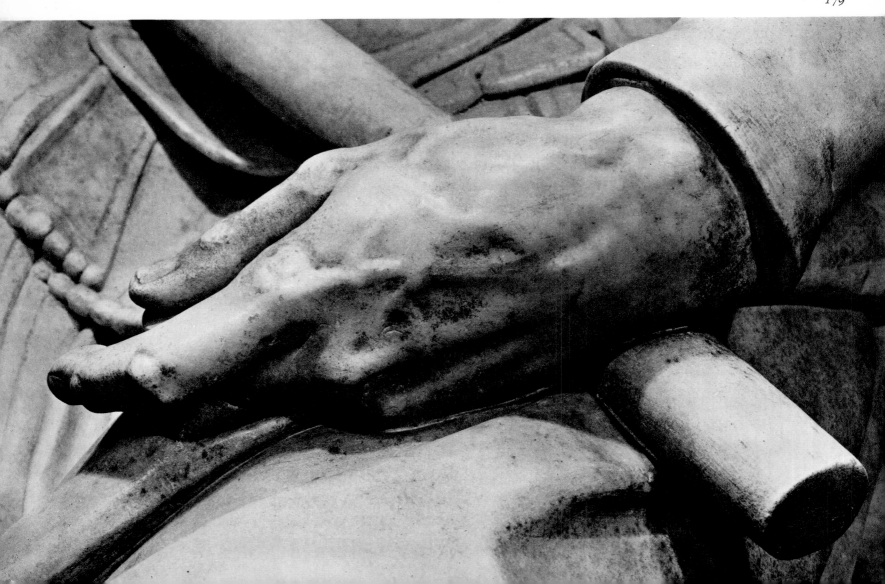

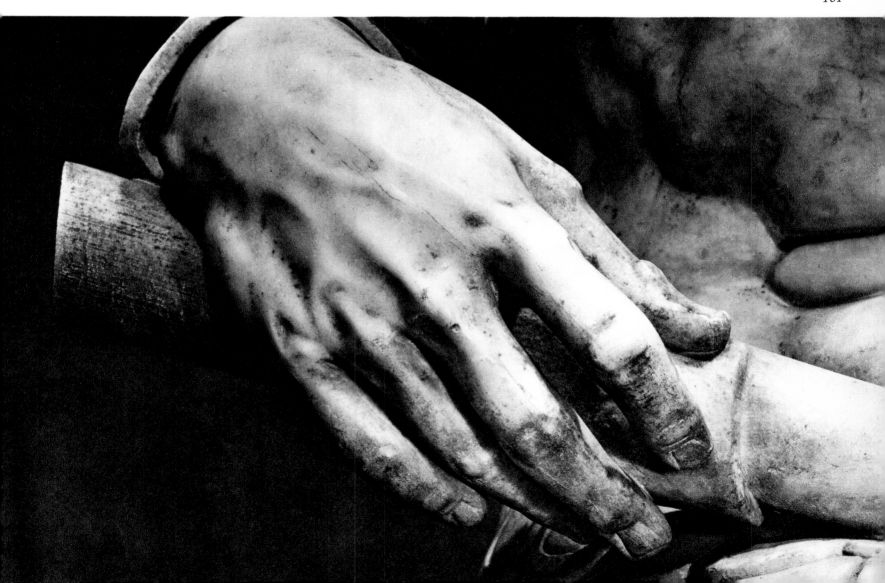

19. GIORNO (Day)

Marble; length 72¾″, depth 34¼″
See discussion of date on pages 168–70
The Medici Chapel (Tomb of Giuliano), San Lorenzo, Florence

Held by no other bonds than those of his pose and his own excessive musculature, this gigantic figure is nonetheless completely tied; and the more he tries to escape, the more inextricable (judo-fashion) becomes his position. Not even the *Rebellious Slave* seems so securely bound. It is as if the artist were trying, in the spirit of his great prose fragment (see page 173), to tell us that *Night* and *Day* themselves rage helplessly in the bonds of the death to which they have vainly tried to consign Giuliano, who has escaped to an ideal realm of serene and relaxed power. The true impotence of the figure becomes painfully apparent when it is seen from above and from the back—views invisible to the observer, but carefully worked out by the artist, and essential to the realization of the principal aspect. In contrast to the earthquake power of the side of the statue exposed to the spectator, the concealed views suggest foetal positions, or the crumpled shapes in which the dying fell at Pompeii. Not that Michelangelo had the former in mind or knew anything about the latter; rather that these comparisons reveal the mood of paralytic frustration to which the great artist was chronically subject, and never more so than in the period during which he was at work on the Medici Chapel. "I am poor, humble,

colorplate 12

182

192

and mad," he wrote in 1520 to the powerful Cardinal Bibbiena at the Vatican. He complained that he felt old (although he was only in his late forties), and that if he worked one day he had to rest four.

The drapery is looped over the right leg, and was doubtless intended to be continued throughout the now unfinished masses of marble below the bent knee and down to the foot; it seems to represent bed coverings which the figure is throwing off. Nonetheless, such suggestions in Michelangelo's art (David's sling, for instance; fig. 103) are always intended as attributes of a continued state of being or of tension; they should never be taken as indicating a transitory moment of action.

The mighty back, possibly Michelangelo's most arbitrary anatomical statement, is roughly partitioned into huge masses whose surge is not canalized by any linear contours save those of the twisted shoulder over which the roughly blocked-in face peers like that of a wild animal in the forest. Swelling to the bursting point, these pulsating muscles, taut tendons, and distended veins are clearly intended to contrast with the exquisite lassitude of the Captain above, with his soft limbs and hanging hands. One wonders whether so self-involved a figure could

183

187

188

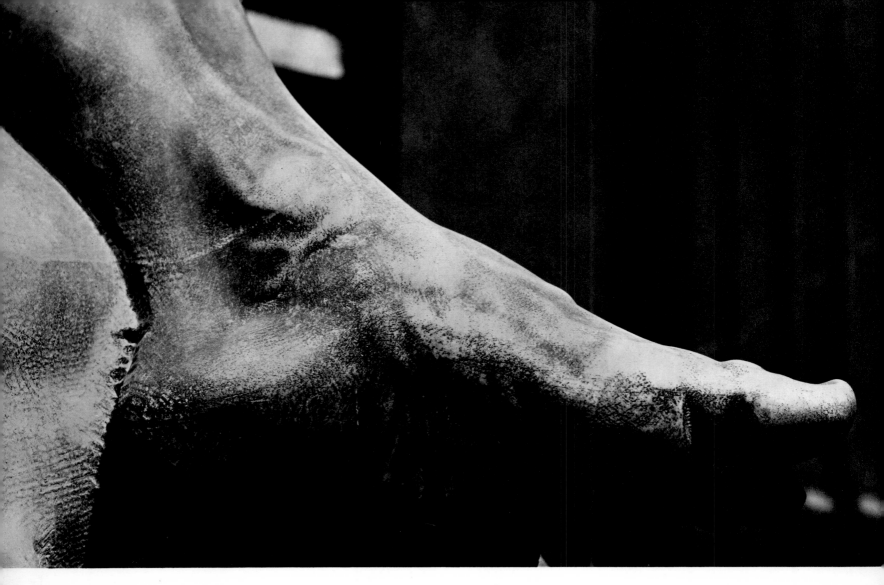

have stood up. Perhaps it could not. It seems caught in some underworld in which all beings are conceived in anguish and foredoomed to torment, as if in fulfillment of the Duke's *vendetta*. "What would he have done to us then had he lived!"

Michelangelo must have realized from the start of his designs for the wall tombs that these figures would be seen not only from head on—the "principal" view—but diagonally as well, since the Chapel was not large, was entered from the corners on either side of the *Medici Madonna*, and contained doors leading, of necessity, to hidden sacristies flanking the altar space. These diagonal views, reminiscent of those in the *Brazen Serpent* spandrel in the Sistine Ceiling, were brilliantly conceived and sensitively exploited. The "angle shots" along the ankles and legs, which would be imitated throughout Mannerist sculpture in Florence, are of the utmost importance to an understanding of the statues as a whole. They would, of course, have contrasted sharply with the reverse views of the foreshortened shoulders and backs of the River Gods (figs. 252–55) placed directly below the Times of Day and going in the other direction, to create the constant opposition and directional variation essential to the composition of the Chapel as a whole.

190 ▶

20. NOTTE (Night)

Marble; length 76⅜", depth 24¾"
See discussions of date on pages 168–70
The Medici Chapel (Tomb of Guiliano), San Lorenzo, Florence

The ambivalance of Michelangelo's feelings during the long ordeal of the Medici Chapel, during which he was torn three ways by his responsibility for the Tomb of Julius II, his contract with the Medici Popes, and his continuing loyalty to the briefly re-established Florentine Republic, is illuminated by a subsequent circumstance. In 1545, when the great artist had been absent from Florence for twelve years, the enigmatic *Notte* became the subject of a number of epigrams, including a famous if insipid one by Giovanni Strozzi, to which Michelangelo replied with a devastating quatrain:

> *Dear to me is sleep, even more being made of stone,*
> *As long as the loss and shame shall last.*
> *Not to see, not to hear, is my good fortune;*
> *Therefore do not wake me, hush, speak softly.*

This attack on the Medici tyranny is no more than a free expression of what must have been

colorplate 13

191

194

the artist's inner feelings during the very period in which he was willing to celebrate Medici power, or so we must assume from his acceptance of the leading role in the defense of Florence against the Medici troops. Yet only a few years after writing those lines, Michelangelo was in cordial correspondence with Duke Cosimo, whose government had been the object of his anger.

According to a mid-sixteenth-century account, the left arm of the *Notte*, now twisted behind her back, was originally bent to support her torso in a far less complex and tormented attitude. Michelangelo seems to have sacrificed the first position of the arm partly to carve the mass of marble which once composed it into the fearful mask disturbing the sleeper, partly to increase the tremendous tension of the pose. Possibly at the same time he carved away the back of the head, producing a distortion of the skull more apparent than real (there is actually quite enough marble for the depth of the head) which has the effect of carrying the tension of the left shoulder over the neck, into the right arm, and down to the left thigh. An examination of the surface shows clearly that the figure was complete, and largely finished and polished, before these changes were made. The polished marble continues over the shoulder, where it is suddenly interrupted by the preliminary blocking in of the newly carved arm. The left hand, which must have been curved to lie along the sarcophagus lid, is now clenched above the mask. Possibly it was designed to clutch some of the drapery, but it is so far from completion that this cannot be stated with any certainty.

The changes converted what must have been a comparatively relaxed figure into a tormented being who makes a worthy pendant for the *Giorno*. The hidden view is by no means so larval as that of the *Giorno*, and the view from above shows clearly the initial elegance of the figure, with its long, clean lines, exquisitely smoothed in every nuance. Michelangelo was

197

198

199

200

201

also evidently somewhat dissatisfied with the dreaming face as it had been first carved, and started to rework that as well. The left eyebrow has been somewhat chiseled back, the tip of the nose cut down in a strange, broken arc, the nostrils pinched, and the lips modeled to give a troubled expression. All of these changes, like those of the left arm and the hair, have remained unfinished.

The original pose of the *Notte* must have resembled very closely that of the *Leda*, a painting, now lost, ordered by Alfonso d'Este, Duke of Ferrara, when Michelangelo visited that city during his flight to Venice in 1529, at a time when the *Notte* was still unfinished. The appearance of torpor, warmly oppressive in the *Leda*, is converted in the *Notte* (largely by means of these changes, made after the *Leda* had taken wing for France) into one of anguish. If the *Notte* shows, as Vasari says, the grief of one who has "lost a great and honored thing," perhaps it is for her own children. Michelangelo in a later poem claimed that

> . . . *shadow serves for the planting of man.*
> *Thus the nights are holier than the days.*

This seems to be the aspect of Night that he has celebrated in the statue. Drugged by her garland of poppies, haunted by the cries of her owl, troubled by the threats of terrible masks, the figure writhes in restless sleep.

With an astonishing combination of clinical accuracy and poetic grace the artist has explored the bodily effects of childbirth and lactation, at once probing and caressing the folds of flesh in the diaphragm and the swollen and pendulous breasts. Again the diagonal view reveals great beauties, in the long, blade-like curves of the ankles and thighs. The almost finished drapery drawn into a point to sharpen and strengthen that of the right foot provides an indication of how the rough marble in the other figures would have looked if it had been brought to completion. The menacing owl fluffing itself up and the savage mask, both hideous and lovely, give an indication of the effect the apes of the Tomb of Julius II might have had, if the artist really intended to finish them.

21. LORENZO DE' MEDICI

Marble; height 70⅛", width 26¾", depth 28¾"
See discussion of date on pages 168–70
The Medici Chapel (Tomb of Lorenzo), San Lorenzo, Florence

Silent, shadowed, helmeted, closed, the melancholy image of *Lorenzo* constitutes a perfect opposite to that of the sun-warmed, drowsily sensuous *Giuliano* who faces him across the Chapel. He sits there on his block, corroded by sadness, even malevolence, as if he were contemplating the destruction of the world, a prototype not only for Milton's *Il Penseroso* but for Milton's Satan. In the absence of any word on the subject by Michelangelo it is hazardous to attempt interpretation, although the widespread notion of the opposition of jovial to saturnine, active to contemplative types is very attractive. The gesture of silence is an old one, appearing in Fra Angelico's fresco over one of the doors of the monastery of San Marco in Florence, and going back to early medieval sources. The pose of the legs and feet repeats that of the bitter *Isaiah* on the Sistine Ceiling. As with so many of Michelangelo's enigmatic figures, the precise meaning may elude definition, but not the effect. The *Lorenzo* distills a crushing gloom, and must have been intended to do so. This mood, incidentally, is much more intense in photographs in which the face is lighted as Michelangelo intended, with the shadow

of the helmet cutting across the bridge of the nose and leaving the eyes and eyesockets dark.

Although the details of the armor and the helmet were left to Michelangelo's assistant, Montorsoli, as they were in the case of the *Giuliano*, the face, the knees, and the splendid right forearm must have been finished by the master. The left hand, idly holding what appears to be a crumpled handkerchief, still shows the characteristic surface produced by the toothed chisel, and lacks both finish and polish. The neck and the feet are also not entirely finished. The back of the statue—another of those eloquent Michelangelo backs—was of course meant to be hidden.

The fierce little bat- or lynx-face on the money-box held under the Captain's left elbow yields in malevolence to the lion's head of the helmet, whose expression cannot be fully appreciated from the floor. The gloom of the statue itself, equally impressive when seen outside its niche, surpasses them both in intensity.

207

208

209

210

211

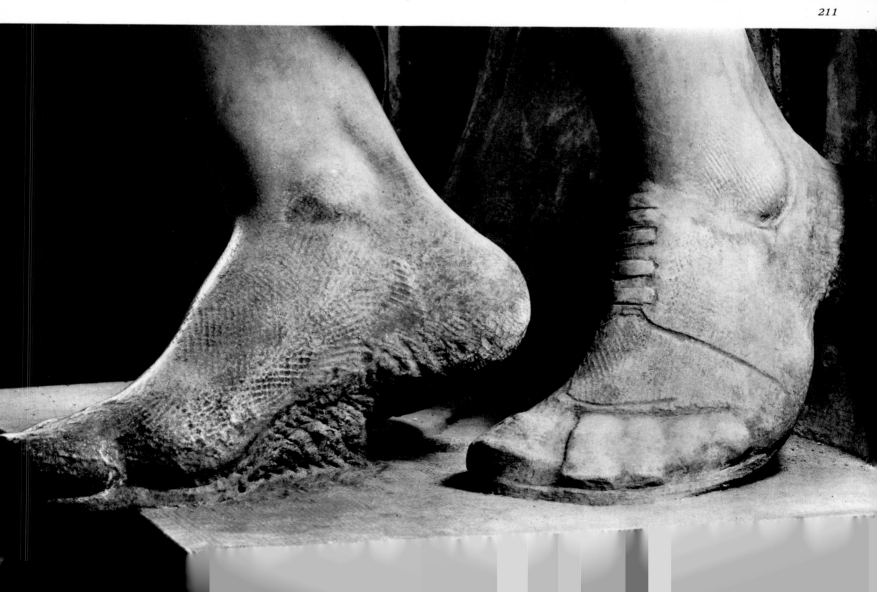

22. CREPUSCOLO (Twilight)

Marble; length 76¾", depth 31½"
See discussion of date on pages 168–70
The Medici Chapel (Tomb of Lorenzo), San Lorenzo, Florence

Twilight is the quietest of the four Times of Day, a quiet induced by fatigue. As in the *Giorno*, Michelangelo has chosen a model in middle life, but the figure's sagging muscles show no such fierce energy. Wistfully, but without bitterness, he seems to contemplate the end of the day, even the end of the road. The unfinished face bears a strong resemblance to Michelangelo's own features, as we see them in later self-portraits. The back, feet, and hands are likewise unfinished, but most of the body has received its final polish, and the legs retain only a few traces of the toothed chisel. In this case, the hidden view apparently held little importance for the artist, who enveloped it almost entirely in jagged folds of drapery, but the view from above, with its long, slender lines, is very delicately studied. Most of all, however, the ample forms of the principal view display a richness and warmth, indeed a weary

212

213 ▷

214

215

216

satisfaction, that one does not often associate with Michelangelo. Yet it is a convincing rendition of the very feelings that must have overcome him at the end of each day passed in the arduous physical labor of stone sculpture.

As in the *Giorno,* the muscular forms flow without linear division, but show none of the fierce tension of that shattering work. Throughout the heavy abdomen, flatter chest forms, and slender legs, the shapes move with ease and grace, endowing—as Michelangelo was to do consistently throughout his later life—maturity with its own beauty.

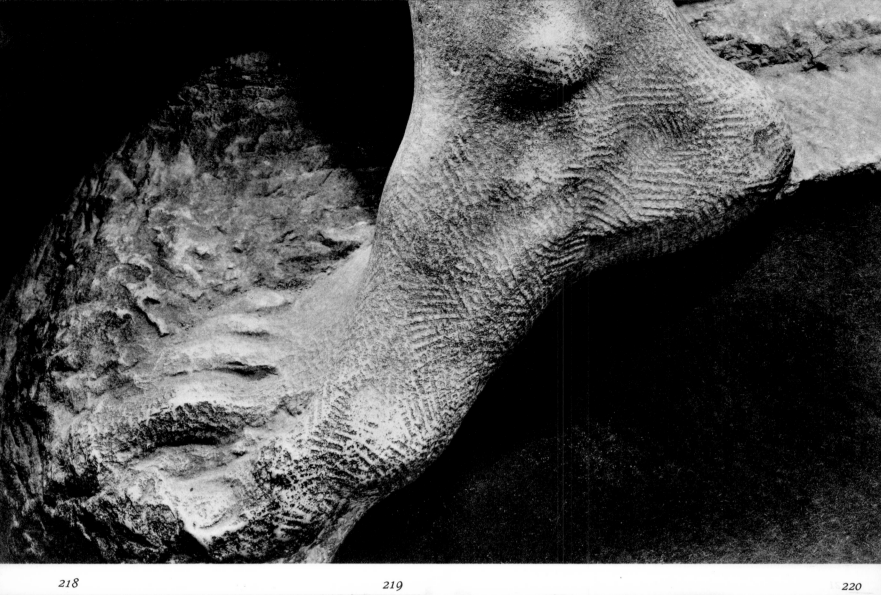

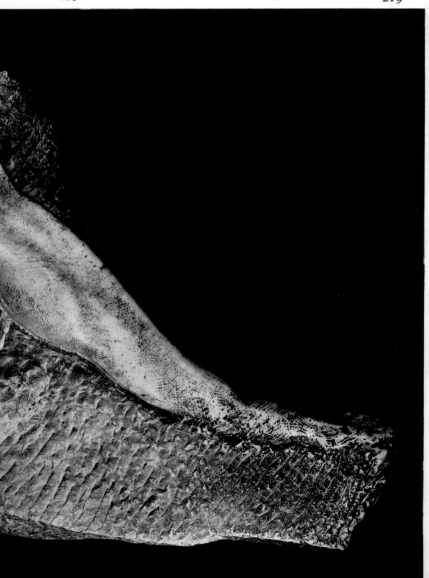

23. AURORA (Dawn)

Marble; length 81", depth 24⅜"
See discussion of date on pages 168–70
The Medici Chapel (Tomb of Lorenzo), San Lorenzo, Florence

Turning on her couch, Michelangelo's personification of *Dawn* looks out upon the world with an expression of inconsolable bitterness. Once seen, neither her pose nor her expression can ever be forgotten. A strange tension runs through every limb and feature. Her smooth, firm muscles and breasts are those of a young girl, made to conform to the athletic ideal of Michelangelo's male figures. From every view, including the usually larval hidden view, her clean, hard beauty is apparent. From above, the figure shows such brilliance of line and crisp sharpness of form that it seems to participate in the quality of the architecture. The angular view, seen of course from the altar, is one of the most striking of all—a magnificent bouquet of taut legs and elegant ankles, surmounted by the anguished face. Only from the front, however, due partially to the inspired diagonal placing across the sarcophagus lid, does the noble roundness of the forms fully emerge. All in all, the figure is unique among the four Times of Day for what one might call the monolithic quality of its conception; it is as unified as a sword blade, in contrast to the tied, twisted, tortured poses of *Notte* and *Giorno* and even the *Crepuscolo* with one leg hooked over the other.

The entire movement of the figure comes to a climax in the headdress, composed of a veil falling over the right shoulder in magnificent folds, partially concealing a strange diadem, whose twin volutes echo those of the sarcophagus below. The area between the volutes is one of the few unfinished portions of the work, and there one can just make out what might have been intended to be the gnawing mouse, symbolizing destructive Time, which Condivi tells us Michelangelo wanted to carve in the Chapel. If this is not mere imagination, the little animal is visible from the back, head down, tail erect, one front paw forward.

colorplate 14

223

224

225

226

227 ▶

222

The face, for all its Hellenism, contains an unexpected trait borrowed from a Greek source closer to home. As can be verified by a comparison with any number of Florentine Madonnas of the thirteenth century dominated by the Byzantine tradition, notably those of Coppo di Marcovaldo and Cimabue, the formation of the eyebrows, especially the spoon-shaped configuration where brows and nose meet, is an Italo-Byzantine feature. The face of *Aurora* is one of the earliest examples of a medievalism very strong in Florence during the 1520s, the era of the so-called Mannerist crisis (see page 32). There is, moreover, no more poignant example of the general mood of despair so important to the formation of Mannerist art than the statues of the Medici Chapel, which were imitated times without number in Florence in the succeeding decade.

In the face of the *Aurora* there also becomes apparent for the first time a new conception of form in Michelangelo's art, a kind of inorganic distortion for the purposes of ornamental beauty and expressive intensity, ignoring, sometimes even defying, actual anatomical structure. As a result, the sculptor is able to provide an effective solution, by way of compromise, to a problem which must have distressed him often—the rendering of the eye (which plays so large a part in Michelangelo's poetry) in such a way as to indicate its glance without resorting to pictorial effects. Instead of an unhappy choice between a blank eyeball modeled to preserve its outer surface, and a delineation of the cornea by means of incision, the sculptor can now merely depress the surface of the eyeball, and suggest its color and direction by manipulated shadow. Perhaps it was such poetic deformation that Pietro Aretino meant when he wrote to Michelangelo:

In your hands lives occult a new nature.

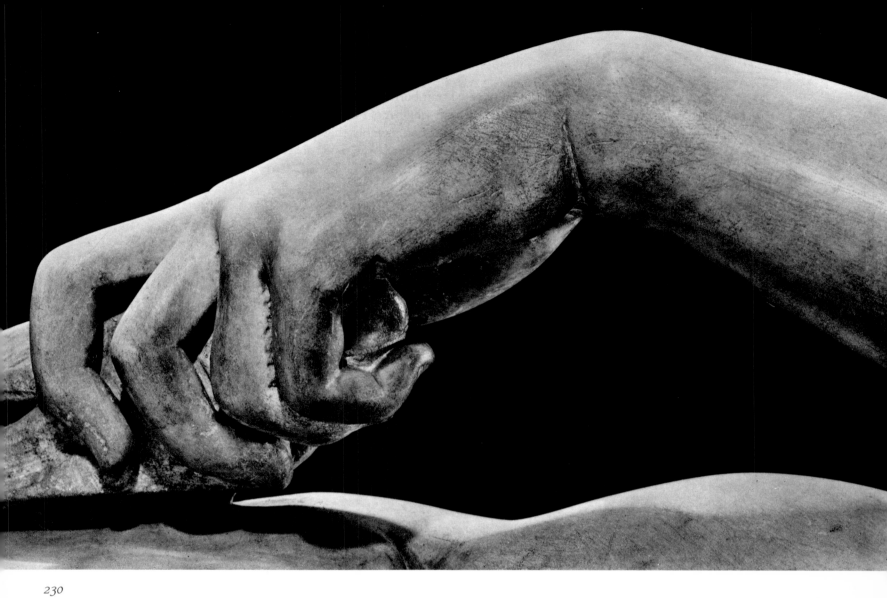

230

231   232

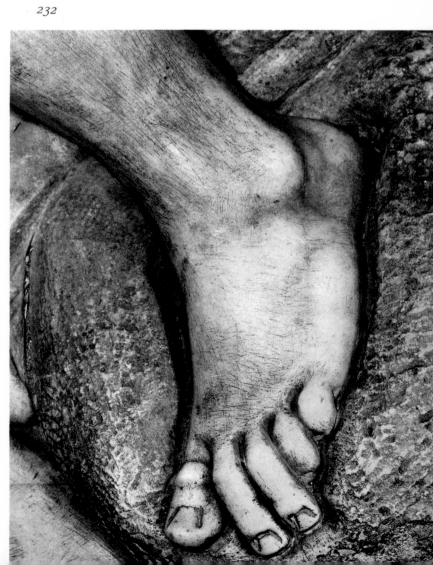

235 ▶

233

234

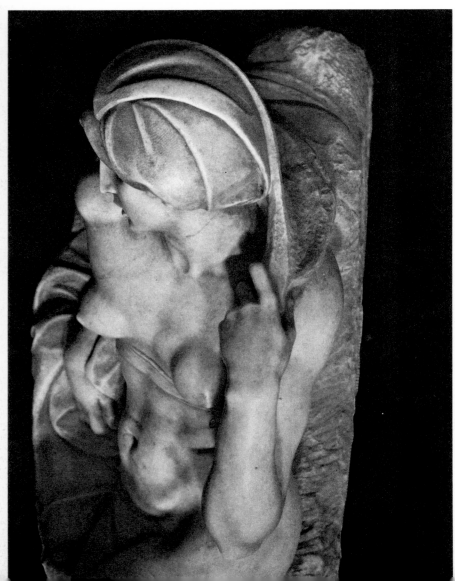

24. THE MEDICI MADONNA

Marble; height (with base) 8' 3½", width 3' 1½", depth 2' 11½"
See discussion of date on pages 168–70
The Medici Chapel, San Lorenzo, Florence

At the head of the Chapel, facing the altar, concentrating in her being all the forces of the complicated monument and its imagery, sits the most beautiful of all Florentine Madonnas. Deprived of her surrounding architecture (never executed), still rough in almost every surface (never finished), the *Medici Madonna* seems to acquire through these very imperfections a lonely grandeur, as if the physical shortcomings intensified her spiritual meaning. No artist of the Renaissance; indeed no artist of the loftiest period of medieval art, ever surpassed Michelangelo's vision of Mary, and only the truly sovereign Virgins of the Gothic cathedrals can compare with her in nobility. All the charm and winsomeness and triviality of so many Florentine Madonnas of the earlier Renaissance have been swept aside—even the classic serenity of those by Fra Bartolommeo and Andrea del Sarto.

The *Medici Madonna* is in the tradition of Cimabue, Giotto, and Masaccio. While this great work fulfills the prophecies of Michelangelo's own earlier Madonnas (figs. 36–39, 82–99, 121–25), it goes far beyond them in its conception of Mary as the mortal vehicle of divine grace. "Humble and lofty, more than any other creature," Dante had sung of Mary in the *Paradiso*, and this is what Michelangelo has shown. The Virgin is neither enthroned in regal splendor

◀ 239 nor surrounded by the attributes of elegant Florentine life. Her legs crossed and her right toe projecting, she sits upon a simple marble block, holding her Child to her breast; she braces herself gently with a slightly quivering right hand, while her left shoulder bends to give her bosom. Solemnly, wistfully, she gazes outward, symbol not only of divine mercy but of mortal motherhood, loving and intense, heroic and quiet, limitless and reserved.

As does the *Madonna of the Stairs* (colorplate I; figs. 36–39), the *Virgo Lactans* seated on the marble block hints at the probably insoluble mysteries of Michelangelo's own psychic past, especially at the memory which seemed to him so important, his drinking in his love of sculptor's tools with the milk of a stonecutter's wife. However this may have affected Michelangelo's inner life, what is left of this circumstance is here transfigured. The sublime conception of Mary has by now become the fountain at which all human longings are assuaged, the source of that peace which alone stills the torment of the Medici Chapel and its anguished population.

The Child, of superhuman force and improbable size, turns in a magnificent *contrapposto* movement, an upward spiral running counter to the gentle, forward inclination of Mary's torso. Apparently Michelangelo wanted to diminish the contrast in power between the nursing Christ Child and the resurrected Saviour above. The forms of His splendid body yield nothing in strength and energy to the grand adult male figures of *Giorno* and *Crepuscolo* who gaze in His direction. The curves of the muscles are contrasted with the jagged shapes of Mary's drapery, that move in a fabric of rich oscillations upward to the perfect peace of her face.

The very subject of the *Virgo lactans*, of course, confronted Michelangelo with a considerable 242 and 243 ▶

240

241

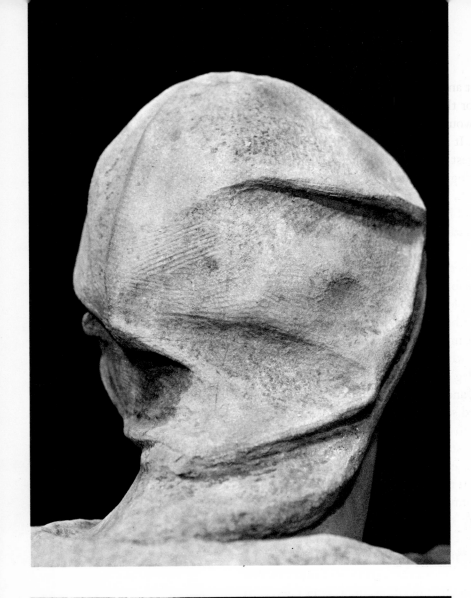

244

245

problem. An actual representation of her bared breast and the phenomenon of nursing, however customary in the Gothic period, was difficult for the Renaissance at best. But realized on the gigantic scale of these figures—the Madonna would be about nine feet tall if she stood up—such a treatment would have become grotesque. It is not the least of the beauties of the *Medici Madonna* that Michelangelo was able to suggest the full psychological and spiritual import of the human and divine theme without running any such risks. From the front, one sees only the Child's head and the curve of His cheek. From the side, His lifted right arm effectively conceals from the floor the actual contact of head and bosom, and the neckline of the Virgin's garment does not dip. Michelangelo never carved the Child's face and the Madonna's breast in detail.

The theme of the Child bestriding His mother's knee, of course, is taken from the *Taddei Madonna*, also left unfinished a score or so of years before. Unusual in Michelangelo's work is the projecting foot of the Virgin, hazardous to complete in marble. One wonders whether he would ever have finished the undercutting, or whether he would have been forced by the nature of the material to leave the marble support. The importance of the pointed toe is readily understandable from the front, the only view from which the figure, enclosed in a niche, would have been completely visible: the foot and the leg carry the eye rapidly upward toward the dominant, if delicately veiled, motive of nursing, and the point of the toe establishes one end of a vertical axis which culminates in the pointed shape of the Virgin's folded veil.

In the handling of the eyes, Michelangelo has used to even greater effect the device of suggestion adopted in the eyes of the *Aurora*. Even if the statue had been finished and polished we would still be able to experience the calm, deep gaze in all its intensity, shorn of the illusionism and emphasis on the momentary which were repulsive to Michelangelo his whole life long. In the flow of surface throughout the columnar neck, the cheeks, and over the strikingly asymmetrical forehead and nose, we may clearly observe how Michelangelo's toothed chisel caressed the marble. Finished or not, it breathes a complete and more than natural life. Vasari was right when he said that in the unfinished work the perfection of the idea was already apparent. The divinely beautiful face is felt as if through a veil of gauzy marble —reminding one of the "mortal veil" Michelangelo so often mentions in his later poetry, to signify the fabric of perishable human flesh that clothes the beauty of God's intention. The head has been carried to the same point of completion all around, even in the simple shapes that are, and were intended to be, completely hidden from view.

From the left side, it can be seen that Michelangelo at first planned a much larger figure. Not only the surface of the block but portions of the left arm, thigh, and back of the original statue still remain. This whittling down of an idea designed for a larger scale is very common in Michelangelo's later sculpture. Several of the figures of the upper story of the Tomb of Julius II, as finally set in place in 1545 (figs. 27–30; also figs. 113, 284), seem to have undergone this process of whittling down, three stages of which are evident in the *Milan Pietà*. The only finished portions of the group are passages in the torso and legs of the Christ Child, and in the shimmering drapery covering the Virgin's knee, which hint at the exquisite surface refinements Michelangelo intended for the finished work.

246 and *247* ▶

25. CROUCHING YOUTH

Marble, height 21¼"
See discussion of date on pages 168–70
The Hermitage, Leningrad

No clear evidence exists to show when or why Michelangelo abandoned the idea of placing eight of these crouching youths above the entablatures of the ducal tombs, flanking the so-called thrones. At any rate, there is no room for them in the Chapel as it stands at present, and only one has ever turned up. The compressed pose and the powerful masses of the figure are convincing enough as the design of Michelangelo, but it has been rightly shown that the soft, uncertain use of the toothed chisel differs sharply from the master's own technique. Unfinished as it remains today, the little figure was probably brought to its present condition by Niccolò Tribolo.

248

249

250

251

26. RIVER GOD

Clay, over tow, wood, and wool; length 70⅞″
See discussion of date on pages 168–70
Accademia di Belle Arti, Florence

The models for at least two of the River Gods were exhibited in the mid-sixteenth century below *Aurora* and *Crepuscolo*, and this battered torso, rediscovered in the early years of the present century, was apparently one of them. The other one has disappeared. The two models, identified as *Tiber* and *Arno* in Porrini's doggerel verse (see page 179), were given by Duke Cosimo de' Medici to the sculptor Bartolommeo Ammanati, and presented by him to the Florentine Academy in 1583. What is shown in figure 252 is really a view of the statue from above. The figure should be turned on its right side, so that the front of the torso faces the observer.

The fragment enjoys the distinction of being the only large-scale clay model by Michelangelo to have survived. Its fierce intensity provides, therefore, a unique insight into Michelangelo's methods of creation (see page 16). Damaged as it is, the surface is instinct with life in every portion. The taut curves of the River Gods must have been intended to project far beyond the limits of the plinths which now stand empty. The model in the Accademia assists in reconstructing the intended effect, essential to the composition of the whole work.

252

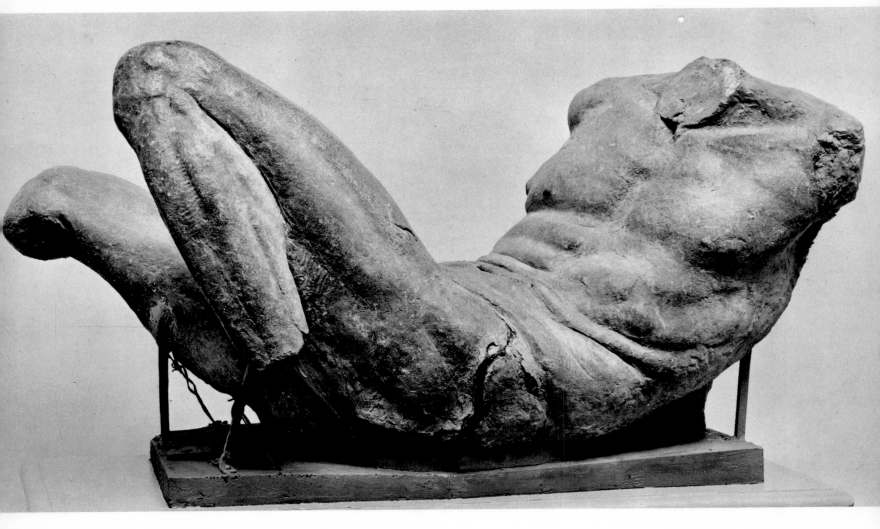

253

254

255

27. DAVID-APOLLO

Marble; height 57⅜″, width 15⅜″, depth 17¾″
Carved 1525–32, possibly at intervals
Museo Nazionale (Bargello), Florence

Described by Vasari as an "Apollo taking an arrow from his quiver," this statue was listed in the inventory of the collections of the Medici Duke Cosimo I as a David. That both identifications were made in Michelangelo's lifetime shows how easy it was to interchange classical with Biblical figures during the Renaissance. Just such an interchange may well have occurred in this case. Quite possibly Michelangelo began the figure as a David in 1525 or 1526, judging by the style, then started to turn it into an Apollo when Baccio Valori, the Medici governor of Florence after the siege of 1529–30, asked him for a statue. That it was this same unsavory patron who had ordered the great artist's assassination as a determined enemy of the Medici can hardly have increased Michelangelo's enthusiasm for the commission.

The round object under the figure's right foot would originally have been intended as the severed head of Goliath; and as in so many Davids of the fifteenth century, the right hand would have held a stone and the left have been reaching for the sling. When recarved, the left hand was apparently to be perceived as drawing an arrow from the quiver, not hard to

256

257

distinguish in the mass of rough marble behind the shoulder. What would have happened to Goliath's head in the second version we can only guess. Perhaps it would have been turned into a helmet, as a trophy for the victorious god.

Regardless of the exact literary meaning of the figure—a matter of demonstrably slight importance to the artist himself—its content is evident enough. The figure is strangely lethargic, in the mood of the statues of the Medici Chapel (with which there has been a not-too-successful attempt to connect it). The soft and strengthless arms are a far cry from the pride and power of the great marble *David* (figs. 100–112) set up twenty-odd years earlier in front of the Palazzo Vecchio. The slow spiral of movement develops, in mirror image, the motion of the Christ Child in the *Bruges Madonna* (figs. 86, 91, 97); but the heavy proportions, unusual in the 1520s, recall such earlier works as the *Bacchus*.

If the *David-Apollo* had been completed, one can imagine its surfaces polished and sensuous as in the *Giuliano* (colorplate 11; figs. 169–77). One can hardly blame Michelangelo for leaving it as it was, considering the identity of the patron. As with the *Medici Madonna*, the surfaces of the flesh seem to shine through the unfinished marble as through gauze.

258

244

28. HERCULES-SAMSON

Clay; height 26½"
See discussion of date below
Casa Buonarroti, Florence

This tiny clay model of two struggling figures perpetuates not only the opposition of ancient demigods and their enemies, Biblical champions and Philistine warriors, Renaissance republics and ambitious Popes, but even, save the mark, twentieth-century scholars against each other.

The most plausible identification of the model is with the ill-fated marble group destined

261

for the terrace in front of the Palazzo Vecchio by the Florentine Republic in 1508, as a pendant to Michelangelo's marble *David*. The original subject was to have been Hercules and Cacus, as a symbol of the fortitude of the government of Florence. The block was quarried in Carrara, but remained there for years, while Michelangelo was occupied with work for Julius II and later Leo X. In 1525 Clement VII, unwilling to release Michelangelo for this work, chose his enemy Baccio Bandinelli to carve the block, which was brought to Florence. The powerless leaders of the now hollow Florentine Republic requested Michelangelo to take over the work, and he apparently wanted to change the subject to Hercules and Antaeus, for which he did several drawings. Nonetheless, the Pope took the block away from Michelangelo definitively, and gave it to Bandinelli, who started carving a Hercules and Cacus from the bottom up, and got as far as the groin. In 1528, after the third expulsion of the Medici, the Signoria gave the unfinished group back to Michelangelo (for the third time), telling him just to make "one figure together or two conjoined with another as it appears to and pleases Michelangelo."

According to Vasari, the group was to have represented Samson and *two* Philistines. Work was prevented by the war and subsequent siege of Florence. After the re-entry of the Medici, Clement VII gave the block to Bandinelli again (for the third time), and he carved the rest of the atrocity we now see in front of the Palazzo Vecchio. The clay model represented either Hercules and Cacus, or Samson and *one* Philistine. In the absence of the raised right arm, which, if it represented Samson, should have held the jawbone of an ass, we will never know. The rough, bearded head, rediscovered some forty years ago, would fit either subject, but not a victory group, counterpart of the slender and youthful *Victory* (figs. 277–83) for the Tomb of Julius II, now in the Palazzo Vecchio.

The group as imagined in the clay model seems to have been conceived for a position in the open rather than for a niche, as it has at least three very beautiful views. The composition of two entwined figures breaks completely with the simple alignments of separate figures common to the rare statuary groups of the earlier Renaissance. This kind of interweaving of human forms, of course, springs from Michelangelo's basic interest in wrestling males, to be found as early as the *Battle of Lapiths and Centaurs* (see page 50), and reappearing throughout his vast pictorial compositions. In this group, however, the interweaving takes on for the first time a complete plastic existence in the round. The little model fairly explodes with violence, yet out of the intricate human knot emerge shapes and rhythms of great ornamental brilliance, such as the rich curve of the left flank of Hercules-Samson as seen from the back. Although never carried out by Michelangelo himself, his revolutionary idea was imitated enthusiastically by a horde of Mannerist sculptors and studied repeatedly by Jacopo Tintoretto.

29. THE TOMB OF JULIUS II (1532)

Project never carried out

After the surrender of Florence to Medici forces in 1530 the stage was set for the fourth act in the tragedy of the Tomb. By April of the following year Francesco Maria della Rovere, back on the throne of Urbino since 1521, had become greatly upset at the endless delays. Although he was willing to pay the 8,500 ducats still outstanding on the 1516 contract, he was afraid of losing both the money and the work. One can hardly blame him. Julius II and his executors had already paid out 8,000 ducats (an enormous sum) and given the artist a house and land rent-free. In twenty-five years they had received nothing. By June the artist was willing to return the house and all the marble, to let other artists finish the work, and to reimburse the estate to the tune of 2,000 ducats. Pope Clement VII was interested in getting as much out of Michelangelo as he could, but at the same time he wanted to placate the Duke. Proposals and counter-proposals went back and forth between Florence and Urbino for months, by way of Rome, with the Pope as arbiter and Sebastiano del Piombo as go-between. By April, 1532, both sides were ready for a new contract—the fourth—and Michelangelo came to Rome for the signing.

Although the Tomb of Julius II is one of the best-documented monuments of the whole Renaissance, the later phases of its sad history are more concealed than elucidated by mountains of correspondence and contracts. The new contract required Michelangelo to refund the 2,000 ducats, but permitted him to keep the house in the Macello dei Corvi as his own property; and indeed it remained so until he died there. He was also to deliver six unfinished but unspecified statues existing in his studios in Rome and Florence, to supply "all other things belonging to the said sepulcher," and to have the remaining statues executed by other artists from his own models and drawings. A model was to be delivered, but is not described. Nothing more definite is known.

The gates are wide open for speculation. We have to account not just for the six statues mentioned, but for eight—the *Moses* and the two Louvre *Slaves* which had remained in the Macello dei Corvi all these years, and the *Victory* and the four Academy *Slaves* done in Florence. Worse yet, we have no idea whether the monument was to project as far as the 1516 version did, or whether it was to be reduced to a simple wall tomb, as had been suggested in 1525. The latter is probable, since the price was cut by more than half, and since the new contract had a penalty clause, putting the 1516 contract back in force if Michelangelo should default again. But the Pope, it must be remembered, wanted Michelangelo to do the larger project, and claimed it would "rejuvenate him by twenty-five years."

As for the statues, the most sensible suggestion so far seems to be the omission of the two Louvre *Slaves* (figs. 134–43), since later on, in 1542, Michelangelo declared they could not possibly go on the wall tomb, having been designed for a much more ambitious project. Even at this juncture, these would scarcely have harmonized with the Academy *Slaves*, which were not only different in proportions and in style, but also much larger. According to this hypothesis, then, the four *Slaves* now in Florence would have stood on the four pedestals of the lower story, now occupied by volutes. At present they are too large for these positions, but the removal of the unfinished stone would have permitted them to fit at least as well as any of the statues in the Medici Chapel, for instance, all of which project. The termini would have been suppressed entirely.

The *Victory* would have been placed in one niche, while *Moses* still remained on the right corner of the second story; and the other *Victory* and the remaining statues of the upper levels, presumably already blocked in, would have been farmed out to other sculptors. The reduction of the project to a wall tomb (fig. 264) would have necessitated the alignment of the effigy of the Pope in its present uncomfortable pose (fig. 30). This suggestion accounts for all the existing statues by Michelangelo himself. It has the further merit of corresponding with the slippery proposals of Sebastiano del Piombo, who argued that the Duke's agents had no idea what was in Michelangelo's two workshops in Florence, and that it was enough if the great artist gave the Tomb "a little of his shadow."

When did Michelangelo actually carve the five statues in Florence? Since they are mentioned as already existing in both correspondence and contract, it seems that by 1532 they must have been completed substantially to the point at which we now see them. The contract required only that Michelangelo *finish* them, and this he has not done. Also, during the next two years he spent at least half his time in Rome. Since in Florence he was heavily overburdened with work for the Medici Chapel and the Laurentian Library, he could scarcely have had time to work on the statues for the Tomb.

We know that Michelangelo had made models for the remaining figures before leaving Rome

264. Tomb of Julius II
Author's reconstruction
of 1532 project

for Florence in 1516 (figs. 1–6) to commence the ill-fated façade of San Lorenzo. It seems reasonable to assume that he took the models with him, especially since two of them are still in the Casa Buonarroti. Not having enough marble for the Tomb, he ordered more blocks in Carrara when he ordered those for the San Lorenzo façade. Although a separate shop was built on Via Mozza for the work on the Tomb, the accounts did get confused, and Michelangelo used a considerable sum of Medici money for these blocks. The *Slaves* may have been blocked in during this period, and possibly even the *Victory*, though still in female form; but certainly little or nothing was done to complete the statues.

Only after the expulsion of the Medici from Florence in May, 1527, would Michelangelo have been able to turn again to the statues for the Tomb. It is noteworthy that the Duke of Urbino passed through Florence that very month at the head of a powerful armed force, and that he returned there in April, 1528. Considering the stress he laid on the completion of the Tomb, it would be strange if he took no time then to inspect the progress of the work. This was the moment when Pope Clement VII, now exiled in Orvieto, was trying unsuccessfully to persuade Michelangelo to resume the unfinished Medici Chapel. From May, 1527, to April, 1529 (when the artist was made governor of the fortifications of Florence), was the only period when he would have had the opportunity to do the finished, or almost finished, portions of the five statues. It would follow, therefore, that the 1532 contract really did little more than formalize what Michelangelo had intended in 1525, and that the statues to be included in it were those planned for the project, for which no contract exists.

The strange *Victory*, with its perplexing content, has often been connected with Michelangelo's passion for the handsome and cultivated young Roman nobleman, Tommaso Cavalieri, and interpreted in terms of the last lines of a famous sonnet:

> *It is no marvel if nude and alone*
> *I remain prisoner of an armed cavalier.*

But the crumpled prisoner is clothed and the nude victor unarmed! Furthermore, the group must have been blocked in, and was probably carved, long before 1532, at which time Michelangelo made the acquaintance of Cavalieri. If there is any relation between sculpture and poem, it goes the other way.

A glance at the new arrangement (fig. 264) makes it clear enough that the meaning of the monument had also changed. The whole idea of resurrection, essential to all three of the previous projects, has now been abandoned. The Pope, deprived of angelic assistants, now reclines on his right elbow in a pose which, although derived from respectable ancient sources, inevitably strikes modern eyes as absurd (fig. 30). The Captives no longer struggle against the bonds of death, since the termini have vanished. In fact, the positions of the arms and heads of the Academy *Slaves*, doubtless considerably changed from the original designs of 1513 and 1516, turn them into caryatids—giant Atlas figures, which have taken over the function of the termini in upholding the cornice; and the modeling now shows them quivering and straining under its enormous weight. These *Slaves* were frequently imitated in the later sixteenth century, and as caryatids. After all, the new representation of the Pope as alive in death necessitated a new conception.

Clearly the meaning of the *Victory* has changed along with its sex. Instead of liberating a Captive, as in the Berlin drawing (fig. 15), the youthful figure seems rather to be engaged in subduing him, yet to be withdrawn in a strange and unaccountable fashion, at the very moment of triumph. A spiritual struggle seems to be raging in this group, suggesting the age-old Christian doctrine of the battle between Virtue and Vice, or Psychomachia (warfare in the soul). Clearly, at such a distance in time and space from the Rome of Julius II, Michelangelo must have felt differently toward the original program of the Tomb. He once said in a moment of despair that the Tomb was likely to become his own, and immediately after his death his devoted pupil, Daniele da Volterra, even suggested that the *Victory* be placed on the artist's tomb in Santa Croce.

Just such a spiritual struggle as we have discerned in the *Victory* seems to have been taking place in newly liberated Florence, which for the third time had thrown off the Medici yoke. On May 31, 1527, the new Gonfaloniere of the Republic of Florence, Niccolò Capponi, whose alternate rises to and falls from power were to make the chronicle of the following years so confusing, gave an extraordinary inaugural address, reported by the humanist Benedetto Varchi, in which he set the keynote for the goal of the resuscitated Republic in terms of a Psychomachia. In so doing, he was recapitulating the same doctrines which, on the part of his predecessors, had colored the heroic works of art of the first Florentine Renaissance of the early fifteenth century, and later the marble *David* of Michelangelo. "Do you hold dear the conquering of your enemies," he said, "or that your enemies do not conquer you? Then conquer yourselves, put down wrath, let hatred go, put aside bitterness." Speaking of the miserable state of the Medici Pope, prisoner in Castel Sant'Angelo, he warned, "Not the words that are said, ignominiously or injuriously, against enemies but the deeds that are done, prudently or valorously, give, won or lost, the victory."

These words, delivered in the great hall of the Palazzo Vecchio, which still may have held the beginnings of Michelangelo's now-lost wall painting of the *Battle of Cascina*, were followed by another such address, this time before eleven hundred citizens in the same great hall, in February of 1528, when Niccolò Capponi was elected for the second time as Gonfaloniere, now for a term of thirteen months. He pointed out that all the great political changes which had taken place in Florence in these years had been accomplished entirely without bloodshed, and this he called a work of God. He also emphasized the fact that the good fortune of the Republic had been due to the same circumstances as the ruin of Rome and the papacy. "To his divine Majesty, therefore, we have to lift the eyes of our mind, recognizing God alone as our King and Lord, hoping firmly in Him, Who has undertaken the protection of this city and of this State, liberating it from the most cruel plague . . . giving us counsel and fortitude to know how to govern ourselves, making Himself our staff and refuge and strength against whoever sought to molest us." After this address, reported by Scipione Ammirato, who was present, the Florentines were required to vote for Christ as their king. Unaccountably, eighteen white beans (contrary ballots) were cast, but Christ was declared the winner, and His name as King of Kings and Lord of Lords was inscribed in letters of gold over the portal of the Palazzo Vecchio where, in a nineteenth-century replacement, it can still be read today. Then ensued a real austerity campaign. Taverns were forbidden to serve food, ladies to wear silver belts and gold chains, gentlemen fine cloth. Gambling and card-playing became illegal.

It would seem reasonable to interpret in terms of the new asceticism of the Third Republic this unarmed and bloodless *Victory*, looking to heaven for his strength in the eternal inner warfare, about which Michelangelo knew so much so bitterly. At the same time such a group could hardly have been displeasing to the principal executor of Julius II, Francesco Maria della Rovere, Duke of Urbino, who held the post of Captain General of the Florentine army, and as we have seen was on hand at the time. The *Victory* is crowned with the Rovere oak leaves. In his niche, he was intended to be flanked by the mighty figures who upheld the great Pope as source of the dynastic power of the Rovere family.

The new conception of the Tomb, then, embodied Michelangelo's profound Christianity and his republican loyalty, as well as the respect owed by his patron, the Duke of Urbino, to the memory of Julius II—in contrast to the Medici, whom the Duke hated as much as Michelangelo despised and feared them.

Such an interpretation would at least seem preferable to the traditional and somewhat appalling one, which is more appropriate to a play by Genêt than to a sculpture by Michelangelo. That the *Victory* should finally, in 1564, have been placed by the Medici Grand Duke, Cosimo I, at the head of the room in which Capponi's orations were delivered, demonstrates only Cosimo's historical detachment in these years of his total and undisputed rule. Neither Michelangelo's *David* nor, incidentally, Donatello's *Judith* (anti-Medicean inscription and all) was ever removed from its traditional position by the Medici princes. But it is just Donatello's *Judith* and his youthful marble *David*, then also still visible in the Palazzo Vecchio, as well as the glorious *St. George* at Orsanmichele, that are most important for the style of Michelangelo's tense and haunting group.

30. THE ACADEMY SLAVES

"BEARDED" SLAVE: *Marble; total height 8' 4¾"; height without base 7' 8½"; width 2' 4¾"; depth 3' ½"*
"BLOCKHEAD" SLAVE: *Marble; total height 8' 7½"; height without base 7' 11⅝"; width 2' 1½"; depth 2' 11"*
"BEARDLESS" SLAVE: *Marble; total height 9' 1"; height without base 7' 11⅝"; width 2' 7½"; depth 3' 6⅛"*
"CROSSED-LEG" SLAVE: *Marble; total height 8' 10⅛"; height without base 7' 9⅝"; width 3' 1¾"; depth 2' 5½"*
Probably carved 1527–28, from blocks cut 1516–20
Accademia di Belle Arti, Florence

As a glance at the dimensions of the four figures now in the Accademia will show, despite the differences in the total heights of the blocks, the real heights of the figures vary only about three inches. Probably they would have substituted for the termini, and would have appeared to uphold the cornice, which may have been intended to project so as to rest upon their lifted

267 ▶

arms, hands, or elbows. As is usual with Michelangelo's figures, the poses bear only a symbolic relation to the function of the figures. (The twenty nudes of the Sistine Ceiling, for example, hold only lightly the straps with which they sustain their medallions.)

After Michelangelo's death in 1564 his nephew, Lionardo Buonarroti, gave the four statues to Grand Duke Cosimo I, who ordered the architect Buontalenti to include them in the structure of the Grotta of the Boboli Gardens, just outside the Pitti Palace, which had become the Grand Ducal residence. They were placed at the four corners of this stucco nightmare, one of the most ingenious creations of Florentine Mannerism, where they appeared to uphold the four corners of a vault that drips with stucco stalactites and is haunted by monstrous shapes. Early in the present century the statues were relieved of their decorative function, and taken to their present home in the Accademia.

It is unrealistic even to guess at what might have been the order of the four statues on the lower story of the 1532 project, or of the 1525 project of which they were really the outgrowth. Some of the poses seem to go back as far as the Berlin drawing (fig. 15), especially that of the Slave with the crossed leg (figs. 274–76), which resembles the second Slave from the right. This, we have seen (page 143), must have been planned for the 1505 version, and of all the poses it is the closest to the Roman sarcophagus which influenced Michelangelo's idea for the composition. When he actually came to carve the statue, however, he made it writhe and

270

twist in a manner completely alien to the original conception, lifting the crossed foot and
lowering the right arm so that the entire weight comes to bear on the upraised left elbow,
and is transmitted through the body to the unaided left foot. The weight, bulk, and power
of the body are enormously increased, and it is provided with a bearded head, tilted back so
that the whole torso arches and the chest lifts as if in pain. The little wax model in the British
Museum (fig. 6) was undoubtedly done for this figure, presumably before 1516, when
Michelangelo thought he could still complete the second version of the Tomb in a relatively
short time.

None of the other Florentine *Slaves* can be so closely connected with the Berlin drawing.
The exquisite, almost Phidian model in the Casa Buonarroti (fig. 5) was certainly designed
for the last figure on the right. The legs of the beardless *Slave* (figs. 271–73) are posed in
somewhat the same way, but there the resemblance stops: perhaps this lithe and beautiful
figure was given up as unsuitable for the new conception of the monument. At any rate,
another model (figs. 2, 3) was made for this beardless slave, and despite its fragmentary and
corroded condition, it shows clearly the soft, almost epicene rhythm of that slumberous youth.

The titanic bearded figure with its right elbow raised (figs. 265–67), was studied very delicately in the other British Museum model (fig. 1), which explores with searching intensity
all the implications of the pose for the heaving, twitching muscles of the torso. But the model

is for a slenderer figure; once Michelangelo actually started to carve, the masses expanded, the tension increased, the muscular violence heightened; the whole feeling of grief and terror comes to an immense climax in the bearded face, with its memories of the *Laocoön*. Only in the legs of this figure do the familiar bonds appear, and even these are questionable, since the lower legs are clumsily cut, possibly not by Michelangelo himself. The heavy band crossing the thighs is a mantle-strap, of course, of the kind constantly to be seen in Michelangelo's sculpture.

In all four statues Michelangelo's chief interest lay in the torsos, which are, from the front at least, fully developed with the toothed chisel, and lack only the surface finish. Sometimes an arm or a leg is brought to a similar condition, but never a head. The heads remain either roughed in or, as in one striking instance (figs. 268–70), still encased in the block, save for features which are faintly visible on one side through a thick cloud of marble. Sometimes the statues have been started from two sides at once, sometimes from three, but in each case the back is still concealed within the block. One can usually follow the contours around the torso with great precision up to the point where the shape suddenly disappears.

What remains somewhat disconcerting, of course, is the leapfrog relation of the statues to the figures of the Medici Chapel. The *Slaves* were probably blocked in first in 1516–20; then in 1526 the Medici figures were roughed in; and in 1527–28 the *Slaves* were brought to their present state. The Medici figures were not finished until 1530–32.

272

273

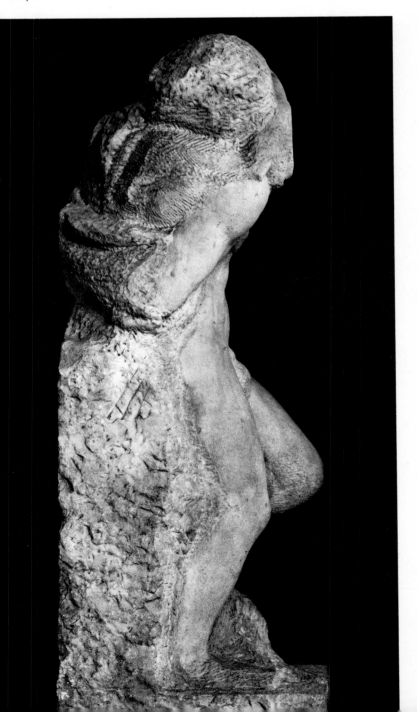 

For all their enormous volume, not to speak of their superhuman strength, the figures are oddly soft. The vast areas of muscle and skin heave, swell, subside, shine silkily, against the drilled blocks of stone. Whatever might have been Michelangelo's conscious intent—and it would seem that he thought or hoped he would finish the statues—their present condition reveals essential aspects of Michelangelo's nature. To watch these giants struggle to free themselves from the surrounding marble has been for viewers during four centuries a strongly empathetic experience. If the great artist could miraculously return and carve away all the rough marble, we would probably miss it.

274

275

31. VICTORY

Marble; height 8' 6¾", width 2' 7⅛", depth 2' 9"
Probably carved 1527–28, from block cut 1516–20
Palazzo Vecchio, Florence

Not all the responsibility for the present disturbing appearance of the *Victory* can be laid at Michelangelo's door. The group was set up in the Salone dei Cinquecento in the Palazzo Vecchio in 1564, and removed in 1868, first to the Bargello, then to the Accademia. In 1921 it was replaced in its present position. In one of these many moves, probably to compensate for placing the statue at a height for which Michelangelo did not intend it, the block was propped sharply forward by cement surfaced to look like rough stone. As a result it has acquired an uncomfortable tilt, and has been deprived of the strong verticality Michelangelo must have intended for it. A mental effort will restore the statue to its original posture, making it clear that it was not intended to lean out of the niche, but to continue the verticals of the architecture, and to contrast, in its unusual slenderness, with the heavy proportions of the flanking *Slaves*.

colorplate 15

277

278

Seen upright, the group loses its strained and tortured appearance, and harmonizes with the architecture for which it was designed. Quite as important, it regains its lofty dignity—a kind of soaring quality, intended not only for its esthetic result but for its moral significance. The unarmed youth has conquered his bearded opponent (characterized as a soldier in armor), and in the moment of victory presses about him his mantle, age-old symbol of divine protection, and gazes slightly upward as if in recognition of divine help. The present position of the statue makes the gaze horizontal, and by rejecting the vertical axis, converts the group into an unrelated assortment of anatomical features.

A single glance at the head of the vanquished soldier, with his low forehead, classical profile, and jutting beard, should suffice to dispel the absurd theory that it is in any way a portrait, spiritual or otherwise, of the sculptor himself. The group is not of Aristotle with a male Campasbe, which would be depressing in any case but unthinkable on a papal tomb. It is an explicit moral allegory belonging to a millennial Christian tradition, realized, however, in corporeal terms long familiar to the Renaissance and essential to Michelangelo's art. The taut quality of the erect and rangy victor is communicated to all his muscles and to his very expression, intent on communication with divinity, like an Abraham or a David. In fact the handling of the features and the curls is closely related to Donatello's earlier marble *David*, which then stood in the Palazzo Vecchio.

279

280

282

While the beard of the vanquished is mostly uncut marble, elsewhere almost all the work with the toothed chisel has been completed. Here and there the splendidly muscled torso has received its finish. The right eye alone, strangely enough, has been given an incised cornea. Possibly Michelangelo was already aware of the logical difficulties in the way of this traditional device, which he was to renounce altogether in finishing the statues of the Medici Chapel.

As beautiful as a Hellenic warrior, as sensitive and proud as Donatello's *St. George*, this athletic figure shimmering with alternately relaxed and contracted muscles remains one of Michelangelo's most penetrative, if least appreciated, creations.

283 ▶

32. THE TOMB OF JULIUS II (1542–1545)

Project of 1542
Completed 1545: elements carved 1505–6, 1513–16, and 1542–45; statues carved 1515–16, and at intervals between 1532–45
San Pietro in Vincoli, Rome

Very little, save the placing of the lower story of the Tomb, had been accomplished to turn the contract of 1532 into reality when Clement VII suddenly died in Rome on September 25, 1534, two days after Michelangelo arrived there from Florence. The new Pope, Paul III, a member of the Farnese family of Parma, was elected on October 13. He not only desired to monopolize the great artist's services for his own projects in the Vatican, but was at outs with the Rovere family as well. The great new commission of the *Last Judgment* effectively prevented Michelangelo from doing anything more on the Tomb, and in 1536, a year after the expiration of the limitations of the fourth contract, the Pope officially absolved Michelangelo from all further obligations to the Rovere family until the completion of the gigantic fresco. While it was in progress, in 1538, Francesco Maria della Rovere, Duke of Urbino, went the way of his illustrious relative Julius II and all the earlier executors of his will, and the responsibility for the Tomb devolved upon Guidobaldo, Francesco Maria's son and successor.

Guidobaldo, reasonably enough, hoped that when the *Last Judgment* was finished in 1541 the artist would be able to return to work on the Tomb, but he reckoned without the imperious personality of Paul III. The Pope now commanded the artist, in spite of his sixty-six years, to start the frescoes of the Pauline Chapel, which were to occupy him off and on for the next nine years. It was obviously out of the question to revive the 1532 contract. The new Duke was asked to content himself with having the six statues and the other still-outstanding work finished by other artists under Michelangelo's supervision. A compromise began to emerge, according to which the artist would provide three, rather than six, statues by his own hand, and supervise the rest. The reduced number also involved a change in identity, since the *Moses* and the two Louvre *Slaves* are now mentioned by name in the documents. Apparently Michelangelo did not wish to face the enormous expense of transporting the four Academy *Slaves* and the *Victory* from Florence to Rome, a move which he would have had to finance himself.

Meanwhile the sculptor had gone ahead even before the completion of a new contract. The lower story of the architecture had been in place in San Pietro in Vincoli for years. Sandro Fancelli, called Scherano, was paid in 1537 for work on the *Madonna and Child* (fig. 28), and in February, 1542, Michelangelo completed an agreement with his old assistant Raffaello da Montelupo to complete this statue, as well as a *Prophet* and a *Sibyl*, both unidentified. Contracts were also let in May to stonecutters for the execution of the upper story of the architecture from the master's drawing and model. In June Michelangelo wrote to the Pope that the two Louvre *Slaves* would be unsuitable (see page 250), and had started work on figures of the *Active Life* and the *Contemplative Life*, to be finished by Montelupo.

On August 20 the fifth and final contract was signed, not only freeing Michelangelo from all previous contracts and from any prosecution on account of them, but even enjoining perpetual silence on the Rovere heirs. The artist had deposited money in a Roman bank to pay the assistants who were to finish the statues and what remained of the architecture. Michelangelo himself was to supply only the *Moses* completely finished by his own hand, but was to retouch the faces of the Pope (fig. 30) and the termini (figs. 31–34). For two or three months Michelangelo was kept on tenterhooks waiting for the Duke's ratification of the contract. The Tomb, after all, had overshadowed more than half of his life, and had become an incubus, especially on account of rumors emanating from Urbino to the effect that he had

284. Upper Story
Tomb of Julius II
Project of 1542–45
San Pietro in Vincoli, Rome

268

simply invested "at usury" all the money received from Pope Julius, and had produced nothing at all. (According to his own account, it had all been spent on marble and on living expenses, and he was actually out of pocket.) By November the Duke seems to have ratified the contract, with the reservation that there must be three statues by Michelangelo's own hand. He therefore proceeded to finish the *Active Life* and the *Contemplative Life* (figs. 285–90) himself, as well as the *Moses*. Since we have no record of any more marble ordered for the statues, it seems reasonable to assume that all the figures now on the Tomb were carved from blocks remaining in Rome from the 1505 and 1513 projects. The *Active Life* and the *Contemplative Life*, now placed in niches designed for the *Victories*, could have been carved from marble intended for the two standing saints of the Berlin drawing (fig. 15); the *Prophet* (fig. 29) and *Sibyl* (fig. 27), much reduced in scale, from blocks intended to flank the *Moses* in its original position; the effigy of the Pope from the block intended for that purpose from the beginning and shipped to Rome in 1508 (see page 126)—only to have its destination changed from inside the monument to outside in 1513, and its position tilted in 1516. The termini (figs. 31–34) would also have remained from earlier versions, but were only carved for this final contract. The positions originally to have been occupied by the Captives are now filled by abstract shapes—two magnificent volutes.

The principal responsibility for the execution of the statues, including the *Madonna* (fig. 27) on which Fancelli had worked in 1537, was given to Michelangelo's pupil Montelupo, but he fell ill and the work had to be farmed out to *his* pupils. Those responsible for the present appearance of the *Madonna*, the *Prophet*, and the *Sibyl* are mercifully unknown. Tommaso di Pietro Boscoli finished the *Pope*, and the termini were done by Jacopo del Duca. It is impossible to state whether Michelangelo ever gave to the faces of the *Pope* and the termini the finishing touches required by the contract. All one can say is that in places their level of execution seems a little better than the mediocre standard of the other figures. The *Active Life* and the *Contemplative Life* are by Michelangelo himself, except for some details, and are very beautiful.

The whole conception of the Tomb by this time had changed beyond recognition. The architecture of the lower story, of course, remained fixed through all the various permutations of the hag-ridden undertaking. But the disappearance of the Captives, which in the 1532 project seem to have replaced the termini, left a clear field for the latters' return. Possibly in reminiscence of the sad Academy *Slaves*, the termini are now exclusively male and bearded, concealing their folded arms in heavy cloaks. Only two are finished, and those are of fairly high quality.

The architecture of the upper story distills a visionary quality all its own. Michelangelo, in this last version, simply abandoned any connection between the styles of the two stories, and produced a structure which seems to soar in the shadows of the transept of San Pietro in Vincoli. This disembodied effect is largely created by the new set of termini (fig. 284), consisting of heads superimposed on long, tapering shafts, which have replaced the pilasters, columns, or any of the other possibilities of the 1513, 1516, and 1532 projects. Together with the lower row of termini (figs. 31–34), these staring masks reinforce the sense of the mystery and terror of death, against which no figure struggles any longer. *Moses*, brought down almost to the level of the spectator, may possibly have been intended by then to convey something of the energy and fire of the departed Pope, but there is no physical resemblance beyond the trimming of the moustache around the lips in the manner of Julius II, the first Pope to wear a beard since early Christian times. The idea of resurrection is suggested only by the position of the Pope (fig. 30), alive in death, and gazing downward as if in meditation. The *Madonna* (fig. 27), about which the less said the better, can show nothing of Michelangelo's intention save in the general lines of the pose. She holds the Child as in the Berlin drawing, but the group is now in mirror image. The Child, in turn, holds a goldfinch, traditional symbol of His Passion and death. In the entire upper level of the monument the feeling of conflict and struggle, which had pervaded every earlier project for the Tomb, is now stilled. This crowning section is devoted to the interplay of abstract architectural forces, whose tone is set by the heads of the termini. The impression on the observer is that of a remote and challenging mystery—the enigma of death which now obsessed the imagination, the writings, and the spiritual life of the aging artist.

As a practical aspect of the completion of the Tomb, it may be noted that Michelangelo carefully incorporated into his design the four small windows of a room behind the monument which could serve as a place for important personages to hear Mass unobserved, and also for the monks' choir. And an ironic epilogue is furnished by the fact that the mighty Julius II, terror of Italy during his lifetime, never made it as far as this tomb, which is nothing but a cenotaph. The great warrior Pope was buried beside his beloved uncle, Sixtus IV, in the so-called Old Sistine Chapel, renamed the Cappella Giulia, in Old St. Peter's; and when this chapel was demolished, under Paul III, both tombs were moved to the Chapel of the Holy Sacrament in the new St. Peter's.

The young artist who had begun the Tomb with high hopes forty years before was by now an old man. Yet at seventy he still had some of his greatest artistic and spiritual achievements ahead of him.

33. THE ACTIVE LIFE (Leah)

Marble; height 7' 1/4"; width 1' 10 3/4"; depth 1' 3 3/4"

THE CONTEMPLATIVE LIFE (Rachel)

Marble; height 6' 5 1/2"; width 1' 10 3/4"; depth 1' 2 7/8"
c. 1542
San Pietro in Vincoli, Rome

In the commanding presence of the universally known *Moses* it is a little difficult to savor the more reserved style of the *Active Life* and the *Contemplative Life* (the unfortunate tourist is never so much as informed that they are by Michelangelo). Yet their grave and quiet music is very affecting on closer attention, and forms a fitting prelude to the personal mysticism of the artist's last years.

Vasari in the 1568 edition of his *Lives* is the first to refer to these two statues as representations of Rachel and Leah, the two wives of Jacob. Exactly how they acquired this further identification is still unclear, but there must have been a tradition in which Leah, whose childbearing activities were a subject of some pride, symbolized the Active Life, and the Contemplative Life was typified by Rachel, who had a fourteen-year wait for her husband and gave birth to her last child, Benjamin, only as she was dying. There is no evidence that Michelangelo himself intended any such meaning; and the further connection with Dante's *Purgatorio* is supported only by the garland in the hand of the supposed Leah. According to Dante, however, Leah should also be holding a mirror, but the object in her right hand is a diadem surmounted by a mask. She is represented as a full-bodied young woman, probably still unmarried, to judge from her firm, high breasts, high virginal zone, and long tresses. The *Contemplative Life* is veiled like a nun, places one knee upon a pedestal, and looks upward as she clasps her hands in prayer.

285 ▶

287 ▶

In both statues the masses are extremely compact and contained, and the treatment of surface astonishingly broad, even blank. Although echoes of the *Last Judgment* style persist in the *Contemplative Life*, which closely resembles some of the figures soaring upward toward heaven on the left of the fresco, the drawing in both figures seems governed by a strong new classicism. The profiles, for example, are severely Hellenic, more so than those in the Medici Chapel, and without a touch of Byzantinism. Yet below this austere surface still pulsates the physical and emotional violence of Michelangelo's nature. The muscles of the left arm of the *Contemplative Life* contract visibly within her modest sleeve. The drapery masses, adhering in many places to the rounded forms of the figures, lift and fall, twist and relax in subtle cadences, still suggesting some of the tumult of the earlier drapery style. Most beautiful of all are the broad surfaces of the faces, in which, as in the faces of the Medici Chapel figures, ornamental forms seem to dominate representation. But the smooth and open flow of volumes is new in Michelangelo's sculptural style, pointing to the new breadth and soaring shapes of the Pauline Chapel frescoes, on which he had embarked during these very years. Through every line and every mass moves the consistent melodious quality that can always be found in Michelangelo's art, but slower now, without the energy of youth. These majestic harmonies are to the turbulence of so much of the artist's earlier work as Milton's *Samson Agonistes* is to *Paradise Lost*. The more we look at these quiet women, the more we can rejoice that Guidobaldo della Rovere insisted that the two figures be finished by the hand of Michelangelo.

34. BRUTUS

Marble; height (without base) 29⅛"
After 1537
Museo Nazionale (Bargello), Florence

Following the recapture of Florence by the Medici in 1530, under Clement VII with the aid of imperial troops, the city and its territory were ruled by a mysterious personage, the young Alessandro de' Medici, who maintained at first the outward appearance of a republic, but then (1532) was openly installed as Duke. This universally detested youth, no more than twenty years old at the time, was passed off as a natural son of the dead Lorenzo de' Medici, Duke of Urbino, for whom Michelangelo was carving the great tomb in the Medici Chapel; but he was generally suspected, and is now believed, to have been the natural son of the Pope himself. On January 6, 1537, Lorenzino de' Medici, Alessandro's cousin, put an end with a dagger to the Duke's life of crime, and fled to Venice. Among the Florentine *fuorusciti* (exiles) in that city and in Rome, Lorenzino was hailed as a new Brutus, and Alessandro was interred,

colorplate 16

291

still dressed in his embroidered nightshirt rather than a shroud, in the Medici Chapel on top of Lorenzo in Michelangelo's sarcophagus—head to foot, in which position the remains were found when the tomb was opened for inspection in 1875.

At some time after the assassination, Donato Giannotti, a close friend of Michelangelo's among the *fuorusciti*, and Cardinal Ridolfi, another exiled Florentine in Rome, whose service Giannotti entered in 1539, had the idea of asking the sculptor to do a bust of Brutus to commemorate the slaying of the tyrant.

It is not possible to date this commission with any accuracy, and even less so to pinpoint Michelangelo's actual work on the bust. Giannotti may have been close to the Cardinal long before entering his service, and the idea may have been born of the elation of the moment. On the other hand, Michelangelo's rancor against the Medici (doubtless influenced by Baccio Valori's assassination order) lasted for years. As late as 1546 he offered to make a colossal equestrian statue of Francis I of France, at his own expense, and to set it up in the Piazza della Signoria, if the King would chase the Medici out of Florence for good.

At any rate the massive conception of the bust and the treatment of the features show strong affinities with both the *Last Judgment* and the frescoes of the Pauline Chapel, especially the latter.

It goes without saying that there is no attempt to give the actual appearance of Lorenzino, a slender youth, in this middle-aged hero. Michelangelo was all his life notoriously averse to portraiture, with the exception of his own features, which keep reappearing in self-revelatory places, and of the devastating caricatures of those he disliked, which turn up in the *Last Judgment*. The sculptor has presented here an ideal image of a great hero, an incarnation of fortitude and resolution who is yet, characteristically, tormented within. But the process of idealization does not subordinate the features to any classical type. The asymmetrical face, the powerful nose and high cheekbones, the tightly compressed lips, convey an impression of rude force more in keeping with the appearance of an Apennine shepherd or charcoal burner than of any personage from antiquity. Its beauty derives from the vibrant strength, the pride, and the corrosive melancholy that succeed each other throughout the pose and the controlled expression. Ironically enough, the one real classical prototype that can be adduced, the famous bust of Caracalla, represents a tyrant whose atrocities, if anything, exceeded those for which Lorenzino murdered Alessandro—but doubtless Michelangelo did not know about that. One wonders what he would have said if he could have known that the bust would be acquired by Gianfrancesco de' Medici, second Grand Duke of Tuscany.

Michelangelo's initial ardor must have cooled somewhat, because he left the bust unfinished, and gave it to his pupil Tiberio Calcagni. Luckily Calcagni did not touch the head. The hair is merely roughed in with a pointed chisel, and just above the right cheekbone the original surface of the block can still be discerned. The face and neck are brought almost to completion with the toothed chisel, and their quivering surfaces, of the utmost beauty of texture, contrast sharply with the meticulous handling of the drapery, in which Calcagni used a flat chisel.

Much of the vitality of the face, and its tragic and poetic overtones, result from the subtle and knowing employment of the systems of distortion which Michelangelo had used with such success in the figures of the Medici Chapel. The eyeballs, for example, are depressed to the point of becoming luminous shadows rather than solid masses, and the planes of the face are manipulated with the sublime disregard for their anatomical structure that is the result of a lifetime's knowledge. In its instinctive understanding of the crystalline structure of marble, in the rude grandeur of its masses and its clifflike pose, this head embodies all Michelangelo's obsessive concern with the "stone Alpine and hard," and brings vividly before us his dream of the mountain mass to be carved into a colossus looking out to sea.

292

293

35. THE FLORENCE PIETÀ

for Colorplate, see Frontispiece
Marble; height 7′ 5″, width 4′ ³⁄₈″, depth 3′ 1″
Before 1555
Cathedral, Florence

That Michelangelo should have attempted to destroy with his own hand this, one of his greatest and most personal works, sheds a special ray of light on the artist's state of mind during the penultimate decade of his long life. That so few of the thousands of visitors to Florence each season should even notice that the left leg is missing furnishes even stronger evidence of the power of Michelangelo's conceptions and the supremacy of his genius.

In the first edition of Vasari's *Lives* (published in 1550 but written three or four years earlier), the group is mentioned as being still incomplete. In 1547 Michelangelo's close friend, Vittoria Colonna, died, to the artist's intense grief, and the inception of the work may be connected with this event. Michelangelo intended the group for his own tomb. When Condivi's *Life of Michelangelo* was written in 1552 (published 1553), it was still unfinished. Vasari tells us

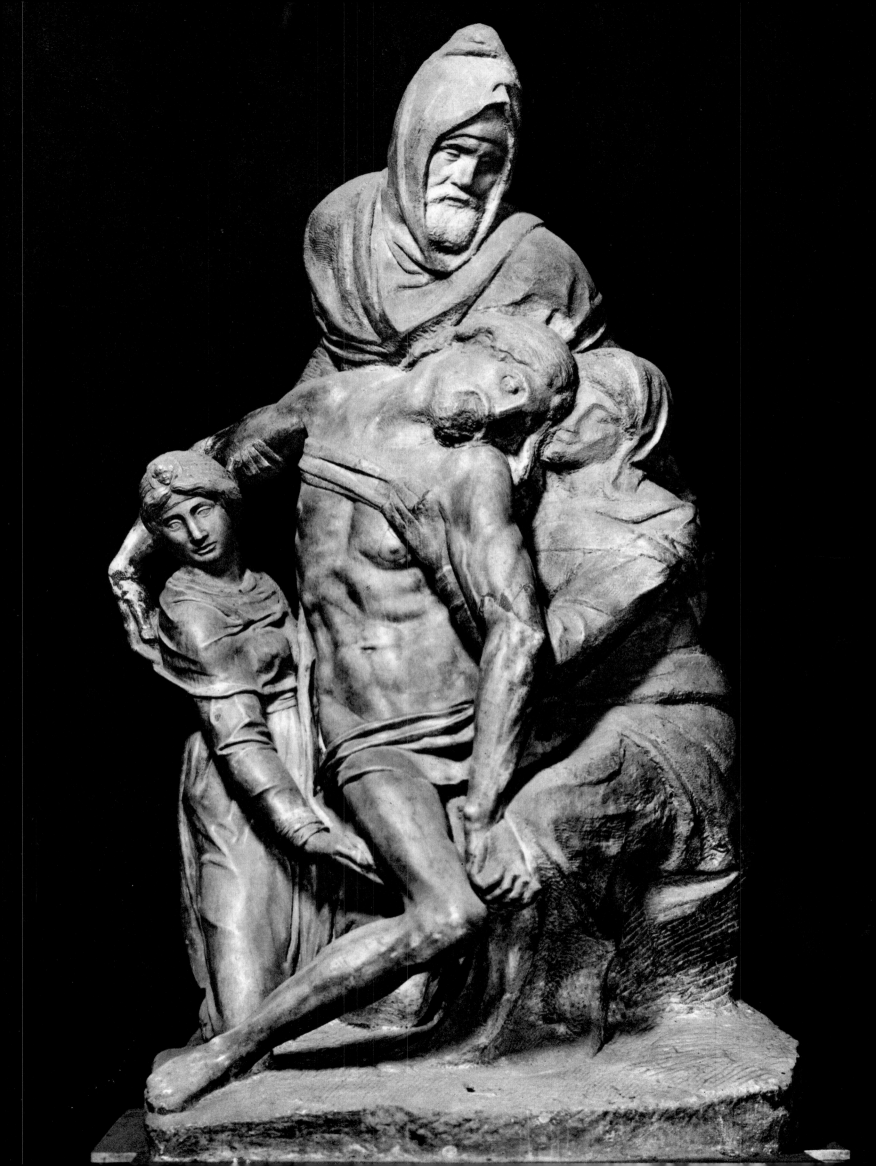

that Michelangelo's servant, assistant, and friend, Urbino, plagued him daily to complete the group, to the point that the artist, in a rage, began to wreck it. Luckily he was prevented by another servant, Antonio del Francese, who then received it as a gift. After the artist's death, the left knee was in the possession of his pupil, the painter Daniele da Volterra, but it has since disappeared. Francesco Bandini bought the group from Antonio, and commissioned still another pupil, Tiberio Calcagni, to complete it from the master's models. At that time Calcagni patched the arms, which had been smashed, and finished the Magdalene. Apparently the left leg was so badly broken that it was necessary to carve what sculptors call a "Roman joint" (a square socket pierced by a metal rod or key) to hold a new leg. This was never made.

After Michelangelo's death Vasari did his best to pry the group away from the Bandini family, so that it could be placed where it seemed to belong—on the great artist's projected tomb in Santa Croce. Not until the middle of the seventeenth century did the Medici Grand Duke Cosimo III finally acquire the work for Florence, where it was first shown in the crypt of San Lorenzo. For two centuries it stood behind the high altar of the Cathedral, but in 1930 it was moved to a chapel in the north transept.

The group has been variously described as a Deposition, a Lamentation, and an Entombment. The time-honored Italian name "Pietà" still seems the best. The subject is related to the image of the dead Christ upheld by saints, which is very common in Italian art of the fourteenth and fifteenth centuries. No Cross was ever intended, nor crown of thorns, nails,

297

298

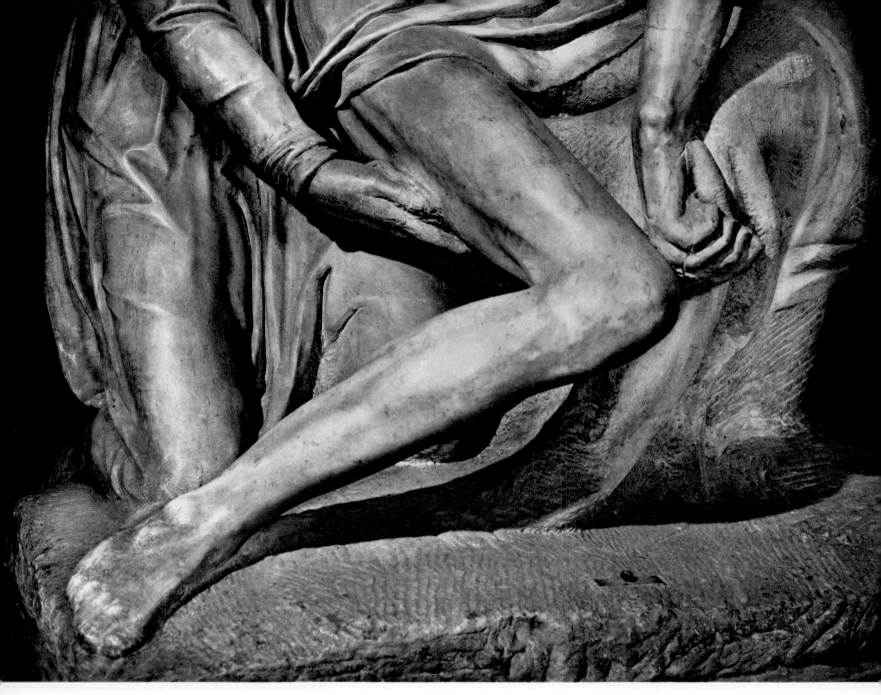

300

basin, sponge, slab of unction, or any other appurtenance of a specific event. Mary is there as Christ's mother; Mary Magdalene because He redeemed her, and she washed His feet (the diadem on her brow, carved by Michelangelo's hand, bears the mask of a smiling *angeletto* —symbol of love—for her of whom Christ had said, "She hath loved greatly, let her go in peace"); Joseph of Arimathea (and this is all-important) because he gave his Lord his own freshly cut, unused tomb. In this respect he is easily identified with Michelangelo himself, who designed the group for *his* sepulcher, and it is in this sense that we must understand the portrayal of the aged artist's own features in those of Joseph of Arimathea. (It has been suggested that the figure really represents Nicodemus, who was believed to be a sculptor. The connection with the artist's own tomb would seem to outweigh this view.)

The familiar grouping is reinterpreted in a deeply personal sense through this mystical identification. The artist, in the person of Joseph of Arimathea, gives his tomb to Christ, Who sinks toward it with a downward motion generally considered one of the most compelling, even irresistible movements in all of man's artistic expression. The mortal figures are powerless against it. Their futile attempts to hold the body of Christ dramatize only the inescapable fact that they, too, are drawn into the grave with Him. The fourteenth-century German mystic, Ludolph of Saxony, whose widely read *Life of Christ* was republished in a splendid

284

edition at about this time in Venice, maintained that we should live in the tomb with Christ, that we might with Him be resurrected. "Certain of death, but not yet of the hour," Michelangelo's last poems are rocked like ships by the enormity of the opening abyss, and by the need for God. Here, too, as in all of Michelangelo's poems, sculpture, and paintings dealing with religious matters, the grandeur of unalterable divine law, subsuming all human essences and desires, dominates the composition as well as the content.

The observer's eye ascends, past the taut and jagged line of the right leg, to the rigid muscles of the torso and the twisted left arm; then to the hanging head, no longer separate from that of Mary as in the *Rome Pietà*, but fused with it in self-obliteration; then to Joseph-Michelangelo, who folds his Redeemer and the Blessed Mother to his bosom. In the union of man and God, which this group celebrates, all individualities are merged to the point of transfusion. The sculptor who drew in the love of his tools from the breast of a stonecutter's wife now uses those tools to carve the meditative drama in which he presses the head of his Saviour to his own breast. It is a transfigured self-portrait. The fire of the *St. Proculus*, the rebelliousness of the *David*, the worldweariness of the *Crepuscolo*, the self-pity of the empty skin of St. Bartholomew in the *Last Judgment* (all in one way or another aspects of the artist's personality), have given way to resignation. The artist's being is dissolved in the currents of sacrificial love which flow throughout the group—currents which increase in depth the longer one gazes.

Small wonder that Michelangelo was irritated by the prodding of Urbino, in spite of his affection for his servant. (When Urbino died, the artist was inconsolable, and wished he had died with him.) But there may well have been other reasons for his attempted destruction of the work. Vasari refers to many flaws in the marble (none is visible) and to its unusual hardness, which made the cutting a defeating task. Perhaps, under such conditions, the exalted nature of the conception may have seemed impossible of attainment. Michelangelo wrote, possibly in those very days,

> *With so much servitude, with so much tedium*
> *And with false concepts and great peril*
> *Of the soul, to sculpture here divine things.*

Tiberio Calcagni did an excellent job in mending the shattered arms of the Christ, a less commendable one in attempting to finish the Magdalene, in whose compressed figure nothing but the general outlines of Michelangelo's design remain. The rest, laboriously cut out with a flat chisel, shows the halting and stiff quality of Calcagni's surface treatment. But in the total composition such feebleness matters little. The body, arms, and legs of the Christ were finished and polished by Michelangelo himself, and in their tension and clarity they show a new and more austere side of his imagination, related to the conception of the Christ of the *Rome Pietà* (fig. 74), but without any of the sensuous sweetness of that work. Everywhere the anguished beauty of the group is overpowering, in the thousand nuances of the slender and shining limbs, in the subtlety of the contours of the total group seen from the side, in the breadth and simplicity of the curving masses seen from the back—in all essentials unchanged since the *Bruges Madonna* (colorplate 5; figs. 85–99). Especially poignant, of course, is the artist's self-image as Joseph of Arimathea, visible like the *Medici Madonna* (figs. 236–47) through a mist of luminous marble. The septuagenarian sculptor has lost neither his poetic eloquence nor his astonishing control: of the broad masses of heads and drapery movements, and of the delicate and vibrant texture of the toothed chisel marks.

The dead Christ—alive in death like all great *Pietàs*, from Giotto to Bellini—shows some startling reminiscences of other works. The band across His chest reminds us of the Captives for the Tomb of Julius II. He, too, in taking on mortal nature, suffered the bonds of death. And, most amazing of all, the pose repeats in mirror image the disposition of the legs (this must have been striking when the figure was intact), the hanging arm, the tense, wiry muscles of one of the most powerful figures in the *Last Judgment* by Lorenzo Maitani (fig. 13). This fourteenth-century relief is carved at hardly above eye level on the façade of the Cathedral of Orvieto, where Michelangelo must often have been able to study it on his trips between

301

302

◀ 304 Florence and Rome. The figure represents a damned soul, held in the jaws of a dragon-like demon, yet, whether consciously or not, Michelangelo has remembered it and converted its pose into that of the Saviour. Such a parallel speaks worlds for the character of the great artist's religiosity. At the moment when he fears death, even the double death of body and soul, he can see no barriers to the saving grace of Christ—even in the depths of Hell. Perhaps he was remembering the promise of the very Psalm (138 : 7–8) which had furnished the Introit for the Mass of St. Peter in Bonds:

> *Whither shall I go from thy spirit? or whither shall I flee from thy face?*
>
> *If I ascend into heaven, thou art there: if I descend into Hell, thou art present.*

36. THE MILAN PIETÀ

Marble; height 6' 4¾"
First version, after 1552; second and third versions, late 1563 and 1564
Castello Sforzesco, Milan

One stands before this last work by Michelangelo with a certain reverence. The successive stages through which the work passed, clearly visible even in the photographs, are artistically beautiful even in their shattered condition—barbarically simple, haltingly stated. They also admit us to the inner world of the artist in the last days of his life.

According to a document dated 1561, Michelangelo gave to his servant Antonio del Francese a *Pietà* which, since it was not mentioned by Condivi in his life of the artist written in 1552, must have been made after that year. Vasari tells us that "it was necessary to find something of marble, so that every day he could pass some time carving, and another piece of marble was set out in which had already been roughed in another *Pietà*, different from that one [the *Florence Pietà*], much smaller." Presumably this was the work already given to Antonio del Francese, who in the 1561 document was given a *Christ with the Cross* (which has now disappeared). Both were in Michelangelo's studio after his death.

colorplate 17

The great sculptor's pupil, Daniele da Volterra, wrote to the nephew, Lionardo Buonarroti, in June, 1564, "I don't remember whether in all that writing I put that Michelangelo worked all the Saturday of the Sunday of Carnival, and he worked standing up, studying on that body of the Pietà." This was February 12. On February 14 Michelangelo was already ill, but refused to go to bed; instead he went out for a walk. By the 15th, sicker than ever and still refusing to be cared for, he sat by the fire. On the 16th he went to bed. He dictated a will in three clauses, leaving his soul to God, his body to the earth, his belongings to his nearest relatives. At the moment of death, he asked his friends to remember the death of Christ. On February 18 he died, in the presence of Daniele da Volterra, Antonio del Francese, two doctors, Diomede Leoni, and his friend Tommaso Cavalieri, the recipient of so many testaments of love more than thirty years before.

It is not known how the *Pietà* came into the Palazzo Rondanini in Rome, where for years it could be seen in the courtyard. After having been taken to a villa outside Rome, the work was acquired in 1952 by the city of Milan, where it is poised on a grimly inappropriate, unfinished, Roman funerary urn, before an ugly stone niche.

The appearance of the version of the *Milan Pietà* as given to Antonio del Francese in 1561 may, to a certain extent, be reconstructed from a drawing in the Ashmolean Museum in Oxford (fig. 35), which shows five sketches for Pietàs. Two of these, representing the dead Christ upheld by two figures, were apparently rejected by the artist, but in the other three one can

307

308

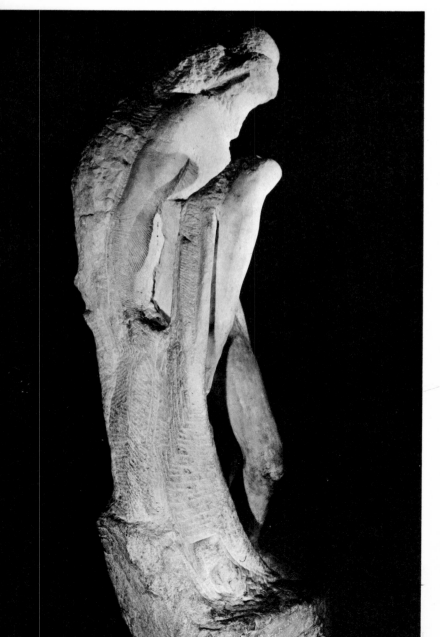

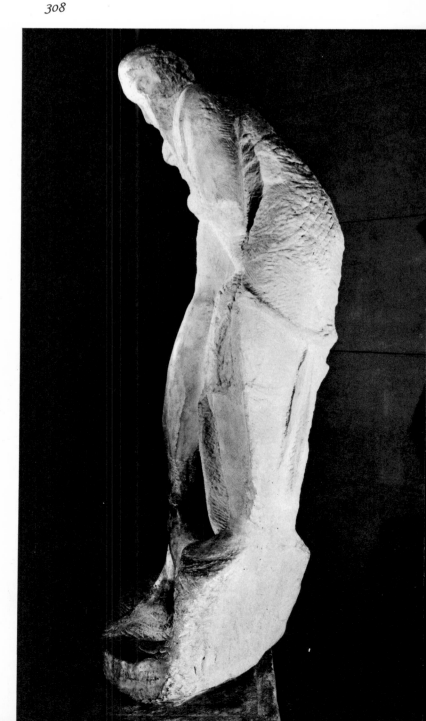

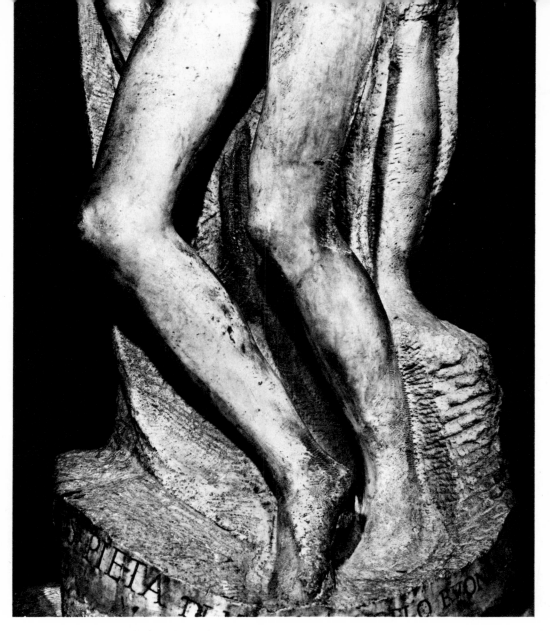

distinguish various ideas for the *Milan Pietà*. The final version, apparently, is that at the left, in which the artist, whether deliberately or not, revived a type which appeared now and then during the fifteenth century, showing one figure, usually God the Father, upholding the dead Saviour. That the Virgin alone should perform this task seems to be almost unprecedented. Never, in fact, before this instance does the entire weight of her Son's dead body rest in her arms.

The version was brought very close to completion, at least in the delicate body of Christ, which was even polished. From the position of the right arm, which remains intact from just below the elbow, it can be seen that the torso leaned forward somewhat, and that the head must have hung sharply forward, as in the Oxford sketch. The proportions of the figure are much slenderer than in the sketch, refined and Botticellian like those of the *Rome Pietà* and the early *Crucifix,* and this conception of the body may well have returned to Michelangelo as he worked—possibly as a way of reducing the emphasis on the physical mass of Mary's burden, which would have rendered her function grotesque. She stands on a higher level to hold her Son as if on the brink of the grave, and she must originally have been much taller than at present, her body bending over somewhat and her head towering above the shoulder and head of Christ and turned outward toward the observer. Judging from the surviving portions of this figure, the version was not finished. From the left side one can still make out the much greater original size of the leg and hip—far too large for the reduced figure.

The meaning of the work at this stage, and the subject of the meditations of Michelangelo

310, 311, 312, 313, and 314 ▶

in his old age (he was somewhere between seventy-eight and eighty-six when he carved the first version) is illuminated by the Salve Regina, the prayer for the dying: "Come, our Advocate, turn upon us thy compassionate eyes, and after this exile show to us Jesus, the blessed fruit of thy body."

During the last weeks of his life, possibly in the winter of 1563–64, when Michelangelo was contemplating this *Pietà*, such a formulation no longer seemed adequate to convey an altered emotional message. Leaving the freestanding legs intact (which could not have been changed), he cut away the head, the right shoulder and upper arm, and the chest of the Christ, straightening the figure considerably. The previous right arm would, of course, have gone completely, along with the crescent curve of the Virgin's mantle moving in such a beautiful shape to Christ's feet. For the moment he retained the fragment, as if to serve as a guide, so that he could reproduce its rhythm in a new right arm, belonging to this second version, which can be clearly seen clinging to Mary's right side—the hand apparently intended to be holding her mantle at about the level of her knee, as if the figure were still alive. What had been Mary's right shoulder has now become Christ's head; and a new shoulder, of necessity much slenderer, has been devised for Mary from what was left of her torso. Mary's original head was completely cut away, and a new head carved from her torso. The veil, the left eye and cheek, and the beginning of the nose of this second head may still be seen above the present face. Mary was looking out toward the spectator and so, by then, was Christ, the top of Whose head in this second version is still preserved. The two heads, parallel but one slightly above the other, would have presented a spectacle less of grief than of that identification with each other, that dissolution of the limits which prevent one personality from merging with another, that takes place to a certain extent in the *Florence Pietà* and in so many of the artist's late drawings.

The second version, which was the work of only a few days (to judge from the roughness of the surviving fragments), did not satisfy the sculptor and again he started in cutting back and cutting down. Now the two figures are drawn together. Mary's head turns to her right and bends down toward her Son, her chin intended to appear just above His head. This too was recarved so as to sink a little, the full beard (Michelangelo had always before portrayed Christ with a youthful beard consisting of no more than a few curls, or with no beard at all) brushing His chest, the substance of His head carved from Mary's bosom—the only marble left for it. As one looks at the concave profile beginning to emerge from the ghostly radiance of the unfinished marble, the suggestion of a self-portrait is again apparent in the shape of nose and beard. Now in extreme old age, the artist identifies himself with Christ rather than Joseph of Arimathea; mystically he becomes the Lord he loves, merges his being in the divine. Such an identification during the Renaissance was not considered irreverent. Dürer, for example, had repeatedly represented himself as Christ, and such meditations were justified by the great religious work of the fifteenth century, the *Imitation of Christ* by Thomas à Kempis. In fact, the dissolution of the self in God has been the object of mystics from time immemorial: a few days after Michelangelo's aged hand could no longer continue carving this face, his voice could still ask his loving friends to remember in his death that of Christ.

Christ's gesture—drawing Mary's mantle, always a symbol of heaven, about Him—recalls the gesture of the *Victory*, similarly appealing for celestial protection. One thinks again of St. Paul's great lines,

> . . . *then shall come to pass the saying that is written: Death shall be swallowed up in victory.*
>
> *O death, where is thy sting? O grave, where is thy victory?*

Not that specific passages were going through Michelangelo's mind at this moment: it is unlikely in his state of increasing detachment, knowing himself to be near death, probably (if we can draw any conclusions from his actions) even wanting death, that anything more than echoes of oft-heard, oft-read doctrine drifted, perhaps just below the level of conscious-

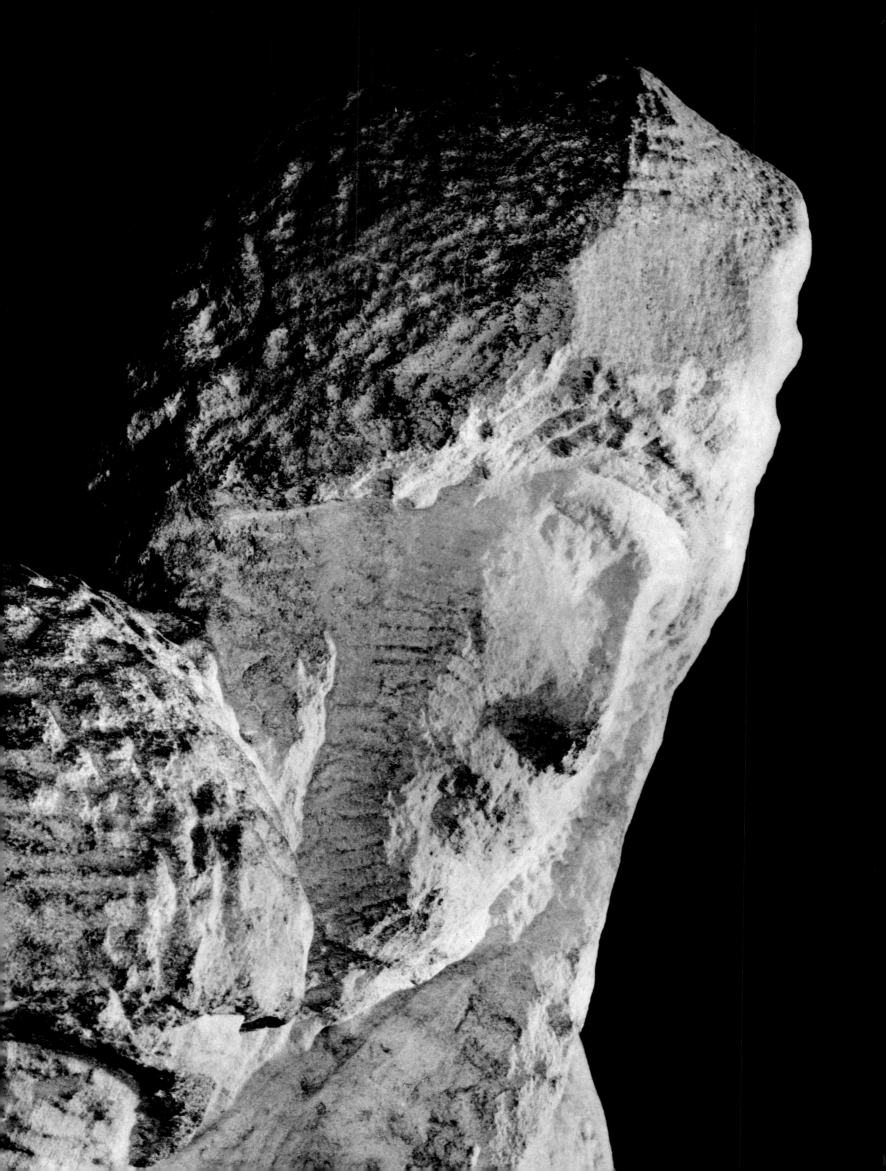

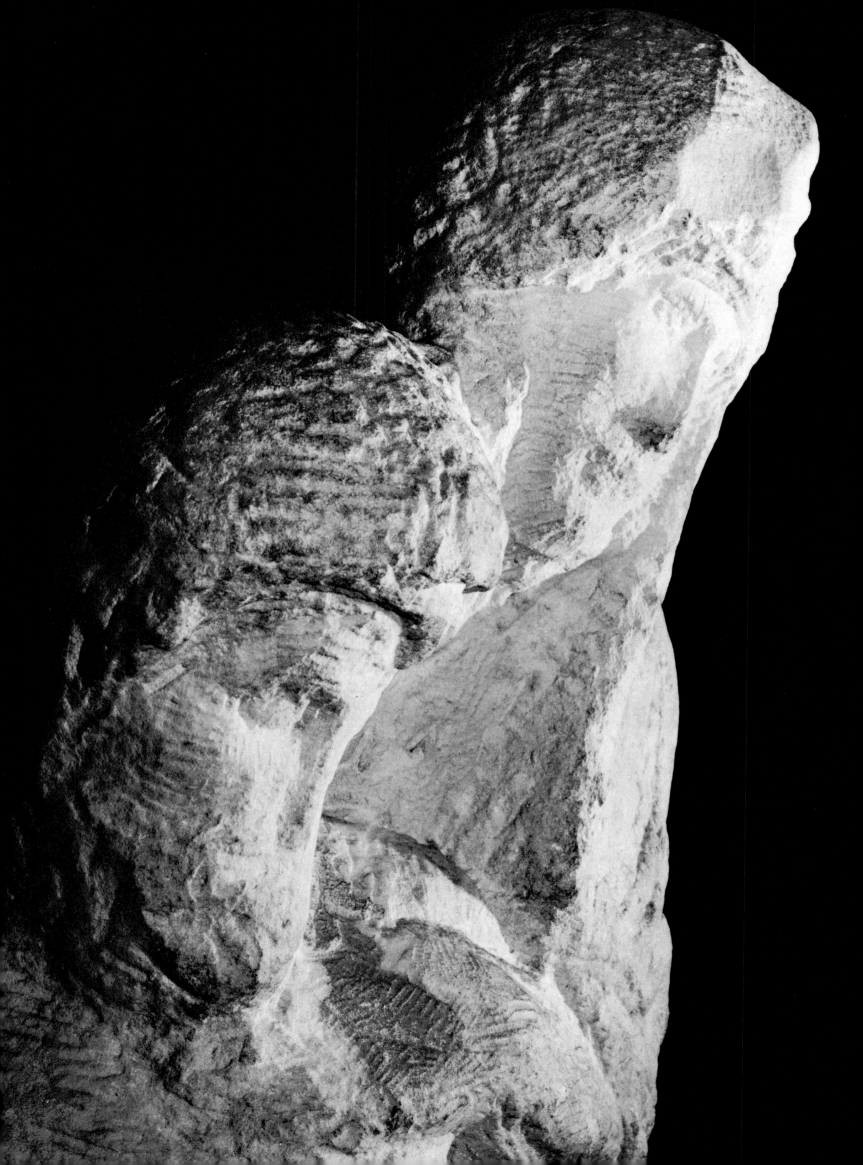

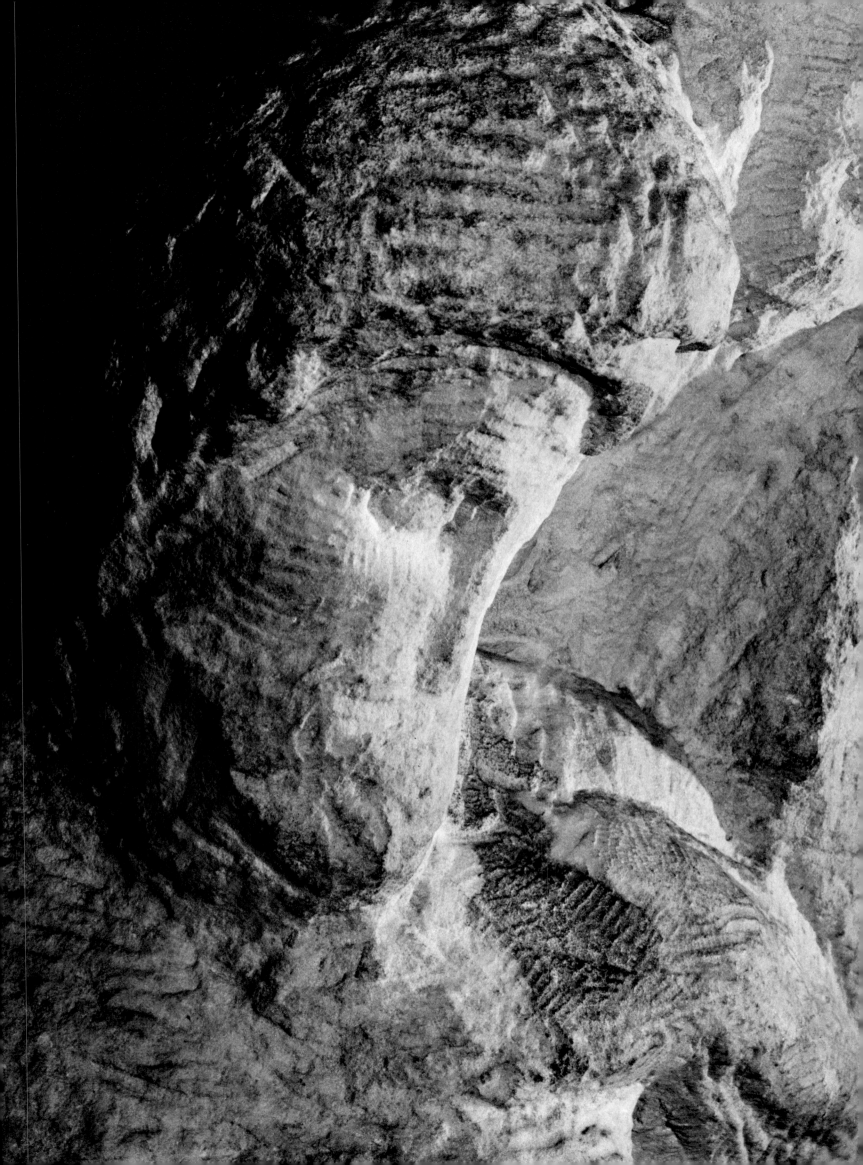

ness. But it is equally improbable that he could have forgotten teachings which were the foundation of the faith he professed his whole life long.

As the gentle, almost smiling Mary holds forth so lightly the wraithlike body of her Son, we think also of St. Paul's words,

> *There is a natural body and there is a spiritual body.*

Lofty, soaring, erect, the recarved group suggests less a Pietà than a Resurrection, the ultimate Christian victory. With every line seeming to lift out of the tomb rather than to sink into it, the *Milan Pietà* is the exact opposite of the *Florence Pietà*. In Michelangelo's last moments the great subject of the Resurrection, which he so often dreamed of carving or painting (no less than fourteen drawings still exist), has infused the spectacle of sacrificial death with the promise of the hereafter.

And now the tools, the love of which he had drunk in at the bosom of a stonecutter's wife, indicate in stone the dim shape of his own head, identified with divinity and drawn with infinite tenderness into the bosom of the Blessed Mother. The group floats. The marble is no longer sufficient for any of its elements. Corporeal beauty, even physical substance, dissolves. The unfinished is at one with the immaterial. Light breaks from its marble prison. We have followed Michelangelo as far as we can follow a mortal. In his death we remember that of Christ—and His resurrection.

The most dedicated and productive of present-day Michelangelo scholars has shown that the *Milan Pietà* represents not grief but blessedness and peace. The nucleus of the work is perhaps to be found deep in Michelangelo's past, in a poem generally dated between 1538 and 1541, in which the process of redemption and the techniques of sculpture are fused:

> *By what biting file*
> *Decreases and grows less each hour thy tired coil,*
> *Infirm soul? Now when shall time be dissolved for thee*
> *By that tool, and thou return where thou wast, to Heaven;*
> *White and glad, as at first,*
> *The perilous and mortal veil laid by?*
> *But although I change my skin,*
> *In these last years and short,*
> *I cannot change my old and ancient use,*
> *That with more days forces and presses me the more.*
> *Love, from thee I will not hide*
> *That I bear envy to the dead,*
> *Dismayed and confused*
> *So that my soul trembles and fears itself with me.*
> *Lord, in the extreme hours,*
> *Extend to me Thy pitying arms,*
> *Take me from myself and make of me one to please Thee.*

BIOGRAPHICAL OUTLINE

1475 MARCH 6: Michelangelo di Lodovico di Lionardo Buonarroti Simoni born at Caprese, a tiny village in the Apennines (now in Arezzo province), the second son of Lodovico (1444–1531), then 169th Podestà (Florentine Commissioner) of Caprese, and Francesca di Neri di Miniato del Sera.

MARCH 31 (?): Lodovico's term as Podestà concluded, the ancient but impoverished family returns to Florence, where for centuries they had lived in the Quarter of Santa Croce. Michelangelo given to a wet nurse, the wife of a stonecutter, at Settignano near Florence, where the family owned a farm.

1481 Lodovico Buonarroti, with his brother Francesco (1434–1508), a money-changer, rents brother-in-law's house in the Via dei Bentaccordi (believed to be No. 7, still standing) in the Quarter of Santa Croce. Michelangelo and brothers Lionardo (1473–1510), Buonarroto (1477–1528), Giovansimone (1479–1548), and Sigismondo (1481–1555) move to this house at an unknown date. Michelangelo goes to grammar school taught by one Francesco da Urbino.

1485 Lodovico Buonarroti marries a second time, to Lucrezia di Antonio di Sandro Ubaldini da Gagliano (died 1497). Lodovico and Francesco oppose Michelangelo's desire to become an artist, as unworthy of family's position.

1488 APRIL 1: Lodovico Buonarroti places Michelangelo in the shop of Domenico and David del Ghirlandaio to learn painting; he is to receive salary of 24 florins for 3 years but stays only a year.

1489 Michelangelo introduced by his friend the painter Francesco Granacci to Lorenzo de' Medici, the Magnificent; received into Lorenzo's art school in the Medici Gardens, opposite the monastery of San Marco. Taught by Bertoldo di Giovanni, pupil of Donatello. Opportunity to study from classical sculpture; contact with members of Lorenzo's Neoplatonic Academy; lives in Medici Palace; treated "as Lorenzo's son." Carves *Madonna of the Stairs* and *Battle of Lapiths and Centaurs*. Draws from Masaccio's frescoes in the Brancacci Chapel, Church of the Carmine; receives a disfiguring blow from young sculptor, Pietro Torrigiani.

1492 APRIL 8: Death of Lorenzo de' Medici. Michelangelo returns to father's house, but later invited back to Medici Palace.

MONTH UNKNOWN: Buys marble block for a larger-than-lifesize statue of Hercules, completed before 1494; sold by the Strozzi family to King Francis I of France in 1529; lost since 1731. Reported to have dissected corpses at the monastery of Santo Spirito. Carves a smaller-than-lifesize wooden crucifix for the prior of Santo Spirito; lost in the early 19th century, this crucifix was rediscovered in 1963.

1494 JANUARY 20 (?): Receives only commission from Piero de' Medici,

the Unfortunate, son and successor of Lorenzo the Magnificent: a statue in snow.

Before OCTOBER 14: Flees to Venice for fear of the invading French, then to Bologna. Carves small marble figures of *St. Petronius, St. Proculus,* and candle-bearing *Angel* for the tomb of St. Dominic at San Domenico in Bologna, started by Nicola Pisano in the 13th century and remodeled by Niccolò dell'Arca. Lives in the house of Gianfrancesco Aldrovandi; studies Dante, Petrarch, and Boccaccio.

NOVEMBER 9: Piero de' Medici is banished from Florence; the Ferrarese monk Girolamo Savonarola, prior of San Marco, takes over the government.

1495 LATE IN YEAR: Returns to Florence; possibly lives with Lorenzo di Pierfrancesco de' Medici and brother Giovanni, members of the younger branch of the Medici family, next to the Medici Gardens. Carves two small statues, *St. John the Baptist* and *Sleeping Cupid* (both lost). *Cupid* sold to a dealer, Baldassare del Milanese in Rome, who offers it as a work of ancient sculpture; Michelangelo tries in vain to buy it back.

1496 JUNE 25: Arrives in Rome, where he lives in great poverty.

JULY 5: Begins work on a marble block bought for him by Cardinal Riario, nephew of the late Pope Sixtus IV and cousin of Michelangelo's future patron Cardinal Giuliano della Rovere, later Pope Julius II. This block is probably that of the *Bacchus*. Lives with a nobleman near the palace of Cardinal Riario; works in the house of Jacopo Galli, a rich banker who had a collection of ancient sculpture.

1497 JULY 1: Refuses to leave Rome for Florence until Cardinal Riario has paid him for recent work, *Bacchus,* eventually bought by Galli.

AUGUST 19: Writes to his father that he is "at times in a great passion for many reasons that happen to him who is away from home."

1498 MONTH UNKNOWN: Makes a cartoon for a painting of the *Stigmatization of St. Francis,* for Cardinal Riario, to be painted by his barber; cartoon and painting are both lost.

MONTH UNKNOWN: Carves a statue of Cupid or Apollo for Galli; now lost.

MONTH UNKNOWN: Lodovico Buonarroti moves to an apartment in the Via San Proculo in Florence.

MARCH (?): Arrives in Carrara to oversee quarrying of marble block for the *Pietà,* for which the French Cardinal Jean Bilhères de Lagraulas had negotiated since November, 1497.

AUGUST 27: Signs contract arranged by Galli with Cardinal Bilhères de Lagraulas to carve *Pietà* in one year for 450 ducats; to be "the most beautiful work in marble which exists today in Rome . . . no master would do it better today." First in church of Santa Petronilla attached to south side of Old St. Peter's, the group has occupied three other sites in St. Peter's.

1499–1500 Probably at work on *Pietà*.

1501 SPRING: Returns to Florence.

JUNE 19: Signs contract for the Piccolomini altar, signed June 5 by Cardinal Francesco Todeschini-Piccolomini, later Pope Pius III. Agrees to complete 15 statuettes in 3 years, for 500 gold ducats. Four statuettes delivered 1504, probably carved by pupils. Michelangelo threatened with lawsuit as late as 1561; after his death, nephew Lionardo repays 100 ducats to Piccolomini heirs.

AUGUST 16: Commissioned to execute the marble *David* in 2 years, from block cut in 1464 by Agostino di Duccio for one of the buttresses of the Duomo of Florence, at monthly salary of 6 gold florins. Begins work September 13.

1501–5 Paints *Madonna* for Angelo Doni (Uffizi). Carves *Bruges Madonna*, and Madonna *tondo* for Taddeo Taddei (London, Royal Academy).

1502 FEBRUARY 28: Price of marble *David* now 400 gold florins.

AUGUST 12: Signs contract for bronze *David*, 2½ braccia high (53 in.), for Pierre de Rohan, Maréchal de Gié, for 50 gold florins.

NOVEMBER 1: Piero Soderini installed for life as Gonfaloniere of the Republic of Florence.

1503 APRIL 24: Signs contract with the Consuls of the Arte della Lana to carve 12 over-lifesize Apostles for the Duomo in 12 years for 2 gold florins a month.

APRIL 29 and OCTOBER 10: Receives 2 payments of 20 gold florins each for bronze *David*, which was probably poured by that date.

JUNE 12: Operai del Duomo (Cathedral Board of Works) decides to build a dwelling and studio for Michelangelo at the corner of Borgo Pinti and Via della Colonna, from a model by Simone del Pollaiuolo called Il Cronaca.

1504 JANUARY 25: Commission of 30, including Andrea della Robbia, David del Ghirlandaio, Filippino Lippi, Botticelli, Giuliano and Antonio da Sangallo, Leonardo da Vinci, Perugino, Andrea Sansovino, and other artists, is appointed to decide on a place for the marble *David*.

APRIL: Marble *David* finished.

JUNE 8: Marble *David* placed on the terrace in front of entrance to Palazzo Vecchio.

AUGUST–DECEMBER: Payments to stonecutters in Carrara for block for *St. Matthew*, one of 12 Apostles for the Duomo.

OCTOBER 31: Payment for paper for cartoon of the great fresco, *Battle of Cascina*, for Sala del Cinquecento in the Palazzo Vecchio, facing Leonardo's *Battle of Anghiari*.

DECEMBER 31: Payment for mounting the pieces of paper; Michelangelo is already at work on the cartoon.

1505 FEBRUARY 28: The Signoria of Florence pays Michelangelo 280 lire advance on the painting of the *Battle of Cascina*.

MARCH: Called to Rome for the first contract for the Tomb of Julius II; planned to be freestanding with approximately 40 over-lifesize marble statues and several reliefs, all to be executed in 5 years for 10,000 ducats.

APRIL–DECEMBER: In Carrara supervising quarrying of the marble for the Tomb. Wants to carve a mountain overlooking the sea into a colossus.

NOVEMBER 12: Engages shipowners to bring 34 wagonloads of marble to Rome.

DECEMBER 10: Contracts for delivery of 60 wagonloads of marble; blocks to be cut to Michelangelo's specifications sent from Florence.

DECEMBER 18: In Florence, voids the contract for the 12 Apostles for the Duomo.

1506 JANUARY: Returns to Rome; takes house near St. Peter's for work on Tomb.

JANUARY 14: The *Laocoön* group discovered in Rome.

JANUARY 27: From Rome, buys a property with vineyards, woods, orchards, and house at Pozzolatico near Florence.

JANUARY 31: Marble from Carrara held up by bad weather; whole boatload of blocks flooded by overflowing Tiber.

APRIL 11–17: Tries unsuccessfully to obtain money from the Pope: according to his own later account he was "chased away" from the papal court. Leaves in anger for Florence.

APRIL 18: Cornerstone of Bramante's St. Peter's laid.

MAY: At work again in Florence, possibly on *St. Matthew* and Madonna *tondo* for Bartolommeo Pitti (Bargello).

MAY 2: Replies to a letter from Giuliano da Sangallo containing Pope Julius II's offer to hold to the original agreement if Michelangelo is willing; proposes to continue work in Florence on the Tomb, sending finished statues to Rome.

MAY 9: Giovanni Balducci writes recommending that Michelangelo return to Rome.

MAY 10: Pietro Roselli writes Michelangelo of the Pope's plan to have him paint ceiling of Sistine Chapel; says Bramante declared Michelangelo would not accept the job.

JULY 8: Papal *breve* summons Michelangelo to Rome.

JULY–AUGUST: Negotiations for Michelangelo's return involve Piero Soderini, head of the Florentine Republic, his brother, the Cardinal of Volterra, and Cardinal Alidosi. Michelangelo meanwhile is apparently at work on the *Battle of Cascina*.

NOVEMBER 21: Pope Julius II, who has by now outflanked the Florentine Republic to the east and north, and entered Bologna in triumph, summons Michelangelo to Bologna, by a letter from Cardinal Alidosi to the Signoria of Florence.

NOVEMBER 27: Piero Soderini writes, "Michelangelo has commenced a painting for the palace (*Battle of Cascina*) which will be an admirable thing." Date of destruction of the fresco is unknown. Cartoon was eventually cut up, fragments dispersed, all are now lost. Michelangelo leaves for Bologna, probably meeting Pope Julius II there on November 29 "with a rope around his neck." Pope pardons Michelangelo; commissions over-lifesize bronze statue of himself.

1507 JANUARY 29: Pope visits Michelangelo in his studio behind San Petronio. Trouble with assistants; Michelangelo dismisses one, who takes the other with him.

MAY 26: Maestro Bernardino, armorer of the Republic of Florence, arrives in Bologna to superintend casting of the statue. Michelangelo writes that he lives "with great discomfort and extreme labor"; shares bed with three assistants; finds the heat intolerable and the wine bad.

JULY 6: Statue of Julius II is cast; pouring successful only up to the waist. Kiln has to be destroyed and remade.

JULY 9: Second, successful pouring.

1507 JULY–MARCH 1508: At work finishing statue of Julius II.

1508 Before MARCH 11: Returns to Florence; believes himself "free of Rome."

MARCH 18: Rents for a year the house constructed by the Operai del Duomo in the Borgo Pinti. Statue of Julius II unveiled in Bologna.

Late MARCH or early APRIL: Julius II calls him to Rome to work on the Sistine Ceiling. First contract calls for 12 Apostles in 12 spandrels, and ornament covering central section, for 3,000 ducats. Rents workshop near St. Peter's. Uncomfortable and always in difficulties with servants.

MAY 10: Receives 500 ducats on account; begins preliminary work.

MAY 11–JULY 27: Makes payments through Francesco Granacci to Jacopo di Piero Roselli to apply rough preliminary coat of plaster (*arricciato*) to the ceiling.

MAY 13: Writes to Fra Jacopo Gesuato in Florence to send a specially fine blue.

JUNE (?): Second contract, for the ceiling as executed. Prepares drawings and cartoons. Complains to Lodovico that he is discontented, unwell, and penniless.

JUNE 10: Cardinals unable to conduct services of the Vigil of Pentecost in the Sistine Chapel on account of the noise, and the dust from the scaffolding.

JUNE: Michelangelo's brother Giovansimone visits Rome.

JULY 22: Giovanni Michi writes from Florence offering the services of Raffaellino del Garbo as assistant.

JULY 29: Writes Lodovico Buonarroti to send Giovanni Michi from Florence to help with the work.

JULY or AUGUST: Records deposit of 20 ducats each for 5 assistants to come from Florence.

AUGUST 7 (?): Francesco Granacci writes from Florence concerning other possible assistants.

SEPTEMBER 2: Buonarroto Buonarroti sends his brother Michelangelo a 2½-pound bag of colors from Florence.

DECEMBER 26: Bronze *David*, poured by Michelangelo but left unfinished, completed by Benedetto da Rovezzano in Florence, is finally shipped to France. Benedetto is paid the remaining 10 florins.

1509 JANUARY 27: Writes to Lodovico that "it is now a year that I haven't had a *grosso* from this Pope, and I don't ask anything because my work is not proceeding in such a way that it seems to me would merit it. And this is the difficulty of the work, and it is still not my profession. And thus I waste my time without result. God help me."

Before JUNE 3: Albertini in his book on Rome mentions painting well under way in the Sistine Chapel.

JUNE: Writes Lodovico Buonarroti he is not dead as had been reported in Florence, but still alive, although "it doesn't matter much. . . . Don't speak about me to anyone, because there are bad men." Letters throughout the period of the Sistine Ceiling deal with his family's financial necessities, transfer of funds, advice in buying land and choosing wives, and attempts to set two brothers up in business by the purchase of a shop. "Life matters more than belongings."

JUNE: Sends devastating reprimand to Giovansimone for apparent acts of arson and for threats to Lodovico: ". . . for the last twelve years I have trudged all over Italy; supported every shame; suffered every want; lacerated my body with every labor; placed my own life in a thousand dangers, only to help my family; . . . you alone want to overturn and ruin in one hour what I have done in so many years and with such labor; by the body of Christ it will not be true."

SEPTEMBER 15: Sends Lodovico 350 ducats, apparently from payment for first portion of the Sistine Ceiling.

SEPTEMBER: Lodovico, now Podestà of San Casciano near Florence, embezzles 100 florins belonging to Michelangelo.

SEPTEMBER 22–25: Goes to Bologna to appeal for money from Pope Julius II, who had left Rome about September 1 to conduct his campaign against the French in the Po Valley; stops in Florence to visit with his family.

OCTOBER 17: Writes from Rome to his brother Buonarroto in Florence to dissuade his brother Sigismondo from visiting him in Rome: "I am here in great distress and the greatest physical labor, and I have no friends of any kind and I don't want any; I don't have the time that I can eat what I need: therefore let me have no more trouble for I cannot stand another ounce." Probably the second section of the Sistine Ceiling had reached a crucial stage.

NOVEMBER–DECEMBER: Sigismondo comes to Rome anyway.

1510 DECEMBER–JANUARY 7, 1511: Second trip to Bologna for money, which is paid to him on his return to Rome. Apparently he then paints third section of the Sistine Ceiling.

1511 FEBRUARY 23: Contemplates third trip to Bologna for money.

AUGUST 14: Unveiling of the Sistine Ceiling; lunettes remain to be executed. Mass of the Vigil of the Assumption is celebrated by Pope Julius II in the Sistine Chapel.

DECEMBER 30: The statue of Julius II is destroyed in Bologna by the Bentivoglio family, who had captured the city in May. The bronze fragments are sent to Alfonso d'Este, Duke of Ferrara, to be melted down for cannon.

1512 MAY and JUNE: Acquires property in parish of Santo Stefano, outside Florence.

JULY 4–19: Alfonso d'Este, in Rome to ask the Pope's pardon, visits the scaffolding of the Sistine Chapel.

SEPTEMBER 5: Advises his family to flee Florence for safety, after the Sack of Prato.

SEPTEMBER 18: After the triumphal entry of Cardinal Giovanni de' Medici into Florence, advises his brother Buonarroto: ". . . don't make friends or familiars of anyone except God; and don't speak of anyone either well or ill. . . ."

OCTOBER: Writes to Lodovico: "Attend to living; and if you cannot have the honors of the Territory like other citizens, suffice it that you have bread and live well with Christ and poorly as I do here; for I live meanly and I care neither for life nor honor, that is of the world, and I live with the greatest labors and with a thousand suspicions. And already it is about fifteen years that I have never had an hour of well-being, and all this I have done to help you, nor have you ever known it or believed it."

OCTOBER 31: The Sistine Chapel is reopened.

1513 FEBRUARY: Entreats Lodovico to have the father of a pestiferous pupil send for him to come home to Florence.

FEBRUARY 21: Pope Julius II dies at the age of 69.

MARCH 11: Michelangelo's childhood friend, Cardinal Giovanni de' Medici, son of Lorenzo the Magnificent, is elected Pope Leo X. Has no work for Michelangelo.

MAY 6: Second contract for the Tomb of Julius II signed with the dead Pope's executors, Lorenzo Pucci, Cardinal Santiquattro, and Leonardo Grosso della Rovere, Cardinal Aginensis. To be completed in seven years and reduced somewhat in scope, projecting on three sides only, but to culminate in a statue of the Virgin and Child.

JULY 30: Writes bitter letter to his brother Buonarroto accusing him of ingratitude: ". . . but you have never known me and you do not know me."

1513–16 Works in Rome, in a house in the Macello dei Corvi (a section since completely destroyed for the Victor Emmanuel Monument). Carves the *Moses* and two *Slaves*, later given to Ruberto Strozzi who presented them to King Francis I of France. Designs a small chapel façade for Pope Leo X at Castel Sant' Angelo.

1514 JUNE 14: Signs contract for *Resurrected Christ* of Santa Maria sopra Minerva, with Canon Bernardo Cencio, Maria Scapucci, and Metello Vari Porcari; to be executed in 4 years for 200 gold ducats. First version left incomplete, because of a bad vein in marble; now lost.

1515 OCTOBER 20: Mentions a painting he agreed to do for Pierfrancesco Borgherini; eventually refers the commission to Andrea del Sarto.

LATE IN YEAR: Probable first interest of Michelangelo in Leo X's projected façade for San Lorenzo in Florence.

DECEMBER: Pope Leo X confers the title of Counts Palatine on Michelangelo's family.

1516 JULY 8: Signs third, greatly reduced contract for the Tomb of Julius II to be executed in 9 years, wherever he liked. Workshop is put at his disposal, in the Regione Trevi, near Santa Maria di Loreto, apparently connected with house in the Macello dei Corvi.

SEPTEMBER: In Carrara for marble for Tomb of Julius II.

OCTOBER: Pope Leo X agrees to give the commission for the façade of San Lorenzo to Michelangelo and Baccio d'Agnolo.

NOVEMBER 23: Writes to Buonarroto directing that all care be taken of their father Lodovico in his serious illness; no money to be spared from Michelangelo's account in Florence; in case of danger, the sacraments of the Church to be assured.

1516–20 Makes sketches for a *ballatoio* (outer gallery) for the drum of the dome of the Cathedral of Florence. Sends figure drawings to Sebastiano del Piombo for use in his paintings.

DECEMBER 1 or 5: Leaves Carrara for Rome to confer with Pope Leo X about the façade of San Lorenzo.

Before DECEMBER 22: Returns to Florence to superintend the clay model for the façade. Existing foundations inspected and considered too weak.

DECEMBER 31: Leaves for Carrara.

1517 (?) Designs windows for the lower story of the Medici (now Riccardi) Palace, Florence.

1517 MARCH 20: After visits to Florence in January and February, rejects façade model as "childish"; begins own clay model.

APRIL 17: Buys a house in Via Mozza (now Via San Zanobi) as workshop for San Lorenzo façade and Tomb of Julius II; buys additional land in July.

MAY 2: Clay model is misshapen "like pastry," and Pope Leo X asks for a wooden one. Cost is raised from 25,000 to 35,000 ducats. The new design is to be "the mirror of all architecture and sculpture of Italy."

AUGUST 31–DECEMBER 22: Supervises in Florence the wooden model for the San Lorenzo façade, with 24 wax figures by Pietro Urbano. New foundations finished in December.

SEPTEMBER: Vari reminds Michelangelo of his obligation to finish statue of *Resurrected Christ* for Santa Maria sopra Minerva, Rome; Michelangelo demands his first payment of 150 scudi; received December 17.

1518 Piero Soderini asks Michelangelo's advice for an altar and reliquary for the head of St. John the Baptist and two tombs, for the church of San Silvestro in Capite.

JANUARY 19: Contract signed with Pope Leo X obligates Michelangelo to complete façade of San Lorenzo in 8 years for 40,000 ducats including all costs, project inevitably conflicting with Tomb of Julius II. Two-story design was to frame 8 standing statues in marble and 4 seated ones in bronze, all over-lifesize, and 11 large and 4 small reliefs.

FEBRUARY (?): Pope Leo X insists on transferring the excavations to Pietrasanta and Seravezza in Florentine territory, requiring Michelangelo to build a new road in unworked territory and train new crews.

1518–19 Almost overwhelmed by troubles in the quarries: the ignorance of the new stonecutters, the strike of the bargemen egged on by the stonecutters from Carrara, the permission granted by Cardinal Giulio de' Medici to the Operai del Duomo to raid the new quarries for the Cathedral pavement, the death of a workman in a stoneslide, the serious illness of an assistant, a completed column shattered by a fall to the bottom of a ravine, the complaints from Cardinal Aginensis about the Tomb of Julius II. Writes to his brother Buonarroto: "I have undertaken to raise the dead in trying to domesticate these mountains and bring art to this village." Quarries new block of marble for Vari's *Resurrected Christ*.

1519 JUNE: Cardinal Giulio de' Medici takes G. B. Figiovanni, canon of San Lorenzo, from lunch, giving him charge of spending 50,000 scudi for additions to San Lorenzo—library, and tomb chapel for Magnifici Lorenzo and Giuliano and Dukes Lorenzo and Giuliano.

NOVEMBER 4: Medici Chapel begun; some walls of San Lorenzo destroyed, and two houses of Nelli family. Chief architect Michelangelo Simoni, "for whom Job having had patience would not have had it with that man one day."

1520 MARCH 10: Contract for the façade of San Lorenzo suddenly and inexplicably annulled and marbles abandoned. Confused and bitter artist writes of "great humiliation." Has lost three years in mechanical struggles.

APRIL: Reports that *Resurrected Christ* is finished, and requests balance due him.

JUNE: Intervening with Cardinal Bibbiena to obtain the commission of the frescoes in the Sala di Costantino in the Vatican for his friend and follower Sebastiano del Piombo, refers to himself as a "man poor, vile, and mad."

DECEMBER: Model for the Medici Chapel completed.

1521 MARCH 21: Vari's *Resurrected Christ* finally sent from Florence; arrives In Rome in June; much retouching required.

APRIL 10: Goes to Carrara to measure the blocks for the tombs, the architecture, and the figures; quarrying and roughcutting continues until January, 1526.

APRIL 21: Medici Chapel completed to level of cornice.

SEPTEMBER (?): In Florence briefly; writes to Lodovico in Settignano protesting he cannot understand why Lodovico should have thought Michelangelo "chased him away." "You have made trial of me thirty years already, you and your sons, and you know that I have always, when I could, thought and done good for you."

DECEMBER 6: Death of Pope Leo X; new Dutch Pope, Hadrian VI, has no work for Michelangelo.

1522 MARCH 17: Frizzi asks Michelangelo to make drawings for a tomb in Bologna.

MAY: Cardinal Fiesco asks for a statue of the Virgin.

SEPTEMBER: Executors of Julius II complain to Pope Hadrian VI, who orders Michelangelo to fulfill his obligations with regard to the Tomb.

MONTH UNKNOWN: Michelangelo's friend Leonardo Sellaio asks for a drawing for a painting to be executed by his servant Gobbo (the Hunchback).

1523 MONTH UNKNOWN: Senate of Genoa asks for a statue of Andrea Doria.

JUNE: Cardinal Grimani, Patriarch of Aquileia, asks for a work, either in painting or in sculpture.

JUNE: Angry letter to Lodovico, who had accused him of diverting income from his mother's dowry: ". . . If I annoy you by living, you have found the way to remedy it . . . say whatever you will about me, but don't write me any more, because you don't let me work. . . . You die only once, and you don't come back to repair things badly done."

JULY: Writes to Bartolommeo Angelini, "I am old and in bad shape; if I work one day I have to rest four."

NOVEMBER 19: Cardinal Giulio de' Medici elected Pope; assumes name of Clement VII.

DECEMBER: Michelangelo goes to Rome for an audience with the new Pope, who renews proposal of new library for San Lorenzo. Negotiations with the executors of Julius II under threat of lawsuit; first proposal for a simple wall tomb made and rejected. Negotiations continue in succeeding years.

1524 JANUARY 12–MAY 12: Wooden models for the architectural portions of the Medici Tombs executed in Florence.

JANUARY: Writes Pope Clement VII that lantern of cupola of the Medici Chapel is finished; calls himself "crazy and bad."

MARCH 29: Finer execution of rough-hewn blocks for the tombs begun in Florence under the stonecutter Andrea Ferrucci da Fiesole.

Before APRIL 21: Commences carving the figures; four blocks still missing.

MAY: Pope Clement VII proposes tombs for Leo X and for himself; no room for them in the Medici Chapel, as one of the ducal tombs was too far along to be changed. Michelangelo's proposal to put them in the anteroom rejected.

1525 Pope Clement VII wants a ciborium for the high altar of San Lorenzo; the Duke of Suessa wants a tomb for himself and his wife; Bartolommeo Barbazzi, canon of San Petronio in Bologna, wants a tomb for his father.

MAY: Writes to Sebastiano about a dinner party which gave him "the greatest pleasure, because I got out of my melancholy a little, or my madness. . . ."

DECEMBER: Writes to Giovanni Fattucci in Rome ridiculing Pope Clement VII's proposal for a colossus 40 braccia high (approximately 70 feet) for the Piazza San Lorenzo, suggesting that it be placed on the opposite corner from the Medici Palace, enclosing the barbershop so as not to lose the rent; smoke would come out of a horn of plenty in the statue's hand, and Michelangelo's costermonger friend suggested (very secretly) that the head would make a nice dovecote. Or, since San Lorenzo needed a campanile, bells could go in the head and the sound would come out of the open mouth, so that on feast days when the biggest bells were rung the statue would seem to be crying for mercy.

1526 MARCH 10: The *Medici Madonna*, *Crepuscolo*, *Aurora*, and *Lorenzo* apparently nearing completion for Medici Chapel.

JUNE: Architecture of one Medici tomb completed. Clement VII in financial difficulties due to war with Charles V.

OCTOBER: Construction reduced in the Laurentian Library.

1527 APRIL 29: Michelangelo gives the key to the Medici Chapel to his friend Piero Gondi as a hiding-place for his belongings; all work stops.

MAY 7: Rome sacked by imperial troops.

MAY 21: Republic proclaimed in Florence.

JUNE 7: Pope Clement VII captured and imprisoned in Castel Sant' Angelo.

DECEMBER 6: Pope Clement VII escapes to Orvieto.

1528 EARLY IN YEAR: Pope Clement VII offers Michelangelo 500 ducats to continue working for him.

APRIL 22: Receives commission from Florentine Republic for colossal statue of *Hercules* to flank marble *David*; the block was originally quarried for Michelangelo in 1508, but assigned by Leo X to Baccio Bandinelli in 1515.

1529 Prior of San Martino in Bologna wants a painting or a cartoon of the Virgin and Child with four saints, for Matteo Malvezzi, 8 braccia high and 5 wide (18 by 9½ ft.).

JANUARY 10: Appointed member of the Nove della Milizia, for the defense of Florence.

APRIL 6: Made Governor and Procurator General of the Florentine fortifications.

JUNE: Inspects citadels of Pisa and Livorno.

JULY (?): Painting of *Leda* commissioned by Alfonso I d'Este, Duke of Ferrara.

SEPTEMBER 21: Flees Florence with his money to save it from requisition by Republic for prosecution of the war. Arrives Ferrara the 23rd, Venice the 25th. Wants to go to France with Battista della Palla; Francis I's offer of a house and a pension arrives after Michelangelo had left Venice.

OCTOBER: Republic of Florence sends repeated requests for Michelangelo's return.

NOVEMBER 9: Goes to Ferrara, arriving in Florence about the 20th. Renews activity on fortifications.

1530 AUGUST 2: Baglioni betrays Florence to the Medici forces.

AUGUST 12: Florence capitulates; the papal commissioner Baccio Valori begins political persecutions, issuing order for Michelangelo's assassination. G. B. Figiovanni, canon of San Lorenzo, hides artist to protect his life.

OCTOBER: Completes *Leda* for Alfonso d'Este; offended by the tactlessness of the Duke's envoy, Michelangelo refuses to give up the painting.

NOVEMBER: Pope Clement VII orders friendly treatment of Michelangelo, who resumes work on the Medici Chapel.

1531 Federigo Gonzaga, Duke of Mantua, requests work of any sort for the Palazzo del Te; Baccio Valori wants a design for his house; Cardinal Cybò wants a design for his tomb.

EARLY IN YEAR: Lodovico Buonarroti dies in Florence at age 87.

APRIL: Francesco Maria della Rovere, Duke of Urbino and heir of Julius II, reported angry because of the noncompletion of the Tomb.

JUNE: Michelangelo offers to return the house in Rome, repay 2,000 ducats to the executors, and finish the monument in 3 years.

JUNE 16: One figure for the Medici Chapel, presumably the *Aurora*, finished.

JUNE 26: Renews offer to return 2,000 ducats to the Rovere executors, give drawings, models, finished statues and marble friezes, and blocks to younger artists to complete the work.

AUGUST 19: Second figure for the Medici Chapel completed, probably the *Notte*.

SEPTEMBER 28: Giovanni Battista Mini notes that Michelangelo has lost weight sharply through excessive work; fears for his life.

NOVEMBER: Gives the *Leda* to his pupil Antonio Mini, to furnish dowries for his sisters and to provide him funds; Mini went to France where he was flooded with orders for copies but never succeeded in selling the original, which cannot be traced after the 18th century.

NOVEMBER 21: Pope Clement VII issues a *breve* forbidding Michelangelo on pain of excommunication to undertake any work other than the commissions for him and the completion of the Tomb of Julius II.

1531–32 Working on unfinished *David-Apollo* for Baccio Valori.

1531 NOVEMBER–APRIL 1532: Negotiations for a reduced version of the Tomb of Julius II; goes to Rome in early April for 4th contract for a wall tomb in San Pietro in Vincoli; agrees to pay 3,000 ducats in 3 years and bear working expenses, to work 2 months each year in Rome, ratified June 13.

1532 JUNE 13: Leaves for Florence. Still working on Medici Chapel, and possibly on *Victory* for the Tomb of Julius II.

AUGUST: Returns to Rome. Probable time of meeting with Tommaso Cavalieri.

1533 JANUARY 1: Writes to Tommaso Cavalieri a letter which exists in three separate drafts, comparing their relationship to a little river at the start, which one could cross with dry feet, but now to an ocean in which he is submerged; calls Cavalieri "light of our century, unique in the world." Writes in drafts that Cavalieri seems to have been "many other times in the world," and that he, Michelangelo, would be born dead "and in disgrace with heaven and earth" if Cavalieri did not accept some of his works.

JUNE: Returns to Florence; at work on the Medici Chapel, the Laurentian Library, and probably the *Victory* (now in the Palazzo Vecchio) and the four *Slaves* (now in the Accademia) for the Tomb of Julius II.

JULY 25: Montorsoli commissioned to finish the *Giuliano de' Medici* for the Medici Chapel.

JULY 28: Writes to Cavalieri of his great, "even measureless love"; ". . . I can no sooner forget your name than the food on which I live; in fact sooner . . . food . . . which nourishes only the body unhappily than your name, which nourishes body and soul . . . so that while my memory lasts I can feel neither pain nor fear of death."

OCTOBER 11: Writes to Bartolommeo Angelini that his heart is in Rome with Tommaso Cavalieri. "Therefore if I desire without intermission night and day to be there, it is for nothing else than to return to life, which cannot be without the soul"; his is in the hands of Cavalieri.

OCTOBER: Returns to Rome. Possible discussion with Pope Clement VII of a *Resurrection* for the Sistine Chapel.

1534 FEBRUARY: Pope Clement VII persuades Michelangelo to paint a *Resurrection*; scaffolding erected.

MAY or JUNE: In Florence; continues on the same projects.

SEPTEMBER 23: Arrives in Rome two days before the death of Pope Clement VII, leaving statues strewn about the Medici Chapel; never returns to Florence.

1535 Before APRIL 16: End wall of Sistine Chapel prepared for *Last Judgment* ordered by new Pope, Paul III; preparations for painting in oil directed by Sebastiano del Piombo.

SEPTEMBER 1: Appointed by Pope Paul III "supreme architect, sculp-

tor, and painter of the Apostolic Palace."

1536 JANUARY 25: Preparation for oil painting removed.

APRIL: Brick wall and new plaster completed for painting the *Last Judgment* in fresco.

APRIL 10–MAY 18: Commences painting.

NOVEMBER 17: Pope Paul III frees Michelangelo from all obligations to the Rovere executors and heirs until the *Last Judgment* is completed.

1537 JANUARY: Pope Paul III urges finishing of the *Last Judgment*.

JANUARY 6: Lorenzino de' Medici assassinates the tyrant Alessandro de' Medici, his cousin, first Duke of Florence. At the request of Donato Giannotti, chief of the Florentine exiles in Rome, Michelangelo carves at some time during the next few years a commemorative bust of *Brutus* as tyrant-slayer, for Cardinal Ridolfi.

FEBRUARY 2: Begins bronze horse for the Duke of Urbino.

FEBRUARY 4: Pope Paul III visits the Sistine Chapel.

JULY 4: Mention of a salt cellar for the Duke of Urbino.

SEPTEMBER 15: Pietro Aretino offers his advice about the subject and composition of the *Last Judgment*. Michelangelo gently turns it down, saying the work is largely completed.

OCTOBER 12: Bronze horse for Duke of Urbino finished unsuccessfully; the Duke asks for the wax model, but Michelangelo will not relinquish it.

NOVEMBER 26: G. M. della Porta writes that Michelangelo is continuously busy with the painting in the Sistine Chapel.

DECEMBER: Sandro Fancelli called Scherano paid for work on the *Madonna and Child* for the Tomb of Julius II.

1538 (?) Meets Vittoria Colonna, Marchioness of Pescara.

1538 NOVEMBER: Interruption in the *Last Judgment*.

1538–39 Projects for remodeling and new constructions for civic center on Capitoline Hill; except between 1555–59, the work continues until long after Michelangelo's death.

1540 JULY: Writes ill-tempered letter to his nephew Lionardo Buonarroti in Florence complaining of the poor quality of the shirts Lionardo sent him, and warning Lionardo he will leave him nothing unless he leads a respectable life.

DECEMBER 15: Upper part of the *Last Judgment* complete; carpenter Lodovico paid for lowering the scaffolding, probably to the lower cornice level of the side walls.

1541 MONTH UNKNOWN: Falls from the scaffolding in the Sistine Chapel, slightly injured.

AUGUST 20: In a letter to Lionardo Buonarroti mentions the intensity of his work and asks him not to come to Rome.

OCTOBER 12: Letter from Alessandro Farnese, nephew of Pope Paul III, indicates the Pope's wish to have his new chapel painted by Michelangelo.

OCTOBER 31: All Saints Eve; *Last Judgment* unveiled; Pope Paul III says High Mass.

1542 FEBRUARY 27: Signs contract with Raffaello da Montelupo to finish 3 figures by Michelangelo for Tomb of Julius II.

MAY: Sends Luigi del Riccio a madrigal, probably on youth Cecchino Bracci: ". . . so that if you like you can give it to the fire, that is, to that which burns me. . . . last night, greeting our idol in a dream, it seemed that while smiling he threatened me; and not knowing which of the two things I should believe, I ask you to find out from him. . . . "

MAY 16: Signs contract with stonecutters for the architecture of the upper story of the Tomb; a new contract had to be drawn up and signed June 1.

JULY 20: Petitions Pope Paul III for release from the 1532 contract, and declares the two *Bound Slaves* (Louvre, Paris) no longer suitable for the work.

AUGUST 20: Fifth and final contract for the Tomb of Julius II signed; statues of *Active Life* and *Contemplative Life* to be finished by Raffaello da Montelupo.

AUGUST 23: Arranges that Raffaello da Montelupo will complete the *Active Life* and *Contemplative Life*.

OCTOBER: Writes his friend Luigi del Riccio: "I have been much entreated by Messer Pier Giovanni to begin painting [in the Pauline Chapel]: as one can see, for four to six days I do not think I can, because the plaster is not dry enough so that one can begin. But there is another thing that gives me more trouble than the plaster, and that, much less paint, does not let me live, and that is the ratification [of

the contract] which does not come . . . so that I am in great despair."
". . . sculpture, painting, work, and good faith have ruined me. . . . Better would it have been in the early years if I had been put to making sulphur matches, I would not now be in such a passion." Writes to Cardinal Alessandro Farnese: "I have lost all my youth tied to this tomb. . . . All the discords which arose between Pope Julius and me were due to the envy of Bramante and Raphael of Urbino and this was the reason why he did not follow through with the tomb in his lifetime; to ruin me: and Raphael was right, because everything he had in art he got from me." (Note that in 1506, when the Tomb was halted, Raphael had not arrived in Rome.)

NOVEMBER: Mentions that he is finishing the *Active Life* and *Contemplative Life* (the present *Rachel* and *Leah*). Duke of Urbino finally ratifies the contract.

NOVEMBER: One fresco begun in the Pauline Chapel, probably the *Conversion of St. Paul.*

NOVEMBER 16: Michelangelo's servant Urbino receives payment for preparation of colors.

1543   APRIL 14: Writes to Lionardo Buonarroti: ". . . when you write me, don't put: *Michelangelo Simoni,* nor *sculptor;* just say Michelangelo Buonarroti, for thus I am known here."

1544   MARCH 29: Turns down commission for bust of Duke Cosimo de' Medici on account of "the trouble I have, but more because of old age, because I do not see light."

JUNE: Exhausted, and seriously ill. Taken by Luigi del Riccio to the house of Ruberto Strozzi, nursed with care and saved from death.

JUNE 21: Offers through Ruberto Strozzi to erect a statue of King Francis I of France in the Piazza della Signoria at his own expense if he will liberate Florence from the Medici.

JULY 11: Writes to Lionardo Buonarroti: "I have been sick: and you have come to bring death to me . . . and to see if I will leave you something. Isn't there enough of mine in Florence to satisfy you? You cannot deny that you resemble your father [Buonarroto], who in Florence chased me from my house. Know that I have made my will in such a way that you won't have to worry about what I have in Rome. Therefore go with God and don't arrive in front of me and don't write me again."

1545   Niccolò Tribolo and Raffaello da Montelupo finish Medici Chapel, several statues left incomplete; now open to public.

JANUARY 25: Statues finished by Raffaello da Montelupo put in place on the upper story of the Tomb of Julius II.

FEBRUARY: Three statues by Michelangelo, *Moses, Rachel,* and *Leah,* placed on the Tomb of Julius II.

JULY 12: Pope Paul III visits the Pauline Chapel; *Conversion of St. Paul* probably finished.

AUGUST 10: Assistant Urbino reimbursed for expenses in plastering second wall of Pauline Chapel.

1546   JANUARY: Again ill in house of Ruberto Strozzi; again nursed by Luigi del Riccio.

FEBRUARY 6: Writes another bitter letter to Lionardo Buonarroti berating him for rushing to Rome, throwing his money away, and being too anxious for his inheritance. ". . . the love you bear me: the love of the graveworm! . . . You have all lived off me for forty years now, and never have I had from you as much as a good word."

MARCH: Payments for scaffolding and colors.

APRIL 26: Promises King Francis I to do a work for him in marble, another in bronze, another in painting. "And if death interrupts this desire of mine, and one can still carve and paint in the other life, I will not fail from there, where one no longer grows old."

JUNE 5: Writes to Lionardo Buonarroti: ". . . don't write me any more; every time I get one of your letters I have a fever, such hard work to read it."

AUTUMN: Appointed architect of Farnese Palace; finishes top story and cornice; work continues into 17th century.

NOVEMBER: Accepts the commission for the building of St. Peter's, only under direct orders from Pope Paul III; works for the love of God, without fee.

DECEMBER: First clay model for St. Peter's.

DECEMBER 4: Insists Lionardo Buonarroti buy a house in the family quarter, offering him from 1,500 to 2,000 scudi for the purpose. ". . . an honorable house in the city brings much honor . . . we are citizens descended from a noble line. I have always tried to resuscitate my house, but I did not have brothers for that. . . . Gismondo must

come back and live in Florence, so that they will not say any more to my shame here that I have a brother who in Settignano goes behind the oxen."

1547   MARCH: Involved in Vatican fortifications for about a year.

MONTH UNKNOWN: Begins work on the *Pietà,* now in the Cathedral of Florence, intended for his own tomb, with his self-portrait as Joseph of Arimathea.

AUGUST: Receives at his own request a Florentine *braccio* (cubit) from Lionardo Buonarroti; complains because it is made of brass like one that a mason or carpenter might use; "I was ashamed to have it in the house and gave it away."

AUTUMN: Completes wooden scale model for St. Peter's. Construction continues with interruptions and delays until his death, and into the 17th century. Due to age and infirmities, work largely directed from studio in the Macello dei Corvi by messenger and letter; results sometimes catastrophic.

1547   Probable date for the writing of the first Life of Michelangelo by Giorgio Vasari, in *Lives of the Painters, Sculptors, and Architects,* published 1550.

1548   JANUARY 16: Saddened by the death of his brother Giovansimone in Florence. Wants particularly to know whether his brother confessed and received the sacraments.

MARCH: Thanks Lionardo for informing him of Duke Cosimo de' Medici's severe proscriptions against Florentine exiles and their families. ". . . I am always alone, I go about little and I speak to no one and especially not to Florentines. . . ."

APRIL 7: Writes to Lionardo Buonarroti his advice to make a pilgrimage to Loreto for the rest of his father's soul, rather than Masses, ". . . because giving the money to priests God knows what they do with it."

MAY 2: Complains to Lionardo of urinary blockage. Repeats that he must not be addressed as sculptor; ". . . I was never a painter or a sculptor like those who keep shops. I always kept the honor of my father and my brothers, although I have served three Popes [actually four] it was through force." Later frequently complains of kidney stone.

1549–50   Designs ceiling, floor, and desks for the Laurentian Library in Florence.

1549   OCTOBER 13: Pope Paul III visits the Pauline Chapel.

NOVEMBER 10: Pope dies; Chapel still unfinished on the 29th.

1550   MARCH: *Crucifixion of St. Peter* now finished. No further evidence of Michelangelo's participation in the Farnese Palace.

SEPTEMBER: Commences stairway in the upper garden of the Vatican Belvedere.

DECEMBER 20: Writes to Lionardo Buonarroti to pick a wife for her family, character, and health of body and soul, not dowry, for if he chooses a poor girl he will not be obligated to all the "show and foolishness of women . . . as for beauty, since you are not the best-looking boy in Florence, you shouldn't care too much as long as she is not deformed or repulsive." This advice starts in 1547; Lionardo marries Cassandra Ridolfi in 1553, to his uncle's great satisfaction.

1555 (?)   Begins to carve the first version of the *Milan Pietà.* Late, mystical drawings (*Annunciation, Crucifixion, Agony in the Garden,* etc.) date from this time.

MAY 11: Refuses to go to Florence to work for Duke Cosimo because it would be a sin to abandon St. Peter's.

JUNE 22: Writes to Giorgio Vasari, "No thought is born in me in which death is not sculptured."

SEPTEMBER 28: Designs stairway for Laurentian Library.

Before DECEMBER: Mutilates the *Pietà* (now in Florence Cathedral); stopped by his pupils, he gives it to Tiberio Calcagni who tries to finish it.

DECEMBER 3: Death of Urbino, Michelangelo's faithful servant and assistant.

1556   FEBRUARY 23: Writes of Urbino to Vasari: ". . . in life he kept me alive, dying he taught me how to die, not with displeasure but with desire for death . . . he was sorry to leave me alive in this traitorous world, with so much distress . . . nothing remains for me but infinite misery." Requests Lionardo Buonarroti to come to see him in Rome.

DECEMBER 18: Writes to Vasari about his sojourn with the hermit monks in the mountains above Spoleto: ". . . one cannot find peace except in the woods. . . ."

1557   MAY: Writes Duke Cosimo I of his wish to "repose with death, with whom I seek day and night to familiarize myself, so that she will treat me no worse than other old men."

JUNE 16: Writes to Lionardo Buonarroti that he could not come to Florence because of ill-health: ". . . if I left the comforts I have here I would not live three days."

1558   DECEMBER 16–JANUARY 29, 1559: New design for the Laurentian Library staircase comes to him in a dream; model built and sent to Vasari in Florence for execution.

1559   Florentine colony in Rome persuades Michelangelo to submit designs for their national church, San Giovanni dei Fiorentini. After elaborate design, approved by Duke Cosimo, work stops in 1562. Church completed in the 17th century by other architects with other designs.

c. 1560   Designs chapel for Cardinal Guido Ascanio Sforza in Santa Maria Maggiore.

1560–61   Leone Leoni's medal depicts a blind old man with a dog, groping his way; subject suggested by Michelangelo, from Psalm 51: 15, "Thou shalt lead the sinner."

1561   Designs partial remodeling of great hall of the Baths of Diocletian, Rome, for church of Santa Maria degli Angeli.

Before MARCH 24: Preliminary designs for the Porta Pia, Rome. Construction continues after Michelangelo's death, until 1565.

1563   DECEMBER 28: Last letter to Lionardo Buonarroti, thanking him for his customary gift of sheep cheeses; his hand no longer obeys him.

1564   FEBRUARY 12: Still at work recarving the *Milan Pietà*.

FEBRUARY 14: Ill, refuses to go to bed; goes out of doors.

FEBRUARY 15: Weakened, sits by the fire with a high fever.

FEBRUARY 16: Finally goes to bed; desires his body to be sent to Florence. Dictates a will in three clauses: his soul to God, his body to the earth, his belongings to his nearest relatives. In the moment of his death his friends are to remember the death of Christ.

FEBRUARY 18: Dies in presence of Tommaso Cavalieri, his pupil Daniele da Volterra, Diomede Leoni, his servant Antonio del Francese, and his two doctors.

FEBRUARY 19: Inventory of his belongings by the Governor of Rome shows few possessions. Most drawings apparently burned by his own hand; only three statues still remained, the *Milan Pietà*, a *St. Peter*, and a small *Christ Carrying the Cross*, latter two now lost; also ten cartoons. Michelangelo's body conveyed to church of the Santi Apostoli.

FEBRUARY 21: Lionardo Buonarroti arrives in Rome. He makes arrangements to transport the body to Florence concealed as a bale of merchandise.

MARCH 10: Body arrives in Florence; when coffin is opened in sacristy of Santa Croce, in presence of Vincenzo Borghini, director of the Academy, the body is intact; burial in Santa Croce in tomb designed by Vasari, finished 1572.

JULY 14: Memorial services in San Lorenzo with a splendid catafalque decorated with sculpture and paintings by city's leading artists, in presence of leading citizens and 80 artists.

LIST OF ILLUSTRATIONS

The literature on Michelangelo is so enormous that it is possible to give only a few of the most important titles. The following list includes those most readily available, as well as some, notably the collections of letters and other documents, to be found only in well-equipped art libraries. Michelangelo's leading position in the art of the High and Late Renaissance means that all general works on the period discuss his art in greater or less detail. The literature on special problems has largely been selected with a view to its relevance to the artist's sculpture. Through the bibliography of Steinmann and Wittkower, and the bibliographies in the other starred items below, it should be possible for the interested reader to pursue on his own any major problem connected with Michelangelo's life and work.

GENERAL WORKS

*FREEDBERG, SYDNEY J., *Painting of the High Renaissance in Rome and Florence*, 2 vols., Cambridge, Mass., 1961. The only thorough, systematic, and successful attempt to place Michelangelo's stylistic development through the Sistine Ceiling into the general context of the evolution of the High Renaissance.

*POPE-HENNESSY, JOHN, *Italian High Renaissance and Baroque Sculpture*, 3 vols., New York and London, 1963. Despite its critical dullness, capricious judgments, and unaccountable omissions, this book remains a convenient guide to documentary material, early literature, and recent opinion on Michelangelo.

VENTURI, ADOLFO, *Storia dell'arte italiana*, vol. IX, pt. 1, and vol. X, pt. 2, Milan, 1901–38.

WÖLFFLIN, HEINRICH, *Classic Art*, translated by Peter and Linda Murray, London and New York, 1952 (from the 8th German edition; subsequent English editions 1953 and 1959).

BIBLIOGRAPHY

STEINMANN, ERNST, and WITTKOWER, RUDOLF, *Michelangelo-Bibliographie*, Leipzig, 1927.

DOCUMENTS

BOTTARI, GIOVANNI, *Raccolta di lettere sulla pittura, scultura ed architettura*, 2nd edition, Milan, 1822–25.

DAELLI, GIOVANNI, *Carte Michelangiolesche inedite*, Milan, 1865.

DOREZ, LÉON, *La Cour du Pape Paul III, d'après les registres de la trésorerie secrète*, Paris, 1932.

FREY, KARL, *Sammlung ausgewählter Briefe an Michelagniolo Buonarroti*, Berlin, 1899. The most important collection of letters written by others to Michelangelo.

GAYE, GIOVANNI, *Carteggio inedito d'artisti dei secoli XIV. XV. XVI.*, Florence, 1839–40.

MILANESI, GAETANO, *Les correspondants de Michel-Ange, I: Sebastiano del Piombo*, Paris, 1890.

———, *Le lettere di Michelangelo Buonarroti*, Florence, 1875. The complete edition of Michelangelo's letters in the original Italian. Authoritative save for a number of instances in which dates have had to be changed, and two spurious letters.

*RAMSDEN, E. H., *The Letters of Michelangelo*, 2 vols., Stanford, 1963. The only reliable English translation, with dates corrected and voluminous notes and appendices on many related aspects of Renaissance history and economic life.

SOURCES

ALBERTINI, FRANCESCO, *Memoriale di molte statue et picture nella città di Firenze*, 1510 (edition Milanesi, Florence, 1863).

———, *Opusculum de mirabilibus novae urbis Romae*, Rome, 1510. These two little guide-books by Albertini contain the first printed notices of Michelangelo and his works.

BORGHINI, RAFAELLO, *Il Riposo*, 5th edition, Reggio, 1826–27.

CELLINI, BENVENUTO, *La vita*, Rome, 1911; English translation by John Addington Symonds, Modern Library, New York, n. d.

CONDIVI, ASCANIO, *Le vite di Michelagniolo Buonarroti scritte da Giorgio Vasari e da Ascanio Condivi*, edition Karl Frey, Berlin, 1887. Condivi, artist and friend of Michelangelo's during his old age, published his life in 1553. The edition cited here contains also the first version of Vasari's life of Michelangelo, published in 1550, and the second, which appeared in 1568, altered in many respects according to Condivi.

HOLLANDA, FRANCISCO DE, *I dialoghi michelangioleschi di Francisco d'Olanda*, edition Antonietta Maria Bessone Aureli, Rome, 1953. An account by a Portuguese painter of conversations he claims to have had with Michelangelo on the subject of painting. Their authenticity is still controversial, and they contain, at the very least, many personal interpolations by Francisco de Hollanda, out of keeping with what we know of Michelangelo's style and ideas.

LANDUCCI, LUCA, *Diario fiorentino dal 1450 al 1516*, edition Florence, 1883.

VASARI, GIORGIO, *Vita di Michelangelo Buonarroti*. In addition to the edition of both the 1550 and 1568 lives, cited above under Condivi, there is the standard edition of Vasari's *Vite de' più eccellenti pittori, scultori ed architettori*, with notes by Gaetano Milanesi, Florence, 1885, vol. VII, pp. 135–404. A standard English translation is that by Gaston du C. De Vere, London, 1912–14.

BIOGRAPHIES

GOTTI, AURELIO, *Vita di Michelangelo Buonarroti*, 2 vols., Florence, 1875.

GRIMM, HERMAN, *Leben Michelangelos*, 19th edition, Stuttgart, 1922.

HOLROYD, CHARLES, *Michael Angelo Buonarroti*, 2nd edition, London 1911.

SYMONDS, JOHN ADDINGTON, *Life and Works of Michelangelo Buonarroti* 2 vols., London, 1893, and many subsequent editions.

MONOGRAPHS

*BAROCCHI, PAOLA (ed.), *Giorgio Vasari, La Vita di Michelangelo nelle redazioni del 1550 e del 1568*, 5 vols., Milan–Naples, 1962. By means of notes to Vasari's *Lives*, the editor has succeeded in assembling an astonishingly complete array of passages illustrating the history of every major problem and idea in Michelangelo scholarship and criticism.

JUSTI, CARL, *Michelangelo. Beiträge zur Erklärung der Werke und des Menschen*, Leipzig, 1900; also *Neue Beiträge*, Vienna and Leipzig, 1908.

KNAPP, FRITZ, *Michelangelo* (Klassiker der Kunst), 4th edition, Stuttgart and Leipzig, 1912.

MACKOWSKY, HANS, *Michelangelo*, 6th edition, Berlin, 1939.

SPRINGER, ANTON, *Raffael und Michelangelo*, 3rd edition, Leipzig, 1895.

THODE, HENRY, *Michelangelo. Kritische Untersuchungen über seine Werke*, 3 vols., Berlin, 1908–13.

———, *Michelangelo und das Ende der Renaissance*, 3 vols., Berlin, 1908–13.

*TOLNAY, CHARLES DE, *Michelangelo*, 6 vols., Princeton, 1943–. This immense work is the most thorough study of Michelangelo's art ever attempted, and the only good complete monograph on the artist in English. The final volume, on Michelangelo's architecture, will be published shortly.

DRAWINGS

*BAROCCHI, PAOLA, *Michelangelo e la sua scuola, I disegni di Casa Buonarroti e degli Uffizi*, 2 vols., Florence, 1962. Well-nigh exhaustive study of the largest body of Michelangelo's drawings preserved in one place, amounting to nearly half of his surviving graphic work. All drawings are illustrated, some with several details.

BERENSON, BERNARD, *The Drawings of the Florentine Painters*, esp. 2nd edition, Chicago, 1938, and 3rd edition. Berenson's great work represents a pioneer attempt to bring order into the mass of drawings attributed to Michelangelo. Some of his conclusions he himself reversed in later editions and others have been contested, but the book remains a study of first importance.

BRINCKMANN, A. E., *Michelangelo-Zeichnungen*, Munich, 1925.

*DUSSLER, LUITPOLD, *Die Zeichnungen des Michelangelo*, Berlin, 1959. The most recent general study, treating in detail 722 sheets by Michelangelo or his school, with only 275 illustrations. Representing almost the extreme of the revisionist school, Dussler's opinions are frequently in sharp contrast with those of Barocchi and Wilde.

FREY, KARL, *Die Handzeichnungen Michelagniolos Buonarroti*, 3 vols., Berlin, 1909–11. The classic catalogue of Michelangelo's drawings. Supplement published by F. Knapp, Berlin, 1925.

GOLDSCHEIDER, LUDWIG, *Michelangelo Drawings*, London, 1951. The best treatment of Michelangelo's drawings for the general public.

PANOFSKY, ERWIN, *Die Handzeichnungen Michelangelos*, Leipzig, 1922.

PARKER, K. T., *Catalogue of the Collection of Drawings in the Ashmolean Museum*, vol. II, *Italian Schools*, Oxford, 1956.

POPHAM, A. E., and WILDE, JOHANNES, *Italian Drawings of the XV and XVI Centuries . . . at Windsor Castle*, London, 1949.

WILDE, JOHANNES, *Italian Drawings in the Department of Prints and Drawings in the British Museum: Michelangelo and His Studio*, London, 1953. The work of Johannes Wilde in the Windsor and British Museum catalogues represents the first attempt by a major scholar to reverse the revisionist trend which had been rejecting important original drawings along with schoolwork. Many of Wilde's reattributions have been accepted by Tolnay, although there are still major areas of disagreement.

ARCHITECTURE

*ACKERMAN, JAMES S., *The Architecture of Michelangelo*, 2 vols., London, 1961. An unusually well-written and convincing survey of Michelangelo's architectural style and the development of his architectural works, followed by a catalogue of all the supporting evidence; of first importance.

*PORTOGHESI, PAOLO, and ZEVI, BRUNO (eds.), *Michelangelo Architetto*, Turin, 1964. This collection of essays and a catalogue by 10 Italian scholars has something of the flavor of an anti-Ackerman committee. The essays, though contentious, are often revealing, and the array of brilliant, largely new photographs of Michelangelo's architecture, measured drawings of his buildings, and color facsimiles of his architectural drawings is astonishing in quality and completeness.

REPRODUCTIONS

GOLDSCHEIDER, LUDWIG, *The Paintings of Michelangelo*, London, 1939.
———, *The Sculptures of Michelangelo*, London, 1940.

SPECIAL STUDIES

BROCKHAUS, H., *Michelangelo und die Medici-Kapelle*, 2nd edition, Leipzig, 1911.

HARTT, FREDERICK, "The Meaning of Michelangelo's Medici Chapel," *Festschrift für Georg Swarzenski*, Berlin and Chicago, 1951, pp. 145–55.

KRIEGBAUM, FRIEDRICH, *Michelangelo Buonarroti, Die Bildwerke*, Berlin, 1940. A new general treatment, with some striking ideas.

PANOFSKY, ERWIN, "The First Two Projects of Michelangelo's Tomb of Julius II," *The Art Bulletin*, XIX, 1937, pp. 561ff.

———, "The Neoplatonic Movement and Michelangelo," *Studies in Iconology* (Chapter VI), New York, 1939. Crucial and enormously influential interpretation of the content of Michelangelo's art, especially important for its analysis of the Tomb of Julius II, the Medici Chapel, and the allegorical drawings. Unsurpassed statement of the principles of Michelangelo's style.

———, *Tomb Sculpture*, New York, 1964. The Tomb of Julius II and the Medici Chapel are analyzed in the light of the history of the funeral monument since ancient times.

POPP, A. E., *Die Medici Kapelle Michelangelos*, Munich, 1922. Important and controversial attempt to reconstruct the history and final appearance of the unfinished Medici Chapel.

SEYMOUR, CHARLES, JR., *Michelangelo's David, A Search for Identity*, Pittsburgh, 1967. Exceptionally thorough and sensitive study of the meaning of the *David* and its relation to the tradition of colossal sculpture.

WILDE, JOHANNES, "Michelangelo's Designs for the Medici Tombs," *Journal of the Warburg and Courtauld Institutes*, XVIII, 1955, pp. 54–66.

PHOTOGRAPHIC CREDITS